Women, Power, and Rape Culture

Recent Titles in
Gender Matters in U.S. Politics

Sex Scandals, Gender, and Power in Contemporary American Politics
Hinda Mandell

The Right Women: Republican Party Activists, Candidates, and Legislators
Malliga Och and Shauna L. Shames, Editors

Sex and Gender in the 2016 Presidential Election
Caroline Heldman, Meredith Conroy, and Alissa R. Ackerman

Understanding How Women Vote: Gender Identity and Political Choices
Kelly L. Winfrey

Women, Power, and Rape Culture

The Politics and Policy of Underrepresentation

Bonnie Stabile and Aubrey Leigh Grant

Gender Matters in U.S. Politics
Juliet A. Williams, Series Editor

BLOOMSBURY ACADEMIC
NEW YORK • LONDON • OXFORD • NEW DELHI • SYDNEY

BLOOMSBURY ACADEMIC
Bloomsbury Publishing Inc
1385 Broadway, New York, NY 10018, USA
50 Bedford Square, London, WC1B 3DP, UK
29 Earlsfort Terrace, Dublin 2, Ireland

BLOOMSBURY, BLOOMSBURY ACADEMIC and the Diana logo
are trademarks of Bloomsbury Publishing Plc

First published in the United States of America by ABC-CLIO 2022
Paperback edition published by Bloomsbury Academic 2024

Cover photo: (Jr Korpa/Unsplash)

Library of Congress Cataloging-in-Publication Data
Names: Stabile, Bonnie, author. | Grant, Aubrey Leigh, author.
Title: Women, power, and rape culture : the politics and policy of
underrepresentation : gender matters in U.S. politics / Bonnie Stabile
and Aubrey Leigh Grant.
Description: First Edition. | Santa Barbara, California : Praeger, An
Imprint of ABC-CLIO, LLC, [2022] | Series: Gender matters
in u.s. politics | Includes bibliographical references and index.
Identifiers: LCCN 2022021041 | ISBN 9781440876974 (hardcover) |
ISBN 9781440876981 (ebook)
Subjects: LCSH: Women—Political activity—United States—21st century. |
Rape—Social aspects—United States—21st century. | Sexual
harassment—United States—21st century. | Marginality, Social—United
States--21st century. | BISAC: POLITICAL SCIENCE / Public Policy /
General | SOCIAL SCIENCE / Sexual Abuse & Harassment
Classification: LCC HQ1236.5.U6 S725 2022 | DDC 305.420973—dc23/eng/20220604
LC record available at https://lccn.loc.gov/2022021041

ISBN: HB: 978-1-4408-7697-4
PB: 979-8-7651-3119-0
ePDF: 978-1-4408-7698-1
eBook: 979-8-2161-8420-1

Series: Gender Matters in U.S. Politics

To find out more about our authors and books visit www.bloomsbury.com
and sign up for our newsletters.

To those who choose silence
Flourishing in the face of adversity
Still waters run deep and strong
To those who spill into the streets
Forging healing in solidarity
Mighty rivers rage righteously
For advocates, analysists, activists, and allies
Powerfully embodying the world we envision

Contents

Series Foreword   ix

Acknowledgments   xi

1. Introduction   1

2. The Commander in Chief and the Bully Pulpit   17

3. The Campus Context: Proving Ground for Power   73

4. Who's Holding Court? A Tale of Two Justices   115

5. Congressional Culpability and Legislative Legacy   169

6. Epilogue   203

Index   209

Series Foreword

From the nearly century-long campaign for women's suffrage, to ongoing contestation over reproductive rights, to 2012 presidential candidate Mitt Romney's meme-worthy claim of having "binders full of women," politics has been a central staging ground in the United States for debates about gender. The 2016 presidential campaign was no exception. For the first time in the nation's history, a woman received a major party nomination to head the ticket as candidate for president. As it happens, the Republican Party nominee also served as a lightning rod for discussions of gender issues, particularly in the days following revelations of his vulgar boasting about the sexual assault of women. The eventual outcome of the 2016 presidential election took many experts by surprise, revealing that many observers had badly misjudged how women would cast their votes. In the end, the 2016 campaign season confirmed not just the ongoing centrality of gender in U.S. politics, but that we still have a long way to go in understanding *how* gender matters—to each of us as individuals and as members of a shared polity.

The *Gender Matters in U.S. Politics* series pushes the boundaries of existing research on gender and politics. Traditionally, political scientists have engaged the subject of gender primarily by looking at differences in the way men and women behave—as voters, candidates, leaders, policy makers, activists, and citizens. Today, there is growing recognition—within the field of political science and beyond—of the critical need to think more broadly and more deeply about gender. Across the social sciences, researchers now recognize that gender is not only an individual attribute but a "socially constructed stratification system" that plays a central role in determining an individual's place in the social order.[1] At the same time, scholars are bringing a more intersectional perspective to the study of gender in recognition of the influence of race, sexuality, and other axes of social difference on gender identity and gender politics.[2] These new ways of conceptualizing gender have far-reaching implications for political scientists with interests in topics ranging from electoral behavior, to social movement mobilization, to media and politics.

The books in this series address a wide array of topics—from conservative women pundits to political cartoons—to demonstrate the farreaching, and sometimes quite unexpected, ways that gender is mobilized in contemporary political discourse. Some authors bring new insight to the study of gender in familiar settings, such as grassroots political campaigning. Others take a closer look at gender politics in less well-studied contexts, such as media coverage of political sex scandals—thereby reminding us that that politics doesn't stay neatly within the boundaries of official institutions. And while some books in this series highlight the persistence of gender inequalities, others draw attention to the distinctive ways women's political roles have changed in the wake of second-wave political activism and legal reforms as well as technological advances that have given new forms of voice and visibility to historically marginalized groups.

Finally, while the terms "women and politics" and "gender and politics" have in the past sometimes been used synonymously, the authors in this series emphasize that gender impacts the lives of women *and* men. The books presented in this series are intended to inform, engage, and inspire readers to think in new ways about issues of deep importance to all of us. In making clearly written, empirically grounded, and thoughtfully argued research available to interested audiences, this series aims to spark conversation and produce new understanding.

—Juliet A. Williams
Department of Gender Studies, UCLA

Notes

1. Barbara Risman, "Gender as a Social Structure: Theory Wrestling with Activism," *Gender & Society* 18 (2004): 429–450.
2. See, for example, Leslie McCall, "The Complexity of Intersectionality," *Signs* 30 (2005): 1771–1800.

Acknowledgments

We didn't really want to write a book with the words "rape culture" in the title, but here we are. We could find no better way to encapsulate what we conceptualized as a catchall category of structural impediments to women's advancement in the public sphere with a common theme of violence against women. Along a spectrum from gendered jokes questioning women's competence, and cultural beliefs characterizing women as untrustworthy, to targeted harassment and sexual assault, we observed a policy landscape that had responded inadequately, with abjectly unjust policy outcomes and persisting underrepresentation of women in positions of power across society.

The book project traces its inception to outreach—for which we are most thankful—from Jessica Gribble, Senior Acquisitions Editor at Praeger, who saw our Midwest Political Science Association (MPSA) paper, "She Lied: Rape Myth Relevance in Social Media and Social Construction in Sexual Assault Policy," in 2018 and suggested that it might be a good basis for a title in the book series "Gender Matters in U.S. Politics."

We are grateful to the scholars who informed our thinking, especially philosophers Kate Manne and Martha Nussbaum, who explain the bases and manifestations of misogyny, shame, and entitlement, and political scientists Anne Schneider and Helen Igram, whose social construction frame explains how policy benefits and burdens are apportioned.

We have been inspired by the work of activists and advocates, like those we have interviewed and profiled in these pages, including Ally Coll, cofounder of the Purple Campaign, tackling sexual harassment in government and private enterprise, and Nora Gallo and Lilly James of Every

Voice Coalition, innovating state legislative responses to campus sexual assault by involving students themselves.

The Schar School of Policy and Government made space for us to pursue this research through a Schar Initiative Award in 2017 with which we founded the Gender and Policy Center, and a Multidisciplinary Research Grant Award from the Provost of George Mason University in 2015 which supported early elements of our work through a multidisciplinary study on mitigating campus sexual assault.

We have benefited from collaboration with colleagues, including Hemant Purohit of the Volgenau School of Engineering, and Heidi Lawrence and Lourdes Fernandez of George Mason's Department of English, who helped us investigate the issue of rape rhetoric in several coauthored articles since 2016; and Angela Hattery, now Director, Center for the Study and Prevention of Gender-Based Violence at the University of Delaware.

Thanks are due to all the graduate research assistants at the Schar School who supported us through various stages of this project, especially Shaune Gilbert, Lilian Medina Romero, and Laura Thorn. We also appreciate the comments of some anonymous reviewers and friends and the feedback we received on two chapters (on the campus and court contexts) presented at MPSA in 2021.

I (Aubrey) am immensely grateful to Bonnie for bringing me along on this journey, but most of all, for being a patient and encouraging mentor. To my writing group, Kirk, Pete, Jennifer, and Geoff, who diligently nudge me to stay on track, I hope this book's publication offers some redemption for my endless procrastination. Thank you to Mercy, who indulged my narrowly focused conversations over the course of this project and always provided encouragement and perspective. I am especially thankful to my dissertation committee, Jennifer Victor, Justin Gest, and Desmond Dinan, for being supportive of me working on something other than my dissertation. My family, a source of my inspiration and enthusiasm, has suffered through many of my monologues and deserves my sincerest gratitude. My late grandmother, Doris, always humored my curiosity and determination, or what some might call defiance. My late grandfather, Victor, instilled in me empathy, compassion, and dedication. My dad, Sid, is my most fervent champion and taught me that barriers were meant to be broken. My mom, Debbie, has shown me what determined women can accomplish. I am grateful for my sister, Keri, and her husband, Adam, who entertain all my interests and adventures; and my brother, Colby, and his wife, Kate, who are always up for sincere, thought-provoking discussions. I would be remiss if I did not thank my supportive extended family—Steve, Janice, Cassie, Rob, Caroline, Ed, Debra, and Lydia—especially my mother-in-law, Pam, who is an ardent supporter of all my endeavors. Thank you to Duncan, my husband and best friend, who has willingly served as my editor, manager, and barista for over fifteen years. And finally, I would like to thank Wally for making sure that I always make time for excessively long walks.

I (Bonnie) am glad for the good fortune to have had Aubrey assigned as my doctoral research assistant half a dozen years ago. Now, as many articles and one book later, I count her as my colleague, coauthor, and friend. My most motivating source of inspiration comes from the force of love and pride I feel for my family: my daughter Nina, whose capabilities, passion, and presence are unparalleled and who embodies power and professionalism with aplomb; my son Alex—intellectual, engineer, and pianist—whose insatiably curious mind and insight fuel hours of conversation expanding my worldview; and Ayla, lyricist, composer, and empath, who rightly suggested that I needed to spend more time with women and gender studies folks, and recommends well-placed fiction and music to sustain my spirit and deepen my understanding of the human condition. For David, Nayantara, and Nadia, I have special gratitude for the love, care, and companionship they share with those most precious to me. When thinking about intractable policy problems brings me down, I am buoyed by the knowledge that love, humor, whimsy, and comfort abide in our midst thanks to all of you. Finally, for my husband Jack, whose constancy and willingness to edit my writing on a moment's notice without complaint are evidence of our enduring love and sustaining partnership.

1

Introduction

On January 21, 2017, one day after Donald Trump's inauguration as president of the United States, people took to the streets in protest in what was widely touted as the largest demonstration in recorded U.S. history.[1] Among the millions of people at hundreds of march sites around the country,[2] crowds were dotted by tens of thousands of women wearing homemade bright-pink hats with pointy cat ears, a uniform promoted by the "Pussyhat Project"—in reference to Trump's recorded boast about grabbing women "by the p—" that had come to light just before the 2016 election.[3] The ballad "I Can't Keep Quiet" was embraced as the unofficial anthem of the Women's March, cowritten by musician and sexual assault survivor Connie Lim, who said she was enraged by the rhetoric that was used to describe women during the election cycle—and she was not alone.[4] Trump often spoke of women disparagingly, sometimes likening them to animals, numerically rating their appearance, and assailing their intelligence. He branded them as liars and threatened to sue the more-than-two-dozen women accusing him of sexual misconduct, including harassment, groping, and rape.[5] Beyond the offensive language and behavior, he backed policy positions favoring the restriction of women's access to health care, contraception, and abortion and rescinding protections for sexual assault survivors on college campuses, and he promised to appoint conservative justices to the Supreme Court to further these goals.[6] These justices would also rule to restrict women's ability to attain equal pay and to report sexual harassment in the workplace. Yet Trump received 45 percent of the popular vote to Hillary Clinton's 48 percent in the 2016 election,[7] so his brand of bullying bravado and constraining policy preferences enjoyed substantial support in the electorate—enough for him to win the electoral college. For opponents, though, more likely to be younger, women and/or people of color,[8] his election was felt as an affront and served as a focusing event that propelled issues of sexual harassment and equity onto the policy agenda. Many women watched in horror and indignation as a blustering, verbally abusive man, widely considered to lack the credentials for the office he sought, won an unexpected, and what many believed to be an undeserved, victory against a more prepared and accomplished female opponent. His ascension to the U.S. presidency promised to make him one of the most powerful people on the planet, with the tangible and symbolic power to roll back women's rights and threaten advancements to women's autonomy that had been hard-won in the preceding decades.

Backlash over Trump's election seemed to help fuel the #MeToo movement, catalyzed later in 2017 when stories surfaced about movie mogul Harvey Weinstein's sexual harassment and assault of dozens of women, leading to his eventual arrest.[9] When actress Alyssa Milano prompted women to share their stories of sexual harassment or assault by replying "me too" to her own testimonial tweet in October 2017,[10] women came out of the woodwork with their own unfettered accounts, telling stories they had previously thought unspeakable, of their own experiences years, or even decades, earlier. Using the hashtag originally devised by activist Tarana Burke in 2006 and building on earlier successes in addressing sexual assault on campuses and in the military,[11] the emboldened #MeToo and #TimesUp movements reacted to the historical injustice of sexual offenses perpetrated by powerful men, as typified by Trump and Weinstein, who had long been able to act with impunity. As a result, hundreds of such men—Democrats and Republicans, Black and white—were publicly called to account for previously undisclosed offenses; hundreds of women threw their hats into the ring for public office; and state legislatures saw an uptick in bills addressing sexual harassment.

Weinstein went to jail, but Trump—true to his "Teflon Don" moniker[12]—escaped legal or material culpability for a spate of alleged offenses, including sexual misconduct, and finished out his term. From the powerful perch of the presidency, he tossed off thousands of tweets and public statements that perpetuated sexist stereotypes and promoted policies that advocates believed would addle women's advancement. He presided over the rollback of interpretations of Title IX that had protected survivors of sexual assault on college campuses, claiming that those accused of rape were the real victims. He appointed hundreds of conservative judges to the federal bench[13] and three to the Supreme Court, including one, Brett Kavanaugh, who had himself been plausibly accused of sexual assault as a student. And he allied with members of Congress who aped his antics, like U.S. Representative Matt Gaetz (R-FL), later reported to have shown fellow lawmakers photos of naked women he had met at parties orchestrated by a county tax collector and to come under investigation beginning in 2020 for having sex with and trafficking a seventeen-year-old girl.[14]

Trump's rhetoric was excused by some, at his own suggestion, as mere "locker-room talk"—something that guys supposedly engage in innocently in the normal course of things. The assault allegation against Supreme Court nominee Kavanaugh was minimized and rationalized by some supporters as just a fumbled attempt by a normal high schooler to make out with a girl, or maybe something she had misremembered or made up from many years ago. As for Congressman Gaetz, those in his own party declined to hold him accountable, as they had done with the president before him.[15]

In the chapters that follow, we examine the principal events, actors, and paradigms in the politics and policy of sexual harassment and sexual assault, as epitomized by and advanced during Trump's tenure as candidate and president. While previous presidents and many lawmakers, including Bill Clinton and "lion of the Senate" Ted Kennedy (D-MA), had also engaged in sexual misconduct while in office, Trump seemed to be the most public and unapologetic about his behavior and rhetoric. "I could stand in the middle of Fifth Avenue and shoot somebody, and I wouldn't lose any voters, OK?" he declared on the campaign trail early in 2016, bragging about his general ability to act with impunity.[16] "When you're a star, they let you do it. You can do anything," he said, referring to his self-professed proclivity to kiss and grab women at will (his, not theirs).[17]

Our primary concern with a climate that tolerates and enables sexual harassment and assault and traffics in sexist rhetoric is that it hampers women's full and equitable participation and treatment in the public sphere. This is particularly true when the majority of those "manning" the primary institutions of public power—the executive, judicial, and legislative branches of government—are, as the word implies, men.

Women are chronically underrepresented in positions of authority. Among elected officials and in academia, international organizations, the cybersecurity field, and film industry, women hold, at best, only between a quarter and a third of leadership positions; only 16 percent of governors and 8 percent of CEOs are women, and the numbers for women of color are far worse.[18,19,20,21,22,23] In a world where women "hold up half the sky," as Mao Zedong famously observed,[24] there is almost nowhere on Earth where women share positions of power equally with men or come close to being proportionally represented, even in so-called representative democracies. Despite advances since the women's movements of the 1960s and '70s, gender equality in the United States has been shown to have slowed or stalled between 1970 and 2018.[25]

Though it has, in general, slowly improved across time, the existence of this disparity is well established, so it is not our intent to belabor this point. Rather, we are interested in examining what we consider to be a substantial systemic factor in the existence and perpetuation of women's underrepresentation, and that is a collection of widely shared beliefs and practices that constitute "rape culture." Since the term can be off-putting to some, we would rather have avoided using it here, for fear of alienating a would-be readership that might be loath to open a book with that phrase on the cover. But as scholars studying sexual assault on college campuses since 2015, witnessing the Women's March in January 2017 and the incendiary expansion of the #MeToo movement later that same year, we came to what for us was an inescapable conclusion: that misogyny and sexual violence, pervasive problems on their own, were also central, blameworthy factors in women's underrepresentation, creating structural impediments to changes in the status quo that would allow women to achieve the equal pay, opportunity, autonomy, justice, authority, and representation that they still lack as the first quarter of the twenty-first century nears completion.

Rape culture can be seen as containing a continuum of threats ranging from verbal sexual harassment to unwanted touching to sexual assault; such a culture condones some degree of subjection of women to these behaviors and the physical and emotional toll they impose.[26] The term "rape culture" is credited as originating in Susan Brownmiller's now classic feminist bestseller, *Against Our Will; Men, Women and Rape*, published in 1973, in which she focuses on cultural practices that perpetuate and justify this environment.[27] While sexual violence is the most virulent manifestation of such a culture, it can also be characterized by its abiding continuous put-downs and objectification of women and worse, restrictions on their autonomy that play out in policy.

We discovered a useful model, designed by counseling psychologists Johnson and Johnson, for explaining the concept of rape culture to include five main elements: (1) traditional gender roles, (2) sexism, (3) adversarial sexual beliefs, (4) hostility toward women, and (5) acceptance of violence.[28] Traditional gender roles, based on cultural norms, include beliefs such as that men should be dominant, aggressive, strong, and sexual, while women should be submissive, passive, fragile, and pure. Accordingly, in such traditional roles, women are expected to be modest, sweet, nice, thin, and faithful, while men are expected to be self-reliant risk-takers who exert power over women, have a propensity for violence and emotional control, and may lack the capacity for sexual fidelity.[29]

Ambitious women seeking positions of public authority, such as in elected office or corporate leadership, have had to ignore gendered expectations and break out of the passive roles that have traditionally boxed them in. Yet those actively pursuing roles of political power or other forms of public authority or influence can expect to feel "the full thrust of social disapproval."[30] When Professor Susan Tolchin (Dr. Stabile's doctoral thesis advisor and mentor), wrote about this phenomenon in 1973 in *Clout: Womanpower and Politics*, a book which she coauthored with her husband, *New York Times* journalist Martin Tolchin, she spoke of women being branded as aggressive, tough or ruthless—attributes associated with respect for male politicians, but which can be damning for women. Half a century later, the social opprobrium for women vying with men for positions of power can also precipitate relentless social media takedowns, including rape and death threats,[31] in addition to more pedestrian unflattering portrayals.[32] Nonviolent, rhetorical means may augment or substitute for threats of sexual violence to defuse the perceived threat posed by powerful women by vilifying, belittling, or lampooning women who challenge or resist existing norms.[33]

Merriam-Webster defines sexism as "behavior, conditions, or attitudes that foster stereotypes of social roles based on sex."[34] Tacit acceptance of such stereotypes supports palpable policy positions that can lead to "discrimination or devaluation based on a person's sex or gender, as in restricted job opportunities, especially such discrimination directed against women."[35] One manifestation of sexism can be observed in the pervasiveness of supposedly humorous one-liners about women. Saying that someone runs like a girl, throws like a girl, or cries like a girl are commonplace put-downs. Jokes about women being bad drivers are a persisting part of popular culture, along with many other "women are bad at stuff" tropes—bad at math, bad at tech, and so forth.[36] Women are also frequently called "hysterical"[37] or "hormonal."[38] Such characterizations cut at women's perceived competence, disqualifying them "from positions of power and a general sense of autonomy" and suggesting that they are innately unfit for public life, which, since the time of Plato and

Hippocrates, has been seen as the province of men, who were seen as rational, while women were seen as hysterical.[39]

Philosopher Kate Manne says sexism can be seen as naturalizing or justifying social arrangements that have privileged men in the long-standing systems of society and government where, historically, they have held sway.[40] The dictionary definition of patriarchy is "broadly: control by men of a disproportionately large share of power."[41] While sexism enables this system, misogyny, Manne says, is its "law enforcement branch," systemically enforcing its governing ideology.[42] One way that this is accomplished, we argue, is through the creation and perpetuation of policies in a system, where the preponderance of leadership roles is held by men, upholding their preexisting primacy.

As public policy scholars, we are particularly interested in policy as a mechanism for mitigating public problems and contributing to just outcomes for members of society. The policy process includes government action, enacted by policy makers and influenced and carried out by individuals, groups, and organizations both within and outside of government.[43] Our focus in this book is on the three branches of government—executive, legislative, and judicial—which, in the United States, comprise its central institutions and structure.[44] We also give attention to the campus context, where young women and men forge foundational relationships and skills and are subject to various experiences that will influence their ability to participate and wield authority in the policy process. The policy environment is also shaped by a wide range of actors—including the media and the entertainment industries, corporations, and communities of faith—and the networks and ideas that influence how events are interpreted and unfold in the policy context.[45] While these forces come under our consideration, we examine them here within a framework of chapters focused on those with the most formal, clearly prescribed roles in shaping policy outcomes: the president, Supreme Court justices, and members of Congress. And, because of its central role as a proving ground for power for those preparing for professional positions of authority, we also include a chapter on the campus context.

Presidential speech has been explicitly acknowledged as a key tool of governance since Theodore Roosevelt famously proclaimed it to be a "bully pulpit"—an excellent platform from which he (at the time of this writing, the only pronoun that applies) could powerfully influence policy dialogue and outcomes. Though technological advance has influenced the means through which that power is wielded—from print media, through radio, television, and social media on the internet—presidents have used it effectively to shape the policy agenda and communicate with the public. Franklin Delano Roosevelt used radio addresses in the form of folksy fireside chats to calm a nation confronting the Great Depression,[46] and John F. Kennedy became "our first television president," with many crediting the medium for his election victory after his televised debate with Richard Nixon in 1960.[47] President Trump favored using Twitter to communicate with the public with direct immediacy, circumventing or preempting the press.[48] In the more than twenty-five thousand tweets he sent during his presidency,[49] he often mocked and pilloried his critics and aggressively promoted his "America First" and "Make America Great Again" (#MAGA) agenda.

In our chapter "The Commander in Chief and the Bully Pulpit," we examine President Trump's use of Twitter with a specific eye toward its implications for women. After identifying a couple of hundred of his most commonly used descriptors, we developed a mnemonic device, dividing them into six categories that spell out the word SILENT: (1) Stature and stamina, (2) Intelligence, (3) Looks and loathsomeness, (4) Emotional state, (5) Necessary qualifications, and (6) Trustworthiness. Though Trump by no means exclusively targeted women for attack with his barbed tweets, his mode of attack employed well-established tactics to discredit women, particularly those who challenged or criticized him. With staccato repetition and reference to sexist stereotypes, Trump's tweets played on prior beliefs that women were not trustworthy or competent, that they lacked the intelligence and stamina of men—himself, in particular—and trivialized them by sizing up their appearance, repeatedly branding some women as ugly, irrational, neurotic, incompetent, and disgusting. As we discuss in the chapter to follow, such characterizations are damaging not only to the individual women who found themselves subject to attack but also to the collective persona of women as effective operators in the public sphere.

Discrediting narratives about women, such as those promulgated in Trump's tweets, can influence policy outcomes that have implications for women's access to justice and treatment under the law. In the campus context, the Trump administration rolled back interpretations of Title IX, established during the Obama era, that had made it easier for students to report and seek redress in cases of campus sexual assault. Much of the dialogue surrounding this policy change was built on beliefs about women lacking trustworthiness or competence when offering testimony about the incidence of sexual assault. Adversarial sexual beliefs and hostility toward women, two elements of Johnson and Johnson's model of rape culture, arguably underpinned the policy change, which offered the solution to a purported problem—false accusations of sexual assault—that was orders of magnitude less prevalent than the problem of sexual assault itself. By defining actionable sexual misconduct as being necessarily "severe, pervasive, and objectively offensive" the preferred Trump administration policy centered men's rights and contributed to silencing survivors of sexual assault, who are mostly women and who mostly don't report anyway, often out of a sense of shame or for fear of being disbelieved.

In our chapter "The Campus Context: Proving Ground for Power," we interview the leaders of half a dozen organizations focused on mitigating the problem of campus sexual assault. We consider various types of policy options—preventative, restorative, and retributive—and the target populations at whom they are aimed, whether survivors or perpetrators. Discussions with these organizational leaders highlighted the fact that the two primary policy instruments in place to address campus sexual assault—the Clery Act and Title IX—were not, in fact, created expressly for that purpose, explaining, in part, their imperfect nature for the task at hand. Neither was designed to prevent sexual violence or to support survivors, two primary goals that our interviewees identified as critical, thus pointing to the need for transformational policy change that doesn't center the assailant, whether for exoneration or punishment (the latter being the carceral approach). In order to implement envisioned change that includes survivor support and prevention along with community accountability, our investigation suggested that better data collection is needed at the local campus level to substantiate the extent of the problem and devise appropriate evidence-based solutions. Further, culture change is needed to address pervasive rape myths and sexism that contribute to advancing policies that fail to prevent the educational setbacks and attendant career obstacles that women experience in the wake of sexual assault.

Those whose interests are privileged by policy and tend to prevail in the campus context can ascend to positions of power as lofty as the presidency, a seat on the Supreme Court, or as a member of Congress. Donald Trump, despite allegations of sexual misconduct in the decades preceding his bid for the presidency, won the post nonetheless and served a term during which he successfully nominated Brett Kavanaugh to serve on the Supreme Court. Kavanaugh succeeded in being confirmed in October 2018, even after allegations that he had committed sexual assault as a high school student. In the economy of credibility, whether in the campus or wider context, men tend to enjoy a surplus, whereas women are often looked at askance. Those holding a gatekeeping role, such as the members of the Senate Judiciary Committee, have routinely looked with favor upon those of similar background and experience to their own, as the principle of homophily attests.[50] In their shared experience of the proverbial "old boys' network," so-called locker-room talk can be the norm. As Senator Arlen Specter expressed during his questioning of Anita Hill in a hearing on Clarence Thomas's nomination process for the Supreme Court in 1991, discussion of "women's large breasts," about which Hill reported with some discomfort, was language that "we use all the time."[51] At a time before the term *sexual harassment* had any currency, the all-male Senate Judiciary Committee was not inclined to give credence to Hill's protestation that such language was not appropriate in the workplace and could be off-putting to women rising through the ranks. Brett Kavanaugh, for his part, had completed a prestigious clerkship for Judge Kozinski of the Ninth Circuit Court, who had resigned after allegations of sexual harassment by more than a dozen of his former staff members came to light in 2017.[52] Kavanaugh personally knew Senator Orrin Hatch (R-UT), who had served as senator and member of the Judiciary Committee for the decades spanning the Thomas and Hill nominations, and with whom he spoke directly before the vote to confirm him on the court.[53] Thomas, teed up for a Supreme Court seat by President Bush, who had appointed him to the U.S. Court of Appeals for the District of Columbia Circuit in 1990, had also had an inside line to Hatch during his confirmation process. As with Kavanaugh, Hatch both voted for Thomas's confirmation and suggested that his accuser was either lying or confused when bringing forth allegations of sexual misconduct.

In our chapter "Who's Holding Court? A Tale of Two Justices," we offer a model of judge's roles in women's underrepresentation in the context of testimonial injustice, considering both the ideological persuasion and individual experiences of members of the judiciary. We include an examination of the circumstances of both Justices Thomas and Hill's ascension to the Supreme Court and an analysis of Thomas's rulings and opinions on cases impacting sexual harassment law. Other categories identified as influencing women's autonomy and capacity to achieve positions of public authority include reproductive rights, violence against women, and workplace equity in pay and treatment. Such policies represent the rules that make workplaces and other public spaces more or less inclusive or exclusionary for women. When then senator Biden asserted that he had not treated Anita Hill badly during the Thomas confirmation process, he demurred that he had only been playing by the rules.[54] Left unsaid was the fact that, as chair of the body presiding over the proceedings, he held substantial responsibility for making the rules, including how long any investigation would proceed and who could give testimony. And in this case, as in many others historically, men both made and benefitted from the rules. Though men might be disadvantaged by their race or other attributes, such as sexual preference, they nonetheless enjoy the privilege of maleness in proximity to power. To wit, Barack Obama beat Hillary Clinton for the Democratic presidential nomination in 2008, and Clarence Thomas prevailed during his nomination process for the Supreme Court in the face of Anita Hill's accusations of sexual harassment, despite each having had to contend with the hurdles of racism and relatively humble beginning as, respectively, the biracial son of a single mother and the grandson of a sharecropper.[55] In such positions, men often defend the status quo of power, sometimes through legal technicalities or other procedural boundaries, such as statutes of limitations, that limit women's opportunities for representation in the public sphere.

The playbook of men in positions of power engaging in sexual misconduct, discrediting their accusers, and favoring policy mechanisms that limit women's ability to report and seek redress can be seen as beginning its narrative arc in the campus context, where star athletes or fraternity brothers enjoy a surplus of concern and credibility, while women who accuse them are often seen as suspect or blameworthy and only rarely see perpetrators held to account. Upon graduation to higher levels of power, the central theme of the playbook is evident in upper echelons of institutions throughout and beyond government. In the legislature, as in the executive branch and the judiciary, accusations and anecdotes of abuses have accrued over time, escalating in the aftermath of the Anita Hill-Clarence Thomas hearings and the MeToo movement tipping point in 2017.

In our chapter "Congressional Culpability and Legislative Legacy," we review a sampling of such cases of sexual misconduct among members of Congress, including senators and congressmen, democrats and republicans, over the time period between the Hill-Thomas hearings and the MeToo era. As in our other chapters, we consider the primary policy mechanisms at play to analyze the advancements and limitations attendant to those policies as they pertain to the potential for improved women's representation. The Congressional Accountability Act of 1995 and its reform in 2018 provided some mechanisms of accountability for discrimination and harassment in the workplace by members of Congress, with the latter reform alleviating some of the onerous reporting mechanisms that characterized the earlier version. We relate data from the Office of Congressional Workplace Rights (OCWR) on the amount and number of related settlement awards to relay some sense of the tangible costs of such misconduct, while noting that the actual number of offenses is likely much higher than the settlement awards indicate, based on what we know about the number of initial reports/counseling requests filed with OCWR and the propensity of victims to remain silent. We consider the role of focusing events and policy entrepreneurs in advancing public awareness and promoting policy solutions to address the problem of sexual misconduct in the Congress, and how such efforts relate to making the legislature more meaningfully representative.

In our examination of women's representation and the role of rape culture in moderating women's access to full autonomy and positions of public authority, we have found two theoretical frames of the policy process to be useful. The first is the social construction frame originally devised for the policy context by Schneider and Ingram in 1993, which explains how those who are positively socially constructed and powerful are likely to reap further benefits through the policy process, while those who are negatively socially constructed and weak are more likely to be assigned burdens.[56] In their various conceptions of the model, those with low power and negative construction include mothers, welfare mothers, and feminists, while those with high power and positive construction feature CEOs and members of the military.[57] As Manne's philosophical consideration of misogyny makes clear, members of historically subjugated groups are most likely to make up those who experience burdens as the result of the policy process and are the least likely to occupy the positions of authority charged with policy making.

The second theoretical frame that has offered us insight is the multiple streams analysis originally conceptualized by Kingdon, which advances understanding of how issues arise and advance on the policy agenda through the confluence of problems, policies, and politics.[58] With a focus on sexual violence broadly defined from rhetoric and harassment to bodily assault, we make use of some central elements of Kingdon's thesis, including the roles of (1) focusing events, like Trump's inauguration, Thomas and Kavanaugh's confirmations, and individual instances of lawmakers' sexual misconduct in the congressional setting; and (2) policy entrepreneurs, such as members of the #MeToo movement, in how problem and policy definitions evolve in the machinations of the policy process.

By employing these analytical frames, along with insights from the field of philosophy on misogyny and testimonial injustice, we investigate how women's power plays out in politics and policy in the primary institutions of governmental authority in the United States and consider the implications of women's underrepresentation.

Notes

1. Erica Chenoweth and Jeremy Pressman, "This Is What We Learned by Counting the Women's Marches," *Washington Post*, accessed August 7, 2021, https://www.washingtonpost.com/news/monkey-cage/wp/2017/02/07/this-is-what-we-learned-by-counting-the-womens-marches/; Natalina Lopez, "The Women's March Was the Largest Protest in US History," *Town & Country*, January 23, 2017, https://www.townandcountrymag.com/society/politics/news/g3209/womens-march-history-of-protest/.

2. Barb Darrow, "More Than 1 in 100 of All Americans Were at Women's March Events," *Fortune*, January 23, 2017, https://fortune.com/2017/01/23/womens-march-crowd-estimates/.

3. Leanna Garfield and Melia Robinson, "Thousands of Women Wore Pink 'Pussy Hats' the Day after Trump's Inauguration," *Business Insider*, January 21, 2017, https://www.businessinsider.com/pussy-hats-womens-march-washington-trump-inauguration-2017-2.

4. Elizabeth Blair, "A Song Called 'Quiet' Struck a Chord with Women. Two Years Later, It's Still Ringing," *NPR.Org*, accessed August 7, 2021, https://www.npr.org/2019/01/14/683694934/milck-quiet-womens-march-american-anthem.

5. Eliza Relman, "The 26 Women Who Have Accused Trump of Sexual Misconduct," September 27, 2020, https://www.businessinsider.com/women-accused-trump-sexual-misconduct-list-2017-12.

6. Michelle Long, Amrutha Ramaswamy, and Alina Salganicoff, "The 2020 Presidential Election: Implications for Women's Health," *KFF* (blog), October 15, 2020, https://www.kff.org/womens-health-policy/issue-brief/the-2020-presidential-election-implications-for-womens-health/.

7. Zola Ray, "One Year Later: How Many People Voted for Trump and Made Him President?" *Newsweek*, January 18, 2018, sec. U.S., https://www.newsweek.com/how-many-voted-trump-president-784019.

8. Alec Tyson and Shiva Maniam, "Behind Trump's Victory: Divisions by Race, Gender, Education," *Pew Research Center* (blog), November 9, 2016, https://www.pewresearch.org/fact-tank/2016/11/09/behind-trumps-victory-divisions-by-race-gender-education/.

9. David Crary and Jocelyn Novek, "Resentment over Trump Election Helped Fuel Weinstein Case," *AP NEWS*, May 25, 2018, sec. Donald Trump, https://apnews.com/article/donald-trump-ap-top-news-elections-movies-entertainment-6bb9d49b24d444c6ab475fad63d3f420.

10. Shamira Ibrahim, "Tarana Burke Is Just Trying to Do Her Work a Long Talk about Black Women, Me Too, and Intentions with the Activist and Founder," *The Cut*, May 10, 2021, https://www.thecut.com/2021/05/tarana-burke-me-too.html.

11. Crary and Novek, "Resentment over Trump Election."

12. Marwan Bishara, "Trump, the Teflon President," *Aljazeera*, September 29, 2020, https://www.aljazeera.com/opinions/2020/9/29/the-teflon.

13. John Gramlich, "How Trump Compares with Other Recent Presidents in Appointing Federal Judges," *Pew Research Center* (blog), accessed September 1, 2021, https://www.pewresearch.org/fact-tank/2021/01/13/how-trump-compares-with-other-recent-presidents-in-appointing-federal-judges/.

14. Jeff Weiner, "Matt Gaetz Showed off Images of Nude Women from Parties with Joel Greenberg: Report," *Orlando Sentinel*, April 5, 2021, sec. Politics, News, National & World News, Joel Greenberg, https://www.orlandosentinel.com/politics/os-ne-matt-gaetz-joel-greenberg-nude-photos-parties-20210405-cdpbemaj3jfnnpfkhjqvft6q5m-story.html.

15. Bess Levin, "Unfortunately, Republicans Accused of Sexual Harassment Will Not Suddenly Grow a Conscience and Resign," *Vanity Fair*, August 10, 2021, https://www.vanityfair.com/news/2021/08/andrew-cuomo-republicans-sexual-harassment.

16. Colin Dwyer, "Donald Trump: 'I Could...Shoot Somebody, and I Wouldn't Lose Any Voters,'" *NPR*, January 23, 2016, sec. America, https://www.npr.org/sections/thetwo-way/2016/01/23/464129029/donald-trump-i-could-shoot-somebody-and-i-wouldnt-lose-any-voters.

17. Dara Lind and Dylan Matthews, "Vox Sentences: 'When You're a Star, They Let You Do It. You Can Do Anything.'—Donald Trump," *Vox* (blog), October 7, 2016, https://www.vox.com/2016/10/7/13206364/vox-sentences-trump-sexual-assault.

18. Bridget Turner Kelly, "Though More Women Are on College Campuses, Climbing the Professor Ladder Remains a Challenge," *Brookings* (blog), March 29, 2019, https://www.brookings.edu/blog/brown-center-chalkboard/2019/03/29/though-more-women-are-on-college-campuses-climbing-the-professor-ladder-remains-a-challenge/.

19. Zawadi Rucks-Ahidiana, "Black Women Face Many Obstacles in Their Efforts to Win Tenure," *Inside Higher Ed* (blog), July 16, 2021, https://www.insidehighered.com/advice/2021/07/16/black-women-face-many-obstacles-their-efforts-win-tenure-opinion.

20. Bex Bastable, "Women Still Underrepresented in Top Sport Jobs, University of Chichester Study Finds," *Chichester Observer*, August 3, 2021, https://www.chichester.co.uk/education/women-still-underrepresented-in-top-sport-jobs-university-of-chichester-study-finds-3333392.

21. Victoria Mosby, "The Cybersecurity Shortage Is Real, and Women May Be the Solution," *Technology Solutions That Drive Business*, accessed August 4, 2021, https://biztechmagazine.com/article/2021/08/cybersecurity-shortage-real-and-women-may-be-solution.

22. Swathi Kella, "Despite a History-Making Oscars, Women's Underrepresentation Behind the Camera Persists—Ms. Magazine," *Ms.*, May 3, 2021,

https://msmagazine.com/2021/05/03/oscars-women-film-awards-gender
-womens-media-center/.

23. Center for American Women and Politics, "Current Numbers," CAWP, June 12, 2015, https://cawp.rutgers.edu/current-numbers.

24. The International Herald Tribune, "Holding Up Half the Sky," *The New York Times*, March 6, 2012, sec. World, https://www.nytimes.com/2012/03/07 /world/asia/holding-up-half-the-sky.html.

25. Paula England, Andrew Levine, and Emma Mishel, "Progress toward Gender Equality in the United States Has Slowed or Stalled," *Proceedings of the National Academy of Sciences* 117, no. 13 (March 31, 2020): 6990–6997, https:// doi.org/10.1073/pnas.1918891117.

26. Carrie A. Rentschler, "Rape Culture and the Feminist Politics of Social Media," *Girlhood Studies* 7, no. 1 (January 1, 2014), https://doi.org/10.3167/ghs .2014.070106.

27. Rentschler, "Rape Culture."

28. Nicole L. Johnson and Dawn M. Johnson, "An Empirical Exploration into the Measurement of Rape Culture," *Journal of Interpersonal Violence* 36, no. 1–2 (2017): 77.

29. Johnson and Johnson, "Measurement of Rape Culture."

30. Susan Tolchin and Martin Tolchin, *Clout: Womanpower and Politics* (New York: Coward, McCann and Geoghegan, Inc., 1973), 91.

31. Dafydd Morgan, "Women in Politics Face 'Daily' Abuse on Social Media," *BBC News*, May 23, 2020, sec. Wales politics, https://www.bbc.com/news/uk -wales-politics-52785157; Catherine Buni and Soraya Chemaly, "The Secret Rules of the Internet: The Murky History of Moderation, and How It's Shaping the Future of Free Speech," *The Verge*, April 13, 2016, https://www.theverge.com/2016/4/13 /11387934/internet-moderator-history-youtube-facebook-reddit-censorship -free-speech.

32. Jessica Valenti, "Why Are Top Women Politicians Still Peppered with Gender-Specific Slurs?," *The Guardian*, December 28, 2015, https://www .theguardian.com/commentisfree/2015/dec/28/top-women-politicians-still -peppered-with-gender-specific-slurs.

33. Kate Manne, *Down Girl: The Logic of Misogyny* (Oxford: Oxford University Press, 2018), 76.

34. *Merriam-Webster*, "Definition of SEXISM," accessed August 16, 2021, https://www.merriam-webster.com/dictionary/sexism.

35. Michelle Konstantinovsky, "What's the Difference between Misogyny and Sexism?" HowStuffWorks, September 11, 2019, https://people.howstuffworks .com/misogyny-and-sexism.htm.

36. Matt Novak, "Jane Jetson and the Origins of the 'Women Are Bad Drivers' Joke," *Smithsonian Magazine*, February 14, 2013, https://www.smithsonianmag .com/history/jane-jetson-and-the-origins-of-the-women-are-bad-drivers-joke -17672597/.

37. Alison Espach, "What It Really Means When You Call a Woman 'Hysterical,'" *Vogue*, March 10, 2017, https://www.vogue.com/article/trump-women-hysteria -and-history.

38. Randi Hutter Epstein, "Stop Calling Women Hormonal," *The New York Times*, June 2, 2018, sec. Opinion, https://www.nytimes.com/2018/06/02/opinion /sunday/women-hormonal-hormones.html.

39. Espach, "'Hysterical.'"

40. Manne, *Down Girl*.

41. Merriam-Webster, "Definition of PATRIARCHY," accessed March 13, 2022, https://www.merriam-webster.com/dictionary/patriarchy.

42. Manne, *Down Girl*.

43. Paul Cairney, "What Is Policy?" *Paul Cairney: Politics & Public Policy* (blog), March 4, 2016, https://paulcairney.wordpress.com/2016/03/04/what-is -policy-3/.

44. Paul Cairney, *Understanding Public Policy: Theories and Issues*, 2nd ed. (London: Red Globe Press, 2019), 76.

45. Paul Cairney, "Policy Concepts in 1000 Words: The Policy Process," *Paul Cairney: Politics & Public Policy* (blog), July 11, 2017, https://paulcairney.wordpress .com/2017/07/11/policy-concepts-in-1000-words-the-policy-process/.

46. Sarah Pruitt, "How FDR's 'Fireside Chats' Helped Calm a Nation in Crisis," HISTORY, April 7, 2020, https://www.history.com/news/fdr-fireside-chats-great -depression-world-war-ii.

47. Bob Schieffer, "John F. Kennedy: Our First Television President," *Cbsnews. Com*, May 29, 2017, https://www.cbsnews.com/news/john-f-kennedy-our-first -television-president/.

48. Tamara Keith, "Commander-In-Tweet: Trump's Social Media Use and Presidential Media Avoidance," *NPR*, November 18, 2016, https://www.npr.org /2016/11/18/502306687/commander-in-tweet-trumps-social-media-use-and -presidential-media-avoidance.

49. Maegan Vazquez, Christopher Hickey, Priya Krishnakumar, and Janie Boschma, "Donald Trump's Presidency by the Numbers," *CNN*, December 18, 2020, https://www.cnn.com/2020/12/18/politics/trump-presidency-by-the-numbers /index.html.

50. Miller McPherson, Lynn Smith-Lovin, and James M Cook, "Birds of a Feather: Homophily in Social Networks," *Annual Review of Sociology* 27, no. 1 (August 1, 2001): 415–444, https://doi.org/10.1146/annurev.soc.27.1.415.

51. Grace Segers, "Here Are Some of the Questions Anita Hill Answered in 1991," September 19, 2018, https://www.cbsnews.com/news/here-are-some -of-the-questions-anita-hill-fielded-in-1991/.

52. Matt Zapotosky, "Nine More Women Say Judge Subjected Them to Inappropriate Behavior, Including Four Who Say He Touched or Kissed Them," *Washington Post*, December 15, 2017, sec. National Security, https://www .washingtonpost.com/world/national-security/nine-more-women-say-judge

-subjected-them-to-inappropriate-behavior-including-four-who-say-he-touched
-or-kissed-them/2017/12/15/8729b736-e105-11e7-8679-a9728984779c_story
.html.

53. Jessica Gresko, "Deja Vu: What These Senators Said Then and What They Say Now," *AP NEWS*, September 27, 2018, sec. Clarence Thomas, https://apnews .com/article/ea7caea1332e4897b3f22e804423392e.

54. Jane Mayer, "What Joe Biden Hasn't Owned up to about Anita Hill," *The New Yorker*, April 27, 2019, https://www.newyorker.com/news/news-desk /what-joe-biden-hasnt-owned-up-to-about-anita-hill.

55. Brent Staples, "Editorial Notebook; Judge Thomas's Grandfather – And Mine," *The New York Times*, September 10, 1991, sec. Opinion, https://www .nytimes.com/1991/09/10/opinion/editorial-notebook-judge-thomas-s-grandfather -and-mine.html.

56. Anne Schneider and Helen Ingram, "Social Construction of Target Populations: Implications for Politics and Policy," *American Political Science Review* 87, no. 2 (June 1993): 334–347, https://doi.org/10.2307/2939044.

57. Anne L. Schneider, Helen Ingram, and Paul deLeon, "Democratic Policy Design: Social Construction of Target Populations," in *Theories of the Policy Process*, 3rd ed., ed. Paul A. Sabatier and Christopher M. Weible (Boulder, CO: Westview Press, a member of the Perseus Books Group, 2014), 105–149.

58. Nikolaos Zahariadis, "Ambiguity and Multiple Streams," in *Theories of the Policy Process*, 3rd ed., ed. Paul A. Sabatier and Christopher M. Weible (Boulder, CO: Westview Press, a member of the Perseus Books Group, 2014), 25–58; Katherine Shaw, "Beyond the Bully Pulpit: Presidential Speech in the Courts," *Texas Law Review* 96, no. 1 (2017): 71–140.

2

The Commander in Chief
and the Bully Pulpit

The President's words play a unique role in American life. No other figure speaks with the reach, range or authority of the President. The President speaks to the entire population about the full range of domestic and international issues we routinely confront, and on behalf of the country to the rest of the world. Speech is also a key tool of presidential governance: For at least a century, Presidents have used the bully pulpit to augment their existing constitutional and statutory authorities.[1]—(Kate Shaw, Professor of Law, Cardozo University)

"Federal Judge throws out Stormy Danials [sic] lawsuit versus Trump. Trump is entitled to full legal fees." @FoxNews Great, now I can go after Horseface and her 3rd rate lawyer in the Great State of Texas. She will confirm the letter she signed! She knows nothing about me, a total con!—(Donald J. Trump (@realDonaldTrump) October 16, 2018, https://www.thetrumparchive.com/)

When you give a crazed, crying lowlife a break, and give her a job at the White House, I guess it just didn't work out. Good work by General Kelly for quickly firing that dog!—(Donald J. Trump (@realDonaldTrump) August 14, 2018, https://www.thetrumparchive.com/)

Lightweight Senator Kirsten Gillibrand, a total flunky for Chuck Schumer and someone who would come to my office "begging" for campaign contributions not so long ago (and would do anything for them), is now in the ring fighting against Trump. Very disloyal to Bill & Crooked-

USED!—(Donald J. Trump (@realDonaldTrump) December 12, 2017, https://www.thetrumparchive.com/)

I heard poorly rated @Morning_Joe speaks badly of me (don't watch anymore). Then how come low I.Q. Crazy Mika, along with Psycho Joe, came . . . to Mar-a-Lago 3 nights in a row around New Year's Eve, and insisted on joining me. She was bleeding badly from a face-lift. I said no!—(Donald J. Trump (@realDonaldTrump) June 29, 2017, https://www.thetrumparchive.com/)

Words with me are instruments. I wish to impress upon the people to whom I talk the fact that I am sincere, that I mean exactly what I say, and that I stand for things that are elemental in civilization.[2]—(Theodore Roosevelt, quoted in Jeffers, 2002)

Introduction

President Theodore Roosevelt coined the term "bully pulpit" in 1909 when speaking with journalists he had invited to the library of the White House to share his thoughts on issues of the day. As related by one of those in attendance, Roosevelt, after reading a paragraph "of a distinctly ethical character . . . suddenly stopped, swung round in his swivel chair and said 'I suppose my critics will call that preaching, but I have got such a bully pulpit!'"[3] For Roosevelt, according to *Merriam-Webster*, bully was an adjective meaning *excellent* or *first-rate*—not the noun *bully* ("a blustering, browbeating person").[4] William Safire, the lexicographer, *New York Times* columnist, and presidential speechwriter, called it "the active use of the president's prestige and high visibility to inspire or moralize."[5] Presidential speech is considered a key tool of governance, as noted by law professor Kate Shaw, with unmatched range and broad power to persuade.[6] Though all presidents have taken advantage of the power of the bully pulpit, for purposes from the lofty to the self-serving, many have remarked that Donald J. Trump put the latter form of bully in the pulpit, speaking from the lectern of his smartphone.

The power of presidential speech has persisted and advanced between the twenty-sixth and forty-fifth presidencies, propelled by evolving media. "What FDR was to radio, and JFK to television, Trump was to Twitter."[7] For Teddy Roosevelt, who was credited with being the first modern president, in part for his media savvy, newspapers and magazines gave him the ability to communicate with the masses.[8] Roosevelt courted journalists for the purpose of controlling his message to the American public and sought to bring them on board for his political agenda by developing "succinct linguistic slogans" like "big-stick diplomacy" and "square deal" domestic policies.[9] As Trump assumed the presidency in 2017, Twitter amplified the power of the bully pulpit by allowing him to bypass traditional media outlets and communicate directly with the public at a time of his choosing,[10] often in the middle of the night or early morning hours. Pronouncements by the president via Twitter regularly became headline-making news themselves in traditional outlets, giving the president augmented impact and tangible agenda-setting capacity.[11]

As the most high-profile person in America, any president's expressed views could be expected to set the tone for national discourse.[12] Trump's tweets arguably exhibited such influence, despite little evidence of high-minded national sentiment beyond occasional all-caps exclamations of "MAKE AMERICA GREAT AGAIN!" (with over one thousand mentions, counting 617 of the full phrase and 599 of "MAGA"). A large number of the twenty-six thousand tweets he fired off during the course of his presidency were personal attacks on individuals. The bullying he exhibited with impunity, toward both women and men, signaled the acceptability of such behavior to some, from private citizens to, even more concerningly, government officials who have the power to make, interpret, and implement policy. That his words could trigger dangerous action was made evident in the insurrection that took place on January 6, 2021, when a riotous mob sought to disrupt the electoral process, laying siege to the U.S. Capitol. It was this turn of events that led to his being impeached for a second time and permanently banned from the platform that had long been his preferred social media outlet. According to a statement by Twitter, the action was taken "due to the risk of further incitement of violence."[13]

A right-wing militia's plot to kidnap Michigan governor Gretchen Whitmer in October 2020 was also believed by many, mostly Democrats, to have been incited by Trump's rhetoric. Trump feuded publicly with Whitmer throughout the spring of 2020 over coronavirus relief funds and measures she had taken to safeguard public health during the pandemic. "LIBERATE MICHIGAN!" he tweeted in response to her mask mandate, restrictions on public gatherings, and restaurant and bar closures, while also assailing her with repeated insults questioning her competence. The Trump campaign's assistant press secretary called Whitmer "a power-hungry hypocrite, establishing rules for others that she refuses to obey herself."[14] The plotting militia group called her a "tyrant" and balked at what they called her "uncontrolled power."[15] When asked if he believed that Trump's rhetoric had emboldened such extremist groups, then-presidential candidate Joe Biden, replied, "Yes, I do . . . the president has to realize the words he utters matter."[16]

Our contention in this chapter is that the words of the president do matter and that, while Trump's prolific insults, innuendos, and lies spared no one, they could be particularly damaging to women, among other underrepresented groups. We consider how insults leveled at women by Trump via Twitter, and echoed in his rally addresses and other public pronouncements, tapped into long-standing stereotypes and prejudices that downplay and doubt women's competencies, especially when they seek or hold positions of power or authority in the public sphere. Our analysis identifies, categorizes, and discusses the implications of Trump's multiplicitous insults according to various gendered classifications that have historically contributed to the silencing of women and their subsequent underrepresentation in the power structures of society.

Women's minority status in positions of power—or as aspirants to such roles—can expose them to harsh, limiting judgments based on stereotypes that can serve to undermine them, including characterizations of women as weak, conniving, emotional, or angry.[17]

"There is overwhelming research evidence that gender-stereotypical expectations influence the way we judge the abilities of women and men" and that competence is widely perceived as a male quality.[18] Trump universally sought to demean, trivialize, and disempower his opponents. His name-calling of men, who were clearly not spared from his barbs, could often be seen as emasculating. One of his favorite monikers for men was "little," notes Debbie Walsh, director of the Rutgers University Center for American Women and Politics.[19] According to Yale University psychologist, Professor Marianne LaFrance, "Once you've referred to a person's size or standing as small or little, then you're trafficking in the realm of gender terminology."[20] We examine the ways in which Trump's tweets exploited gender-related terminology and may have contributed to perpetuating gender stereotypes.

It is the consequences of wielding such stereotypes that concerns us. In and of themselves, the sexist tropes they reference are just a set of beliefs, as Martha Nussbaum lays out in her foreword to Kate Manne's book *Down Girl: The Logic of Misogyny*.[21] But misogyny itself, says Nussbaum, can be considered an enforcement mechanism. Weaponizing the power of the bully pulpit not to inspire but to disparage in this particular way could serve to empower "residual patriarchal forces operating in our culture."[22] These forces can prevent or forestall the advance of women's rights and representation by raising doubts in the public mind as to whether women ought, or are able, to serve as well as men in leadership roles. They also raise the costs associated with women raising their voices by subjecting them to gendered criticism and condemnation, at times intensified by the risk of violence.

Trump, Twitter, and Sexism On and Offline

Trump first tweeted in 2009 when he was host of the reality television show *Celebrity Apprentice*. Eight years later, he sent his first tweet from the @POTUS (president of the United States) account, which had been set up during the Obama administration. Still, he continued to prefer his personal account, @realDonaldTrump, from which he had sent some thirty-five thousand tweets by the beginning of his term as president.[23] Whether using his personal account or his official @POTUS account, though, pronouncements from the president of the United States were demonstrated to receive wide attention and wield considerable influence. An analysis of fourteen thousand of Trump's tweets, reported by Barron's, suggests that they could drive the stock market up and down,[24] and a Brookings Institution case study showed that in the immediate after-math of Trump's tweets targeting particular topics or individuals, "levels of severe toxicity and threats" directed at those individuals increased.[25] A related finding shows that "offensive speech on the internet tends to arise in response to political events on the ground," so, many times when Trump targeted individuals at one of his rallies, his online followers mag-nified his messaging by attacking them online as well.[26] When Twitter suspended his personal account on January 8, 2021, after the insurrection at the U.S. Capitol for which he was widely blamed, Trump's @realDon-aldTrump account had over eighty-eight million followers.[27]

Trump was a prolific user of Twitter—tweeting an average of ten times a day since he became a leading candidate for the presidency in 2016—and it was arguably the platform from which his insults were most frequently hurled.[28] It has been noted that "Twitter promotes discourse that is fre-quently denigrating and dehumanizing,"[29] especially for women. One study found that one-quarter of Trump's tweets during the lead-up to the 2016 election fell into the category of mocking and criticism or attacks on others, while one in ten contained uncivil language.[30] According to communica-tion scholar Brian Ott, Twitter is not only defined by but also demands or promotes three key characteristics: simplicity, impulsivity, and incivility, training users to devalue others[31] and depersonalize interactions.[32] Trump's deployment of such tactics was not confined to Twitter; two key attributes of his debate rhetoric during the Republican presidential primaries before the 2016 election, for instance, were his use of simple language and constant insulting of opponents.[33] During just one week in 2015, for instance, he called his political opponents "stupid" more than thirty times.[34]

While only an estimated 20 percent of tweets are of social or political importance, it seems that emotionally charged tweets are more likely to be shared than those of a more neutral tone, and frequent Twitter users have been shown to "favor negativity and aggressiveness."[35] Sentiment analysis of Trump's tweets in 2016 found them to be 45 percent negative, 27 percent neutral, and 28 percent positive, with 65 percent of the adjectives used being negative.[36] Cultural anthropologist and historian Carole McGranahan[37] characterized Trump's political speech on Twitter as being distinguished by wide-scale use of lies and extreme derogatory comments classifiable as nationalist, racist, and misogynistic[38] and noted that anthropologists have considered his words as a means of mainstreaming such speech in the public sphere.[39]

Rheault et al. find that "women who achieve a high status in politics are more likely to receive uncivil messages than their male counterparts," and "female leaders or candidates for leadership positions have found a disproportionate amount of abusive messages targeting them."[40] Incivility toward women who participate in politics can be viewed "as a form of gender role enforcement."[41] The stereotypic traits associated with leadership overlap considerably with the traits associated with men, such that it is nearly automatic that people link men with politics.[42] "Scholars note the danger in reinforcing the association of women and girls with feminine stereotypes, as this may activate feminine stereotypes of women, reinforcing the gender role incongruity with the agentic nature of political office."[43] Research shows that kids learn gender stereotypes in common social studies sources in elementary school.[44]

Characterizations—some might say character assassinations—that forefront gender stereotypes can be damaging in several ways. Not only do they influence the way the public might see or respond to women but they can also have implications for how women see and conduct themselves. According to Harvard Business School professor Katherine B. Coffman, gender stereotypes can contribute to women's own negative self-images in ways that can set them back professionally.[45] This includes imposter syndrome—the nagging feeling of many in underrepresented groups that they don't belong at the higher echelons of power or elite institutions once they earn their way in—as one manifestation of this phenomenon that can also thwart their advancement.[46]

A litany of studies conducted in the immediate aftermath of the 2016 election found that sexist attitudes were a strong predictor of voting for

Trump over Clinton in 2016.[47] In a recent study, Tufts University's Brian Schaffner found that voters who scored above average on hostile sexism were more likely to vote for Trump and more likely to rate him favorably since "hostile sexism," is "fueled by antagonism and resentment toward women who seek equality or power."[48]

Unpacking the Language (Methods)

In order to investigate how Trump's tweets referenced and played upon gendered stereotypes in the policy context and wider public sphere, we made use of the Trump Twitter Archive.[49] This open-source platform, originally launched in 2016, collected all Trump's tweets in real time as of January 27, 2017, before which it collected tweets several times daily, until January 8, 2021, when Trump was permanently banned from the platform. Scraped tweets recorded by the Trump Twitter Archive are cited by various outlets, including FactCheck.org—a nonpartisan, non-profit, project of the Annenberg Public Policy Center at the University of Pennsylvania—PolitiFact, and Snopes.[50]

Informed by our own and other prior research on Twitter communication, rhetoric, and gender politics, we identified just over 190 words, including insulting descriptors used by Trump in his tweets, ranging alphabetically from "angry" to "zero talent"; of those in our final data set, the ten most frequently used terms were: fake, crooked, corrupt, sad, disaster, crazy, hoax, fraud, little, and failed.

Using an approach informed by grounded theory, we identified six categories of descriptors (see table 2.1) which emerged from the data: (1) Stature and Stamina, (2) Intelligence, (3) Looks, (4) Emotional State, (5) Necessary Qualification, and (6) Trustworthiness. These categories contain 140 of the original 190 words curated for the data set. This classification of criticisms reflects stereotypes and myths that can serve to undermine women's bids for elective office or other positions of authority by calling into question their credentials or attributes in these areas. As a mnemonic device, we arranged them to spell out the word SILENT, using the first letter of each, because it is our contention that these criticisms are deployed with the intention of diminishing women's voices in the public sphere.

Stature and Stamina

"She doesn't have the look. She doesn't have the stamina, I said she doesn't have the stamina, and I don't believe she does have the stamina,"

Table 2.1 Categories of Descriptors: The SILENT Treatment

Stature and Stamina		Intelligence		Looks and Loathsomeness		Emotional State		Necessary Qualifications		Trustworthiness	
Descriptor	Number of Tweets	Descriptor	Number of Tweets	Descriptor	Number of Tweets	Descriptor	Number of Tweets	Descriptor	Number of Tweets	Descriptor	Number of tweets
sad	343	stupid	192	disgusting	80	crazy	306	disaster	319	fake	1,217
little	281	dumb	142	nasty	66	angry	158	failed	268	crooked	450
sleepy	247	clue (as in "no clue" or "doesn't have a clue")	98	ugly	50	vicious*	55	failing	260	corrupt	363
weak	240	dummy	83	like a dog	24	nervous	41	mess	199	hoax	301
loser	158	dopey	70	sloppy	12	psycho	25	incompetent	122	fraud	285
joke	126	fool	64	filthy	11	crazed	21	fail	69	phony	235
pathetic	126	dumbest	44	fat	10	mental	21	incom-petance*	48	dishonest	208
sick	118	dope	39	rude	9	reckless	21	ineffective	36	lies	206
lightweight	110	moron	37	spewing	8	wacko	21	third rate	29	false	191
strength (as in no, none or zero)	100	clueless	25	foul mouthed	4	hostile	20	clown	28	criminal	138
short	99	idiot	19	slob	2	wacky	20	goofy	27	lied	104

desperate		"not smart"		loudmouth		meltdown		"bad judgment"*		lying	
desperate	78	"not smart"	17	loudmouth	1	meltdown	19	"bad judgment"*	25	lying	103
puppet	68	low IQ	12	spew	1	unhinged	19	"no talent"	24	biased	93
overrated	47	"not very bright"	6			deranged	17	hack	21	fraudulent	88
weakness	43	low IQ	6			lunatic	6	inept	14	sham	70
cryin'	42	"bad at math"	2			wack job*	4	stumbling	8	shifty	57
begging	31	"ditzy airhead"	1			incoherent	3	zero talent	7	lyin'	56
stamina (as in no, none, or zero)	23					neurotic	3	"not fit"	6	liar	53
begged	21					unglued	1	competence	6	discredited	41
zero credibility	21							security risk	6	cheating	23
lowlife	15							untalented	6	traitor	23
cry	13							"bad judgment"*	5	cheat	21
flunky	13							"not capable"	2	hypocrite	20
exhausted	12							"off her game"	2	leak	20

(Continued)

Table 2.1 (*Continued*)

Stature and Stamina		Intelligence		Looks and Loathsomeness		Emotional State		Necessary Qualifications		Trustworthiness	
Descriptor	**Number of Tweets**	**Descriptor**	**Number of Tweets**	**Descriptor**	**Number of Tweets**	**Descriptor**	**Number of Tweets**	**Descriptor**	**Number of Tweets**	**Descriptor**	**Number of tweets**
wreck	12									"con job"	18
crying	11									disloyal	18
insecure	10									leaker	18
washed up	6									sleazebag	16
"no	5									"no credi-	15
energy"										bility"	
lonely	5									leakin'	9
coward	4									sleazy	8
basket case	3									slippery	7
embarass-	2									cheater	3
ment*											
low class	1									"con artist"	2
										cheatin'	2

Note: Descriptors with an asterisk indicate words that were misspelled when tweeted.

Trump told moderator Lester Holt during his first presidential debate with Hillary Clinton in September 2016, reiterating his line from an ABC News interview, "I just don't believe she has a presidential look, and you need a presidential look."[51] Linguistics professors George Lakoff and Deborah Tannen have each noted the power of repetition—especially of short, simple words or phrases—to get a message to stick in people's minds, a trick routinely employed in advertising.[52] Trump's tweets regularly repeated insults aimed at opponents. We identified words assailing the stature and stamina of his opponents as the first of six categories of descriptors in our analysis of Trump's tweeted insults. These include terms referencing physical size (lightweight, little); submissive behaviors or demeanor (crying, begging, desperate, pathetic); or weak physical constitution (sick, weak, sleepy, exhausted).

Of the twenty-three times Trump's tweets specifically contained the word *stamina*, almost a dozen were focused on Hillary Clinton and her purported lack of this trait. In several such tweets, Trump touted his own self-professed stamina. On November 5, 2015, referring to himself in the third person, he mused: "What other candidate begins to rival Trump in his knowledge, breadth of issues, stamina?" On December 3, 2015, he declared "I consider my health, stamina and strength one [sic] of my greatest assets. The world has watched me for many years and can so testify-great genes!" And ten days later, he tweeted in all caps, "TRUMP HAS STAMINA, HE IS WORKING HARDER THAN ANY OTHER CANDIDATE. He REALLY loves AMERICA. He deserves to win." Here, Trump aligns himself with the traditional gender attribute of masculine strength and virility, despite his advanced age, overweight status, and apparent aversion to exercise.[53]

While robust stamina and energy are often seen as traditional male attributes, women have been portrayed as weak since at least 400 BCE, when, in ancient Greece, Plato opined that "Women share by nature in every way of life just as men do, but in all of them women are weaker than men."[54] "Historically, the American electorate has identified stamina, strength, and endurance—commonly viewed as masculine traits—as qualities necessary in their Presidents," according to scholars of politics and communication,[55] compelling female candidates to overcome negative assumptions regarding their physical strength.[56] "Framing women as frail or sick is one way that women candidates are portrayed as not up to the task of leading."[57] A 2016 Trump campaign ad called *Dangerous* played up this strategy, featuring grainy images of Clinton coughing, stumbling, and being held up by aides, while a voice-over proclaimed that

"Hillary Clinton doesn't have the fortitude, strength or stamina to lead in our world."[58] On September 6, 2016, Trump tweeted (and was retweeted eleven thousand times), "Mainstream media never covered Hillary's massive 'hacking' or coughing attack, yet it is #1 trending. What's up?" The portrayal by Trump and others of Clinton's brief bout with pneumonia while on the campaign trail has been characterized as "a modern-day hysteria diagnosis" that painted her as fainting and unfit for public leadership, reflecting a bias long identified by scholars in political culture.[59] Indeed Republicans had long sought to suggest that Clinton was physically not up to the task of leading. In 2014, Karl Rove, who had served as George W. Bush's influential deputy chief of staff, suggested that Clinton had suffered brain damage from a December 2012 fall.[60] In June 2016, a video of Clinton shaking her head was doctored by a pro-Trump blogger to look as though she had suffered a seizure, and conservative media outlets picked up the footage, dedicating significant coverage to discussions of Clinton's health.[61]

Clinton was far from the only woman that Trump characterized as weak or lacking in stamina. In speculating that he would be able to replace as many as four Supreme Court judges during his tenure, Trump spoke of two women as likely candidates for replacement, including octogenarian Ruth Bader Ginsburg, of whom he said, "What does she weigh? Sixty pounds?" and the much younger Sonia Sotomayor, whose health he labeled curtly as "No good. Diabetes."[62] Of his nemesis, Speaker of the House Nancy Pelosi (D-CA), Trump tweeted on April 16, 2020, "Crazy Nancy Pelosi, you are a weak person. You are a poor leader. You are the reason America hates career politicians, like yourself . . . totally incompetent & controlled by the Radical Left, a weak and pathetic puppet." In the face of formidable female rivals, whose educational and public service credentials could be said to outstrip his own, Trump did not meet them toe-to-toe with substantive or reasoned argumentation. Instead, he often resorted to staccato, stereotypically gendered insults, many of which actually made their mark. A study focused on fake news during the 2016 election cycle demonstrated that one-quarter of the respondents in a nationally representative survey believed that stories of Clinton's ill health were either "probably" or "definitely" true.[63]

Trump also subjected male opponents to gendered assaults on their stature by characterizing them as "little" or "liddle," "lightweight," "crying," or "weak," thus associating them with attributes more in keeping with disparaging concepts of the feminine versus masculine traditional gender roles. Trump branded Republican Senator Marco Rubio (R-FL) as "little" as they vied for the presidential nomination in 2016. Said Trump of his rival in a tweet on February 26, 2016, "Lightweight choker Marco Rubio looks like a little boy on stage. Not presidential material!" and, two days later, referred to him as "Little Marco Rubio, the lightweight from Florida" in a series of seven tweets in a single day. One read, "While I hear the Koch brothers are in big financial trouble (oil), word is they have chosen little Marco Rubio, the lightweight from Florida." In all, Trump described Senator Rubio as "little" or "lightweight" or both in about three dozen tweets. After Trump used the belittling moniker in a GOP debate, a headline in *US News & World Report* declared, "Donald Trump's #Little-Marco Is the Internet's New Favorite Thing."[64] Rubio retaliated by saying that Trump had "small hands" and implying that their size correlated with other parts of his body.[65] "Not even the best political forecasters could have guessed that Donald Trump's hand and genitalia size would become 2016 presidential campaign topics," ran one subsequent news story after the debate.[66]

Trump also diminutized former New York City Mayor and self-funded 2020 Democratic presidential candidate Michael Bloomberg. The moniker "Mini Mike" appeared in Trump's twitter feed sixty-four times between December 2019 and October 2020. When Trump tweeted that Bloomberg was "a 5'4" mass of dead energy who does not want to be on the debate stage with . . . professional politicians," he was fact-checked by the Associated Press, which found that Bloomberg was actually more like five feet seven.[67] Countered Bloomberg: "Donald, where I come from we measure your height from your neck up."[68] Noting the number of times that Trump tweeted about Bloomberg, a CNN report speculated that Trump was "obsessed" with the former New York City mayor, in part because the size of his wealth surpassed that of Trump's by some $50 billion.[69]

In addition to initiating sparring over height and physical size, Trump pursued further emasculating tactics by portraying other men as crying, begging, or otherwise weak. Stereotyped as feminine, crying, in particular, is still widely stigmatized for men.[70] Theory in feminist masculinity studies suggests that in men's hierarchical relationships "enacting characteristics associated with the devalued group (women) may result in particularly harsh social punishment."[71] And it seems to be just such harsh social punishment that Trump attempted to exact when he gave Senate Minority Leader Chuck Schumer (D-NY) the prefix "Cryin'" in several dozen tweets between May 2017 and October 2020. Trump first tried this barb on Schumer after Schumer told the president that he was "making a big mistake" by firing FBI Director James Comey in the midst of the FBI's investigation of Russia's meddling in the 2016 White House race and any potential connections between Trump's campaign and Moscow.[72] At a campaign rally in Louisiana in November 2019, Trump explained to the crowd in a mocking tone that "I call him Cryin' Chuck because I saw him cry one time while making a speech. I said, 'Isn't that sad?'"[73] According to a story in *Newsweek*, that was in January 2017 "when Schumer shed tears during a speech where he condemned Trump's harsh immigration policies."[74]

A study examining the acceptability of men crying while participating in sports suggested that when men are engaged in what are perceived as manly pursuits, they are given more latitude to exhibit the occasional feminine attribute—such as crying.[75] Since politics is generally perceived as being the rightful domain of powerful men, the shedding of an isolated male tear in that realm can be buffered from the social opprobrium that can often accompany the violation of gender stereotypes elsewhere. For women, though, who are seeking to buck traditional gender norms by aspiring to or advancing positions of public authority, association with stereotypically feminine qualities can be considered damning or disqualifying. And raising gendered stereotypes for use against men can be seen as damaging to both men and women, as it casts both as objects of derision based on their perceived feminine attributes.

Intelligence

There is evidence that biases still exist well into the twenty-first century with regard to women's intelligence relative to men's. Harvard president Lawrence Summers famously argued, while speaking at a conference hosted by the National Bureau of Economic Research in 2005, that women are outperformed by men in math and science due to biological differences.[76] The idea that women's brains are substantively different from men's in ways that account for their underrepresentation in leadership roles across professions is known as "neurosexism," and though it has been thoroughly debunked, according to cognitive neuroscientist Gina Rippon, it continues to surface, such as in the widely shared memo of Google engineer James Damore in 2017, as one example.[77] In it, Damore complained about diversity efforts at the company, most of whose seventy-eight thousand employees are white or Asian men and said that such efforts were unlikely to succeed "because in general, women are more interested in people than ideas. Women are also more prone to anxiety and less tolerant of stress."[78] Damore's subsequent firing led to a far-right harassment campaign of "hateful comments and violent threats" against diversity proponents at Google, including trans women, by groups complaining that Google actually discriminates against white, conservative men.[79]

A 2018 study published in *American Psychologist* found bias against women and girls "in contexts that emphasize intellectual ability" and noted that such bias "emerges early and is a likely obstacle to their success."[80] While research using public opinion polls shows a steady rise in regard for women's intelligence among the general public since the middle of the twentieth century (when only 35 percent of the public believed that women were as intelligent as men—up to over 85 percent in 2018)— women are still considered to be less well suited to leadership roles.[81] And significant vestiges of bias regarding intelligence remain, as we see in people's often expressed dislike for smart women;[82] research showing girls as young as five years old as less likely to see those of their own gender as really smart;[83] and the fact that both "adults and children implicitly associate brilliance with men more than women."[84] The evocation of such implicit biases through explicit speech may serve to revive and unleash them, with potentially tangible implications for targeted individuals or groups who have historically suffered the exclusionary consequences of such stereotyping.

"Congresswoman Maxine Waters, an extraordinarily low IQ person, has become, together with Nancy Pelosi, the Face of the Democrat Party. She has just called for harm to supporters, of which there are many, of the Make America Great Again movement. Be careful what you wish for Max!" tweeted the president of the United States on June 25, 2018. The impetus for this insult and teasing threat from the bully pulpit appears to be payback for Waters, a supporter of efforts to impeach him. Waters told her supporters to publicly call out Trump administration officials to protest the separation of families due to the administration's "zero tolerance" policy.[85] In three of his eighteen tweeted mentions of the specific term "low IQ" (twelve) or "low I.Q." (six), Trump was alluding to women. In addition to Waters, Trump used this particular insult against Senator Elizabeth Warren (D-MA) and conservative *Washington Post* columnist, Jennifer Rubin, when, in December 2015, she suggested that Trump was afraid of debating.[86] "Highly untalented Wash Post blogger, Jennifer Rubin, a real dummy, never writes fairly about me. Why does Wash Post have low IQ people?" he tweeted about Rubin, who holds bachelor of arts and juris doctor degrees from Berkeley and, in addition to her career as a journalist, had spent two decades as a labor lawyer, according to her Post profile.

"If you cross him, oppose him, criticize him, you are a nasty guy or a dummy or a loser, whether you are a reporter or governor or federal judge with lifetime tenure. Trump uses his megaphone to seek to intimidate you as you do your job" said *Washington Post* columnist Ruth Marcus,[87] who had herself appeared in a Trump tweet, in which he exclaimed "She is 3rd rate, a total dummy!" Of comedian Rosie O'Donnell, with whom Trump had long publicly feuded, he said in December 2014, "@Rosie is a mentally sick woman, a bully, a dummy and, above all, a loser. Other than that she is just wonderful!" Another "dummy" woman, according to Trump, was Arianna Huffington, president and editor in chief of the Huffington Post Media Group. Yet another critical female journalist whose intelligence he called into question for her opposition was Mika Brzezinski of MSNBC, whom he variously declared "a ditzy airhead" and a "not very bright mess." When Peggy Noonan, Pulitzer Prize winning columnist for the *Wall Street Journal* and former speech writer for President Reagan, urged Congress to censure Trump for attempting to obstruct FBI Director Mueller's investigation of him, Trump called her "a simplistic writer" who "has no idea what is happening" and "never understood" what was happening with the case.[88] And, of Speaker Pelosi (D-CA), Trump said on April 19, 2020, "Nervous Nancy is an inherently 'dumb' person. She wasted all of her time on the Impeachment Hoax. She will be overthrown, either by inside or out." As to the contention that such words can lead to action and violence, it is notable that, in January of 2021, when insurrectionists stormed the U.S. Capitol in hopes of disrupting the counting of electoral votes, many in the crowd called for Pelosi's assassination and publicly expressed the intent to kill her,[89] including members of the far-right group Proud Boys and individual men, later brought into custody, from New York, Georgia, and Colorado. Trump assailed Pelosi's intelligence and much more in hundreds of tweets over a period of years, contributing to her being targeted with vitriolic coverage and threats.

Trump exhibited a noted propensity to attack the intelligence of women and people of color.[90] Women labeled "not smart" or "not very smart" in Trump tweets include comedian Rosie O'Donnell and former reality television *Celebrity Apprentice* contestant and later political aide to President Trump, Omarosa Manigault Newman, both of whom were regular targets of his ire, appearing by name in sixty-six and sixty-nine of his tweets, respectively. He also said that the four young congresswomen who make up "the Squad"—Alexandria Ocasio-Cortez (D-NY) (also known as

AOC), Rashida Tlaib (D-MI), Ayanna Pressley (D-MA), and Ilhan Omar (D-MN)—were "a very Racist group of troublemakers who are young, inexperienced and not very smart."[91] In January 2020, he retweeted conservative talk show host Mark Levin, who said "AOC is such an embarrassing, barely literate moron."

In August 2018, Trump tweeted that "Lebron James was just interviewed by the dumbest man on television, Don Lemon. He made Lebron look smart, which isn't easy to do." Famed basketball player James had opined in an interview with CNN anchor Lemon (both African Americans) that the president had caused racial divisions in America, evidently provoking Trump's retaliatory remark.[92] Its resonance—retweeted more than fifty thousand times, more than any other Trump tweet calling someone "dumb"[93]—is evidence of the acceptability of such sentiments among the American public, as is Trump's substantial following despite his ongoing diatribe of insults, many with evident racist and sexist overtones. As was the case when Trump sought to label any adversary in derogatory fashion, his jibes at women and people of color were retaliatory and repetitive, for maximum effect. He repeated his "dumbest man on television" line about Don Lemon in half a dozen tweets, and his "low IQ" characterization of Maxine Waters more often than that, including at rallies to cheering crowds.[94]

Looks and Loathsomeness

"When she walked in front of me, believe me, I wasn't impressed" candidate Trump said of his opponent, Hillary Clinton, at a North Carolina campaign event in October 2016, after some had commented on his lurking presence, pacing and following behind her as she spoke during the second presidential debate.[95] "Did Trump Just Say He 'Wasn't Impressed' by Clinton's Butt?" asked one subsequent headline.[96] It might seem like an odd question to ask in the context of a presidential debate, but on Twitter and elsewhere, Trump had long taken a critical, appraising stance toward women and made disparaging remarks, particularly about the appearance of those who challenged or criticized him. In general, female candidates have been found to be subject to more media attention and editorializing based on their appearance.[97] In an interview with *Rolling Stone*, Trump was described as having taken a tone of "disgust" when describing Carly Fiorina, contender for the 2016 Republican presidential nomination and former CEO of Hewlett-Packard; "Look at that face. . . . Would anyone vote for that?" he said of Fiorina.[98] As the former owner of the Miss

Universe, Miss USA, and Miss Teen USA beauty pageants, Trump had presided over official venues for scoring women on their looks, and he made a habit of doing so outside of that role. Without any particular provocation, he said supermodel Heidi Klum was "no longer a 10."[99] Trump also declared former Miss Universe winner Alicia Machado "disgusting," and called her "Miss Piggy" and "Miss Housekeeping" (ostensibly disparaging her ethnicity, as the Venezuelan-born model had become a U.S. citizen) accusing her, without evidence, of having made a sex tape after she accused Trump of racist and sexist behavior during the Miss Universe pageants.[100] Trump opined that Arianna Huffington, founder and editor of the HuffPost, a news outlet that often includes coverage critical of him, "is unattractive both inside and out," adding in retributive fashion, "I fully understand why her former husband left her for a man—he made a good decision."[101] Trump also countered claims of sexual assault made against him by multiple women by implying that the accusers were too unattractive to assault[102] or not his type, perpetuating the false notion that rape is about attraction rather than an expression of power through sexual behavior with the intent to demean or defile victims.[103] Experts note that calling victims "too ugly to rape" not only adds literal insult to injury, but also contributes to keeping women silent about the attacks they have experienced.[104]

Despite his ongoing onslaught of insults, Trump rarely used the specific word "ugly" in his tweets in relation to a woman. Of the fifty times the word appeared in his tweets between April 2012 and December 2020, he applied it to women only twice. His April 2014 tweet describing Arianna Huffington as "ugly both inside and out" also declared the purchase of AOL by the *Huffington Post* "a disaster" (thereby also criticizing her business acumen). In October 2012, he hit back at his longtime critic Bette Midler, saying: "@BetteMidler talks about my hair but I'm not allowed to talk about her ugly face or body—so I won't. Is this a double standard?" In 2013, he twice tweeted that Cher, actress, singer, and longtime Trump critic, was "the 4th ugliest celebrity." More than thirty mentions of the word "ugly," however, referred to wind turbines, likely in relation to their impact on the views from his golf course in Scotland, where he fought a years-long, losing legal battle with the government there to scuttle construction of an offshore wind farm.[105]

Trump's attacks on women's looks were usually retaliatory. Beyond calling them unattractive, Trump also characterized women who spoke out against him as repugnant or loathsome, labeling them foul-mouthed or disgusting or likening them to animals. On July 19, 2019, he called U.S.

representative Ilhan Omar of Minnesota "foul mouthed" in a tweet that also claimed that she was greeted by a "tiny staged crowd" when she was met by hundreds of supporters at the Minneapolis–St. Paul Airport. Her supporters had come out to welcome her home after Trump was criticized for his supporters chanting, "Send her back!" at his campaign rally in North Carolina the same week.[106] On August 31, 2019, he tweeted that Omarosa Manigault Newman, who is African American, was "disgusting and foul mouthed" and noted in the same tweet that he was "suing various people for violating their confidentiality agreements" after she wrote a book that characterized him as racist and incompetent.[107] His raising the nondisclosure agreement as a threat illustrates how such agreements are often used as mechanisms for silencing women.[108] On September 8, 2019, Trump complained about model Chrissy Teigen, whom he identified only as the "filthy mouthed wife" of musician John Legend, for failing to give him credit for criminal justice reform,[109] thus exhibiting another rhetorical tactic of his, the erasure of women by failing to mention them by name.

Assailing women's looks or calling them filthy or foul—especially with regard to what comes out of their mouths in speaking back to prevailing authority—can be seen as a means of "policing or enforcing" patriarchal order[110] by flagging how they are not conforming to a conventional ideal of femininity, which values submission, relative silence, acceptance of traditional gender roles, and a pleasing prettiness. In retribution, and as a means of muzzling them, powerful women are often portrayed as repugnant—variously depicted as nasty, ugly, disgusting, and rude, to name just a few of the descriptors President Trump deployed from his Twitter platform.

Disgust is a powerful human emotion that plays a role in the law, according to philosopher Martha Nussbaum, who has been called the "most prominent female philosopher in America."[111] Alluding to women as disgusting, according to Nussbaum, calls to mind a historical tactic of creating a deliberate construction of subordinate groups in ways that serve a political goal,[112] usually to disempower or provoke aggression against them. Trump has described women who threaten his authority as *nasty*, the dictionary definition of which includes "physically filthy, disgustingly unclean"; "offensive to taste or smell, nauseating"; and "indecent, or obscene."[113] Deploying the term *nasty* more than sixty times in his tweets by the end of 2020, Trump targeted various women, including Hillary Clinton, when she challenged him in a debate; Nancy Pelosi, when she called for his impeachment; Mette Frederiksen, prime minister of Denmark, when she called his proposal to buy Greenland absurd; and Duchess of Sussex Meghan Markle, when she referred to Trump as misogynistic.[114]

At a Republican debate in 2015, then Fox News host Megyn Kelly asked Trump whether he was sexist, given the language he had used to talk about women over the years. "Kelly asked Trump about comments in which he called women he didn't like 'fat pigs, dogs, slobs, and disgusting animals . . . made disparaging comments about women's looks' and told a contestant on *Celebrity Apprentice* that 'it would be a pretty picture to see her on her knees.'"[115] Trump retaliated afterward, saying that during Kelly's "ridiculous" questioning, which he deemed "nasty" and "unfair," "You could see there was blood coming out of her eyes, blood coming out of her—wherever."[116] The widely criticized comment seemed to imply that Kelly was visibly menstruating, an absurd point but one that makes reference to a defining characteristic of womanhood for which women have been banished from public forums in various historical and cultural contexts. In another incident, Trump, after being criticized by Mika Brzezinski, recounted an incident in which he claims she was "bleeding badly from a facelift."[117]

During a deposition in 2011, Trump reportedly called a breastfeeding mother—an attorney representing clients who lost money to him in a real estate deal—"disgusting."[118] When she said that she needed a break to pump breast milk, Trump angrily left the proceeding, spitting the insult at her and halting his testimony for the day.[119] Objecting to the presence of lactating mothers in public and seeing lactation as disgusting has been a mechanism for limiting women's public engagement; it wasn't until 2018 that breastfeeding in public became legal in all fifty states, and some breastfeeding mothers are still asked to leave or cover up in public spaces.[120] Breastfeeding, perceived by some as indecent, sometimes "makes others uncomfortable, evokes disgust, and triggers paternalistic moralizing," resulting in censure, whether legal or social, that causes those practicing it to have less than equal access to public spaces like workplaces, parks, or stores.[121] Trump's revulsion toward the practice might also have had policy consequences: in 2018, the Trump administration's delegation to the World Health Assembly in Geneva opposed a resolution to "protect, promote and support breast-feeding," though their primary purpose for the position was likely in support of infant formula manufacturers.[122]

Misogyny and disgust are closely aligned, and, in many cultures, male disgust with female bodily fluids has been tied up with measures to isolate and punish women.[123] The basis of such measures, according to

Nussbaum in her book *Hiding from Humanity: Disgust, Shame and the Law*, is often an aversion to bodily fluids, expressed in taboos about sex, birth, and menstruation.[124] Referring to women as disgusting and, in particular, to instances of women lactating or bleeding, can trigger this base response of revulsion. The United Nations Population Fund notes that globally, women and girls are subject to taboos surrounding menstruation that contribute to their vulnerability to serious human rights concerns and gender discrimination.[125] In Nepal, the practice of banning menstruating women from sleeping in the home, consigning them to often unsafe outdoor huts because of the belief that menstruation is "spiritually polluting," persists despite a government ban.[126] In the United States, one aspect of the women's movement since 2016 has been to challenge laws that stigmatize menstruation, including tampon taxes, limited access to feminine hygiene products for students and prisoners, and insufficient reproductive health education that leads to entrenched period myths.[127]

Referring to women as disgusting, particularly with reference to their "spewing" something objectionable, can be seen as evoking ideas of their uncleanliness or unfitness to be out in the public sphere, no less in positions of leadership. Most societies have some form of social hierarchy in which disgust historically played an intrinsic role, with some seen as tainted, low, and associated with contamination; women, Jews, people of color, and immigrants have variously filled this role.[128] So Trump's tweet storm in July 2019, in which he claimed that four progressive congresswomen known as "the Squad" were "spewing some of the most vile, hateful, and disgusting things ever said by a politician in the House or Senate" and declaring them to be "running on an agenda that is disgusting" ought not be seen in a historical or cultural vacuum. "So many people are angry at them & their horrible & disgusting actions!" he said during a five-day period (July 14–19), in which he labeled them "disgusting" in half a dozen tweets.

The "Squad"—Congresswomen Omar, Ocasio-Cortez, Tlaib, and Pressley—had all been elected to the House during the 2018 midterm elections. Together, they comprised a series of notable firsts in the U.S. Congress—the first Muslim women (Omar and Tlaib); first woman to wear a hijab in Congress (Omar); youngest woman, at twenty-eight, ever elected to Congress (Ocasio-Cortez); and the first Black woman from Massachusetts to ever win a House seat (Pressley).[129] After winning office, Representative Pressley asserted the need to "be disruptive in our democracy and our policymaking and how we run and win elections," noting that wins such as hers and that of Representative Ocasio-Cortez "challenge narratives about who has a right to run and when, and who can win."[130] Labeling their criticisms of the political status quo as "vile and disgusting statements," Trump said that members of "the Squad" were "Anti-America" and "hate-filled extremists" whom he admonished to "go back and help fix the totally broken and crime infested places from which they came," thereby implying not only that they were not American citizens,[131] but that they have origins in places prone to "infestation"—a word that evokes vermin—in keeping with his "yearslong campaign to paint immigrants as subhuman."[132] Yet all members of the Squad were born in the United States, except for Ilhan Omar, who came to the country as a refugee from Somalia as a child some thirty years ago and is a naturalized citizen.[133] Though it is clear that these women legitimately hold power as democratically elected representatives, the president's feigned or willful ignorance of their origins seemed to play well with his political base, who coined the Twitter hashtag #SendHerBack. Speaking from the White House lawn in July 2019, Trump referred to Representative Omar as a "terrorist sympathizer"—sparking concern for her safety and condemnation from House Democrats, including the chair of the House Homeland Security Committee, Representative Bennie Thompson, who asked for an emergency meeting of the Capitol police urging the reevaluation of security procedures.[134] Representative Ocasio-Cortez was also subject to assassination threats associated with the January 2021 insurrection, resulting in at least one arrest by the FBI.[135] Once again, calling women disgusting can be associated with the constraint of their autonomous actions—in this case, due to the threat of violence against them.

Disgust, in addition to being raised with regard to women exercising leadership or political power, is often leveled at people of color, regardless of gender, and the places from which they come. In July 2019, Trump tweeted that Representative Elijah Cummings, who had criticized the Trump administration's actions on the southern border, presided over a district (Baltimore) "FAR WORSE and more dangerous."[136] Cummings's district, Trump said, "is a disgusting, rat and rodent infested mess" in a tweet on July 27, 2019. "If he spent more time in Baltimore, maybe he could help clean up this very dangerous & filthy place." In a tweet on December 26, 2019, Trump referred to Nancy Pelosi's "filthy dirty District" in apparent retaliation for her role in his impeachment proceedings.[137]

Referring to women and people of color as being so unattractive or loathsome as to warrant disdain or as being from places of infestation is to suggest that they are inhuman. According to philosopher Kate Manne,

"Dehumanizing speech can function to *intimidate, insult, demean, belittle*, and so on since it helps itself to certain powerfully encoded *social meanings*,"[138] implying that "subordinated people are . . . brutes, subhuman, or even nonhuman animals."[139] In some cases, that implication has been made explicitly: Trump referred to Stormy Daniels, to whom he paid $130,000 in hush money to suppress information about a sexual encounter they had, as "Horseface" after her defamation lawsuit against him was dismissed; called Omarosa Manigault Newman, "That dog" after she was ousted from the administration and threatened to provide evidence of Trump having used racial slurs; and defended calling comedian and long-time critic Rosie O'Donnell a "fat pig."[140] When MSNBC host Nicolle Wallace called sexual assault allegations against Joe Biden "a smear campaign" by the right, Trump reacted by lashing out in a tweet calling her a "3rd-rate lapdog." Male political opponents and critics of Trump's have also been subject to this treatment. Of Senator Mitt Romney (R-UT), Trump tweeted in June 2016 that he "had his chance to beat a failed president but he choked like a dog. Now he calls me racist—but I am [the] least racist person there is." And in March 2016, he said "@DavidGregory got thrown off of TV by NBC, fired like a dog! Now he is on @CNN being nasty to me. Not nice!"

In addition to explicitly likening a person to a dog or other animal, the use of some language evokes references to animality, such as referring to people as rabid or vicious. For instance, Trump has referred to Representative Ilhan Omar (D-MN) as a "rabid anti-Semite" (July 10, 2019). He accused Lesley Stahl of the television news show *60 Minutes* of a "vicious attempted 'takeout' interview" in October 2020, while branding his own responses as "full, flowing and magnificently brilliant." In July 2019, Trump tweeted a sarcastic thank you to "the vicious young Socialist Congresswomen" whom he credited with his poll numbers going up by four points in a Rasmussen poll. In August 2018, he referred to Omarosa Manigault Newman as "vicious, but not smart" when she accused him of being racist and using the "N-word."[141] Hillary Clinton is another rival at whom the charge of being vicious was leveled, in July 2016 as the presidential campaign was progressing. And, of a woman who sued him for cheating her in a Chicago real estate deal in 2013, Trump tweeted in May of that year, when the case was settled in his favor, that "The so called 87 year old 'lady' was a vicious and skilled investor who was trying to rip me off with made up facts and a blowhard lawyer." Interestingly, Trump relented on likening his white male presidential opponent in the 2020 election cycle to an animal; he tweeted in November 2020 that "Joe Biden may be Sleepy and Very Slow, but he is not a 'rabid dog.' He is actually somewhat better than that, but I am the only one who can get you where you have to be."

Regardless of whom such dehumanizing speech is leveled at, its purpose seems to be to delegitimize them. For some, though, based on their race, ethnicity, sexual orientation, or gender, being likened to an animal or characterized as repugnant has the potential to be particularly damaging, as this is a trope that can evoke deep-seated historical prejudices and stereotypes.

Emotional State

"The belief that women are more emotional than men is one of the strongest gender stereotypes held in Western cultures," according to Victoria Brescoll, assistant professor of organizational behavior at Yale School of Management and fellow at the Women and Public Policy Program at Harvard's Kennedy School of Government.[142] A principle point of interest from her research, from the point of view of this analysis, is that "gender stereotypes of emotion present a fundamental barrier to women's ability to ascend to and succeed in leadership roles" by calling into question their competence or mental stability.[143] Emotional state is one of the six categories of descriptors identified in the course of our analysis of Trump's Twitter insults, and it includes a few more than a dozen words ranging alphabetically from *angry* and *crazed* to *vicious* and *wacky*. Pointing out the ways in which women are purportedly acting out emotionally or are mentally unstable can be an effective strategy in raising doubts about their leadership potential and engendering dislike or ill will for them among the public. Research has shown, for instance, that men who express anger in professional contexts actually experience an increase in status and hireability, whereas women who do so experience a diminishment in status and perceived competence.[144]

In 2016 Trump labeled three people "neurotic" in his tweets, all of them women: *New York Times* columnist Maureen Dowd, MSNBC host Mika Brzezinski, and U.S. Congresswoman Debbie Wasserman Schultz (D-FL), all of whom had been regularly critical of Trump in their respective spheres of influence. For her part, Dowd had expressed concern about violence at Trump rallies, saying that the president enjoyed the excitement of it.[145] In response, Trump tweeted "Crazy Maureen Dowd, the wacky columnist for the failing @nytimes, pretends she knows me well— wrong!" and "Wacky @NYTimesDowd, who hardly knows me, makes up things that I never said for her boring interviews and column. A neurotic dope!" (Dowd's reproof of Trump fomenting violence among groups of his followers proved to sound more prescient than neurotic after the January 2021 storming of the U.S. Capitol.) Together, these messages were retweeted nine thousand times. And, as an example of how traditional media amplified Trump's tweets and the rhetorical associations he created in them, a headline in *The Hill* just after Dowd was so labeled announced, "Trump Blasts 'Neurotic' New York Times Columnist."[146]

In his nineteen tweeted mentions of someone having a "meltdown," four referred to two different women who were among his favorite targets—Nancy Pelosi and Omarosa Manigault Newman. The dictionary definition of a meltdown is "a breakdown of self-control (as from fatigue or overstimulation)."[147] A tweet exclaiming "Nervous Nancy's unhinged meltdown!" on October 16, 2019, was precipitated by Speaker Pelosi and other Democratic leaders walking out of a White House briefing on Trump's decision to withdraw U.S. troops from Syria; Senator Chuck Schumer (D-NY) related that they had left after the meeting devolved into a diatribe of insults, during which the president called Pelosi a "third-rate politician" and said former defense secretary General James Mattis was "the world's most overrated general."[148] The meeting was the first time Trump and Pelosi had interacted face to face since the launch of the impeachment inquiry led by Pelosi the previous month.[149] In the tweet calling her "unhinged," Trump included a photo of Pelosi, standing at the table of two dozen or so seated men, including the president, her arm outstretched, finger pointed in his direction, looking like she is literally and metaphorically standing up to him. This and other iconic photos of Pelosi appearing to serve Trump his comeuppance exemplifies why Pelosi gained hero status among his feminist opponents and became a key target of ongoing, virulent right-wing attacks.[150]

In an open letter to President Trump, Michigan's attorney general, Dana Nessel, publicly admonished him in advance of his visit to the Ford Motor Company in Ypsilanti, to wear a face mask during his tour of the plant there.[151] By the time of his planned visit to Michigan in May 2020, several months into the coronavirus pandemic, he had yet to be seen wearing a mask in public and so was flouting the advice of his own public health officials. Trump's purpose in visiting the plant was to showcase how manufacturers had pivoted to making ventilators at the behest of his administration, which had received widespread criticism for its insufficient response to the unfolding public health crisis. In spite of, or perhaps in spiteful response to, the letter from Michigan's highest law enforcement official reminding him of his legal, social and moral responsibility to comply with state law to prevent further spread of the virus, Trump refused to wear a mask in public view at the plant, saying he didn't want to give the press the satisfaction.[152] Afterward, Attorney General Nessel called Trump a "petulant child who refuses to follow the rules," adding that he would no longer be welcomed in Michigan.[153]

Turning to a favored outlet of his for retribution, Trump tweeted "The Wacky Do Nothing Attorney General of Michigan, Dana Nessel, is viciously threatening Ford Motor Company for the fact that I inspected a Ventilator plant without a mask. Not their fault, & I did put on a mask. No wonder many auto companies left Michigan, until I came along!" This and another tweet within two days in May 2020 mentioning "The Wacky Do Nothing Attorney General of Michigan, Dana Nessel" were retweeted a total of fifty-eight thousand times. Mainstream media also amplified this by repeating the tagline in headlines and news stories.[154] Nessel's purportedly vicious threat was to warn that she intended to have a "very serious conversation" with Ford for bending the rules for the president.[155] The legal requirement to wear a mask in enclosed spaces in Michigan had been established by executive order of Governor Gretchen Whitmer,[156] who had criticized the Trump administration's response to the pandemic as insufficient in the months preceding his visit. All the Michigan leaders with whom Trump had been sparring over the incident, "namely the governor, the secretary of state and the attorney general, were female Democrats."[157]

According to *Merriam-Webster*, the definition of "wacky" is "absurdly or amusingly eccentric or irrational: *crazy*." The etymology of the word derives from the idea of the mental state that results from being whacked on the head too many times. From October 2015 through November 2020, Trump tweets contained this word on twenty occasions, thirteen of which referred to six different women, half of whom were people of color, with seven tweets aimed at several men. This descriptor is demonstrably used more frequently for women than for men in Trump's lexicon of insults. "AOC is a Wack Job!" Trump tweeted in October 2019 (and was retweeted twenty-three thousand times) about Representative Ocasio-Cortez (D-NY). In 2018, Omarosa Manigault Newman wrote a memoir in which she claimed that Donald Trump had used explicit racial epithets both during and before his time in the White House.[158] After the book's release on August 12, 2018, Trump tweeted four times the next day about "Wacky Omarosa," whom he also labeled as a "lowlife" who was "not smart" and had "begged" him for a job, with "tears in her eyes."[159] In October 2017, Trump called Representative Frederica Wilson (D-Florida), who is African American, "wacky" three times over the course of four days after she criticized Trump on October 18 for how he spoke with a grieving widow of a service member who had been killed in an ambush in Niger; it was reported that Trump told widow Myeshia Johnson that her husband "knew what he had signed up for," and referred to him repeatedly as "her guy" rather than by his name, Sergeant La David T. Johnson.[160]

To be sure, Trump also questioned the emotional state of male adversaries. Prior to his term in office, for instance, he twice expressed concern that President Obama would "do something irrational and dangerous for our country in order to save face" (September 13, 2013 and April 25, 2014). And he took pains to brand MSNBC host Joe Scarborough as "Psycho Joe," tweeting about him with that moniker eighteen times between June 2017 and August 2020. The most concerning of these latter incidents involved the president promoting a conspiracy theory accusing Scarborough of murder, after Scarborough criticized the White House's coronavirus response in May 2020.[161] The intent of conjuring conspiracy theories casting political opponents as villainously "psycho" or merely calling their rationality into question seems to have been to discredit them or do reputational damage that would render them less effective critics.

Casting aspersions on the emotional state of women and calling their rationality or sanity into question references a time-honored and resonant stereotype that can raise disqualifying questions about women operating in the public sphere. Some popular press articles in the last decade or so have acknowledged the role of calling women crazy in delegitimizing them, silencing them, and keeping them in line.[162] Trump used the term *crazy* in his tweets over three hundred times, and he hurled this particular insult most often at one woman—Nancy Pelosi. In an apparent effort to have her speak out less often or to be seen as less credible when doing so, Trump undertook a campaign to associate her name with a smattering of discrediting insults, many of which played upon cultural constructs of women's emotional frailty or volatility, including angry (one tweet, twenty-one thousand retweets); unhinged (one tweet, thirty-one thousand retweets); having a meltdown (one tweet, forty-two thousand retweets); something wrong with her "upstairs" (two tweets, eighty-four thousand retweets); nervous (twenty tweets, 460 thousand retweets), and crazy (about fifty tweets and over 1.4 million retweets).

Necessary Qualification (Competence)

Competence is defined as "the ability to do something successfully or efficiently"[163] with sufficient knowledge, judgment, or skill. Trump's attack tweets variously aimed at undercutting his adversaries by questioning their emotional state, intelligence, stature, trustworthiness, or overall competence. In this category of insults, necessary qualifications, this analysis identifies words that cast doubt on their subject's capabilities, including the terms *bad judgment, failing, ineffective, no talent,* or just plain *incompetent.* As with the other categories of descriptors, competence has gendered implications. The prevalence of political gender stereotypes is well documented and shows that women can be seen as competent in communal areas like education and health care, but men are seen as more competent in all other issue areas, particularly national security.[164]

"Incompetent Hillary, despite the horrible attack in Brussels today, wants borders to be weak and open—and let the Muslims flow in. No way!" tweeted Trump on March 22, 2015 (retweeted eleven thousand times). In other tweets declaring his presidential campaign rival incompetent, he referenced her handling of ISIS and Iran. In the run-up to the presidential debates, on October 9, he tweeted "#CrookedHillary has FAILED all over the world! #BigLeagueTruth #Debates2016." He repeated the phrase "failed all over the world" in another tweet, listing Libya, Syria, Iraq, and Benghazi, and mentioned Benghazi alone in seventy other tweets. In January 2016, Trump tweeted "Hillary Clinton is a major national security risk. Not presidential material!" and, in October, he added, "@HillaryClinton's Careless Use Of A Secret Server Put National Security At Risk." Seeming to have an intuitive grasp of what could be discrediting, especially for women, Trump's barrage of insults via Twitter included declarations of Clinton as "ineffective," "not capable," having "bad judgment," and "unfit to serve the country." A Hillary Clinton presidency, Trump said "would be catastrophic for the future of our country" (June 28, 2016) and a "disaster for jobs and the economy" (June 21, 2016), and called the sixty-seventh U.S. secretary of State and former U.S. senator (D-NY) "totally incompetent as a manager and leader" with "no strength or stamina to be #POTUS!" (November 20, 2015).

In Trump's jabs at critics, he frequently called into question the competence of female politicians, journalists, and celebrities. He labeled Nancy Pelosi "an incompetent, third-rate politician," and "a totally incompetent... weak and pathetic puppet" (April 16, 2020). In July 2019, he said her district in San Francisco was "failing badly" and suggested that she "stop wasting time on the Witch Hunt Hoax"—one of his preferred characterizations of the impeachment efforts against him—"and start focusing on our Country!" Of rival Senator Elizabeth Warren (D-MA), Trump said she was a "Seriously failed presidential candidate" (June 11, 2020) and remarked in May 2016, ironically, given his near constant commentary on Twitter, "Isn't it funny when a failed Senator like goofy Elizabeth Warren can spend a whole day tweeting about Trump & gets nothing done in Senate?" In total, Trump referred to Warren as goofy twenty-three times on Twitter, with a combined total of over one hundred thousand retweets, and the moniker was dutifully repeated in the press, as evidenced by the CNN headline "Donald Trump Hits Back at 'Goofy' Elizabeth Warren."[165]

Trump frequently called into question the necessary qualifications of women whose public service credentials easily surpassed his own. In addition to rivals in the House and Senate, Trump took on Supreme Court Justice Ruth Bader Ginsburg in July 2016 after she publicly expressed concern, in a series of interviews, about the possibility of his assuming the presidency, calling him a "faker."[166] When, he wondered, would the Supreme Court Justice of almost three decades "apologize to me for her misconduct? Big mistake by an incompetent judge!" "Justice Ginsburg of the U.S. Supreme Court has embarrassed all by making very dumb political statements about me. Her mind is shot—resign!" he tweeted on July 13, 2016, with ten thousand retweets. On August 6, 2020, he said that U.S. deputy attorney general Sally Yates was "either lying or grossly incompetent" after she refused to enforce the president's Muslim travel ban, which she said was unconstitutional—a position for which she was fired.[167] He also, in what would eventually be revealed as an ironic turn of events, called out "badly failing presidential candidate @KamalaHarris" in a tweet touting that he himself had "recieved [sic] a major award" of some kind (October 26, 2019). And, years before becoming president, he said, upon the troubled rollout of Obama Care, that then secretary of health and human services and former Kansas governor Kathleen Sebelius was "so sad and pathetic that I almost feel sorry" for her. "She has done great harm to many people and must be fired. Incompetent!" (November 2013).

In addition to targeting women wielding power at the federal level, Trump consistently took aim at various female state and local level officials. Mayor Muriel Bowser "is grossly incompetent, and in no way qualified to be running an important city like Washington, D.C.," he spat out in a series of three tweets between June 5 and 6, 2020. Bowser, "who's [sic] budget is totally out of control and is constantly coming back to us for 'handouts'" according to these tweets, seems to have provoked the president's ire by the unveiling on June 5 of the Black Lives Matter mural painted on Sixteenth Street, just across from the White House, and the announced renaming of that section of the street as "Black Lives Matter Plaza."[168] Governor Gretchen Whitmer was similarly assailed by Trump as the "Failing Michigan Governor" who "must work harder and be much more proactive. We are pushing her to get the job done," he tweeted on March 17, 2020; ten days later he said, "Governor, Gretchen 'Half' Whitmer is way in over her head, she doesn't have a clue. Likes blaming everyone for her own ineptitude! #MAGA." His remarks seem to have been prompted in this case by Whitmer's call for the federal government to provide more support to the states in responding to the coronavirus pandemic, and asserting that the federal government was unprepared for it,[169] an oft repeated assessment that characterized his administration's response as bungled and inadequate.[170] As Whitmer repeatedly pursued federal support and called for transparency in the handling of the national supply of ventilators and personal protective equipment, Trump said he had a "big problem" with the "young, a woman governor."[171] In September, Whitmer remarked that Trump was a "threat to the American people" after he was reported, in an interview with veteran journalist Bob Woodward, to having admitted to downplaying the threat posed by the coronavirus at the outset of the pandemic in the early months of 2020.[172] This contributed to making it the leading cause of death in the United States by December 2020, with almost three thousand COVID-19 deaths occurring every 1.5 days, according to the *Journal of the American Medical Association*.[173] Yet, at a rally hours after her statement, Trump repeated that Whitmer "doesn't have a clue" about the coronavirus or the economy, and said Michigan would be better off if the state "had a governor who knew what the hell she was doing."[174]

Trump's penchant for browbeating his critics, particularly women and people of color, was also evident in his ongoing harassment of San Juan mayor Carmen Yulín Cruz, who had been a vocal critic since the administration's response to Hurricane Maria in Puerto Rico in 2017.[175] In September 2018, as another hurricane was anticipated, Trump complained "We got A Pluses for our recent hurricane work in Texas and Florida (and did an unappreciated great job in Puerto Rico, even though an inaccessible island with very poor electricity and a totally incompetent Mayor of San Juan)," even though nearly three thousand people died and the island was without power for months in the wake of the storm there.[176] On the morning of August 28, 2019 he tweeted, "We are tracking closely tropical storm Dorian as it heads, as usual, to Puerto Rico. FEMA and all others are ready, and will do a great job. When they do, let them know it, and give them a big Thank You—Not like last time. That includes from the incompetent Mayor of San Juan!" Shortly after, he declared Puerto Rico to be "one of the most corrupt places on earth" with what he called a "broken" political system with politicians who "are either Incompetent or Corrupt." "Congress approved Billions of Dollars last time, more than anyplace else has ever gotten, and it is sent to Crooked Pols. No good!" he concluded. When protests broke out in Puerto Rico calling for Governor Ricardo Rosselló to resign in July 2019, Trump tweeted, "A lot of bad things are happening in Puerto Rico. The Governor is under siege, the Mayor of San Juan is a despicable and incompetent person who I wouldn't trust under any circumstance, and the United States Congress foolishly gave 92 Billion Dollars for hurricane relief." Earlier in 2019, Trump tweeted, "The crazed and incompetent Mayor of San Juan have [sic] done such a poor job of bringing the Island back to health. 91 Billion Dollars to Puerto Rico, and now the Dems want to give them more, taking dollars away from our Farmers and so many others. Disgraceful!" (April 1, 2019).

Trump's treatment of Carmen Yulín Cruz and others illustrates some central themes from his playbook of insults. As president of the United States, Trump wielded outsized power relative to virtually any would-be critic. Any disparaging tweet of his was bound to be amplified in the press, which regularly repeated his language verbatim in headline news in print and broadcast. His questioning of the competencies of his critics became the story, sometimes leaving their original criticisms of Trump's own shortcomings or underperformance drowned out or under examined. While it is not possible to know his intent with certainty, the tweets appear to have been fired off in both retributive and preemptive fashion. For those who dared to criticize the president, he hit back hard with personal and eviscerating language designed to discredit and undermine—and he'd hold a grudge long after the original altercation, repeatedly raising his bullying branding to continue eluding culpability for his own actions and inadequacies as events unfolded across time. In the face of natural disasters like Hurricane Maria or national crises like the COVID-19 pandemic, Trump tried to paint his detractors with the very adjectives that might easily have applied to himself, including, with regard to necessary qualifications, charges of being inept, ineffective, failing, or incompetent. Drawing upon long-standing and viscerally held stereotypes about women, minorities, and people with less economic or political authority, his insults could gain traction with the help of confirmation bias elicited from sometimes latent discriminatory beliefs. Like students in a schoolyard watching a bully savage a fellow classmate, the public often stood idly by, entertained by the spectacle, sometimes snickering or egging him on but rarely, if ever, reining him in or coming to the aid of the victim—and often, perhaps, thankful the abuse was directed at someone other than themselves.

Journalists who have the power to persuade often came under fire in Trump's tweets if they publicly called his behavior into question. This was the personal front of his wider-scale war on the media, which he labeled with the "fake news" moniker in nearly one thousand tweets. As for individual journalists, he called *New York Times* columnist Gail Collins "Frumpy and very dumb . . . lucky to even have a job . . . incompetent!" (March 2014). When White House correspondent Maggie Haberman reported that Trump was dissatisfied with press coverage of his visits to Dayton and El Paso to see mass shooting victims in August 2019, he twice tweeted about her "fake reporting" for the "failing" *New York Times*. According to the Times report, the president was angry he had not received adequate or sufficiently positive press on these trips and had "screamed at his aides to begin producing proof that in El Paso, people were happy to see him."[177] *Failing* was a favored descriptor of Trump's for any opponent mounting a legitimate challenge—a term he tweeted a total of 260 times, about half of which referred to the *New York Times* specifically. Trump had earlier referred to Haberman, who was part of a team awarded a Pulitzer Prize for reporting on Trump's Russia connections, as "a third rate reporter" when, in 2018, she predicted (accurately, as it turns out) that his lawyer Michael Cohen would turn against him as he faced federal criminal charges.[178] Trump also repeatedly attacked NBC News correspondent Katy Tur, calling her "Little Katy, third-rate journalist" at a rally in December 2015, and telling her to "be quiet" in a news conference the following summer when she questioned whether he had "qualms about 'asking a foreign government . . . to hack into a system of anybody's in this country' after Trump said he hoped Russia would find more emails from Hillary Clinton or the DNC."[179]

Other female reporters whose competencies he questioned included Jennifer Rubin of the *Washington Post*, whom he declared "highly untalented," and RealClearPolitics associate editor A. B. Stoddard, who said in a Fox News segment that Trump had had disastrous debate performances. "Could somebody at @foxnews please explain to Trump hater A.B. Stoddard (zero talent!) . . . that I won every one of my debates, from beginning to end," Trump tweeted in February 2020. And, exhibiting what some described as "particular ire for minority commentators," Trump said CNN contributor and Republican strategist Ana Navarro "has no talent" and "no TV persona" after she criticized him back in 2015.[180] Trump's advisor Roger Stone later referred to Navarro and her CNN colleague Roland Martin as "quota hires."[181] Of another female journalist critic, he said in November 2019, "Who the hell is Joy-Ann Reid? Never met her, she knows ZERO about me, has NO talent, and truly doesn't have the 'it' factor needed for success in showbiz. Had a bad reputation, and now works for the Comcast/NBC losers making up phony stories about me. Low Ratings. Fake News!" In September 2020, he called MSNBC host and correspondent Reid, who is African American, "very untalented" and said she "should be fired for this horrible use of the words "Muslim Terrorists." Such xenophobia and racism on MSDNC. Anyone else would be gone, and fast!!!" and was retweeted fourteen thousand times. At least one media report headlined Trump's criticism of Reid, leading with his quote before noting that she had not actually used the word "terrorists" and calling it a "misquote" rather than a lie or a smear, when she compared Trump's own followers to foreign extremists.[182] A *Daily Mail* headline read "Trump demands MSNBC fire 'very untalented' Joy Reid,"[183] just as in the previous year, when a story in *The Hill* led with "Trump lashes out at MSNBC's Joy Reid, claims she has 'NO talent,'"[184] which was shared more than thirty-three thousand times, thus broadly perpetuating Trump's preferred frame. About one-third of Trump's three dozen tweets calling someone untalented or no talent referred to women, led by comedian Rosie O'Donnell.

When veteran journalist Katie Couric issued an apology for a misleading scene that appeared in a documentary she made about gun violence in May 2016, Trump tweeted that she was "a third rate reporter, who has been largely forgotten, should be ashamed of herself for the fraudulent editing of her doc." *The Hill* repeated Trump's "Katie Couric should be ashamed" line in a headline,[185] illustrating the propensity of traditional media to advance Trump's damaging branding. Rather than making the story akin to a "truth sandwich," as suggested by Lakoff in order to avoid parroting Trump's over the top characterizations and lies,[186] reporting in this case played to Trump's apparent motives—to discredit media writ large and assail individual critics through personal and excoriating rhetorical attacks. Couric's misstep was to insert an eight-second pause in a video that made it appear as though some gun rights advocates had hesitated in response to a question, when they had, in fact, answered immediately.[187] Her apology, then, seems to have been appropriate. But Trump, who often demanded apologies and cast blame in shameful terms toward his detractors, was hard-pressed to ever admit wrongdoing or offer apologies for his own actions. This discrepancy in contrition and assignation of shame points to a double standard by which "women are treated much more harshly if ever they mess up," as noted by Mary Beard, professor of classics at Cambridge University, who has chronicled the evolution and suppression of women's power since the time of Ancient Greece.[188]

Trustworthiness

"The notion that women are fundamentally untrustworthy snakes through almost every area of our lives," notes feminist author Jessica Valenti, citing studies showing that employers distrust women requesting flextime and people thinking a woman's trustworthiness correlates with the amount of makeup she wears.[189] The widespread belief that women can't be trusted underpins policies that make it hard to report and prosecute sexual assault and domestic violence and fuels resistance to rape and incest exceptions in strict abortion laws.[190] The stereotype of women as untrustworthy has its roots in Greek and Judeo-Christian theology and is related to the pervasive myth that women lie about rape.[191] Referencing that stereotype by accusing women of lying, or being crooked or false, in other contexts can serve to undermine and discredit them, effectively blunting the power of their voice.

An inveterate liar himself, prone to exaggeration and braggadocio, Trump often called out purported falsehoods of his detractors. During the first three years of his presidency, he was shown to have lied more than sixteen thousand times—an average of five lies per day, at an exponentially escalating pace.[192] All presidents have lied at times, of course, but Trump could be said to have easily earned the honorific bestowed on him in one headline: "the King of Lies."[193] According to cultural anthropologist Carole McGranahan, "by all metrics and counting schemes, his lies are off the charts."[194] Such lies, McGranahan says, should be considered not just for their content and context, but for "the work that they do"; when "based on derogatory views of a specific group" their work on the part of the liars can be to convert prejudice to perceived truth, "and in so doing can enable violence, be it symbolic, structural, verbal, or physical."[195]

As Glenn Kessler notes in the introduction to his book *Donald Trump and His Assault on Truth*, social science has long established that people "are receptive to information that confirms their preconceived notions, especially when it comes to politics."[196] This might help explain why, just prior to the fall 2016 U.S. presidential election, an NBC/WSJ poll showed that voters considered Trump more "honest and straightforward" than Clinton by 10 points.[197] Given Trump's evident penchant for lying, it could be considered surprising that *liar* was the word most associated with Clinton, not Trump, in a poll of voters about presidential frontrunners prior to the 2016 election.[198]*Arrogant* was the word most cited to describe Trump in that same Quinnipiac poll.[199] In our own research on the prevalence of rape myths in social media dialog on Twitter in the fall of 2016, we inadvertently found that Clinton's name was associated with deceit and sexual assault twice as often as Trump's.[200] In a subsequent study on the gendered implications of fake news, we found that people are more likely to believe and share fake news stories about women than about men, especially when they leverage gendered stereotypes.[201]

Trump's branding of Clinton as "Crooked Hillary" in 366 tweets over four years and repeated in innumerable headlines and rally speeches could be said to have succeeded in exploiting this belief in the public mind, in part due to the long-standing historical notion that women lie. In the month of July 2016 alone, Trump tweeted, on the 6th, "Crooked Hillary has once again been proven to be a person who is dishonest, incompetent and of very bad judgement"; on the 16th, "Very sad that a person who has made so many mistakes, Crooked Hillary Clinton, can put out such false and vicious ads with her phony money!" and on the 26th, "The invention of email has proven to be a very bad thing for Crooked Hillary in that it has proven her to be both incompetent and a liar!" In total, Trump associated "Clinton" with the words *liar, lied,* and *lies* more than a dozen times, and dozens more with the terms *corrupt, criminal, dishonest,* and *fraud.*

On at least one occasion when Trump accused Clinton of lying, the veracity of her claim was questioned by others. On December 20, 2015, he said "Hillary Clinton spokesperson admitted that their [sic] was no ISIS video of me. Therefore, Hillary LIED at the debate last night. SAD!" In the third debate among Democratic presidential contenders, Clinton had said of Trump, "He is becoming ISIS's greatest recruiter. They are going to people, showing videos of Donald Trump insulting Islam and Muslims in order to recruit more radical jihadists."[202] This statement was rated "false" by Politifact for lack of evidence at the time of that debate, but, five months later, when Clinton said in a CNN interview "We now do have evidence" that Donald Trump was being used as a recruiting tool for terrorists, Politifact rated her statement as "true" due to evidence that had arisen in the interim.[203] In a campaign speech given in August 2016, Trump claimed that Barrack Obama "founded ISIS" and that "the co-founder" was "crooked Hillary Clinton"[204]—a claim rated as "pants on fire" by Politifact, defined as a statement that "is not accurate and makes a ridiculous claim."[205]

Politifact, which fact-checks "the party that holds power or people who repeatedly make attention-getting or misleading statements," rated 73 percent of Trump's statements as some degree of false (20 percent "mostly false," 36 percent "false," and 17 percent "pants on fire"), while only 24 percent of his statements fact-checked by Politifact were rated as some degree truthful (3 percent "true," 9 percent "mostly true," and 12 percent "half true").[206] For comparison, President Obama's statements were inversely rated, with 73 percent as truthful (20 percent "true," 27 percent "mostly true," or 26 percent "half true") and 23 percent false (11 percent "mostly false," 11 percent "false," and just 1 percent "pants on fire").[207] Similarly, Clinton's fact-checked statements were rated as truthful 72 percent of the time ("true," 24 percent; "mostly true," 25 percent; and "half true," 23 percent) and some degree of false 27 percent of the time ("mostly false," 14 percent; "false," 10 percent; and "pants on fire," 3 percent).[208]

By the end of his presidency, Trump's "big lie" was that the election resulting in Joe Biden's victory had actually been stolen and that he himself had won by a "landslide."[209] The work of this lie seems to have been to enable him to hold on to power and subvert the election results. The lie's ability to enable "symbolic, structural, verbal, or physical" violence, to use McGranahan's terms,[210] was made evident in the violent insurrection that took place at the U.S. Capitol on January 6, 2021, which led to loss of life, injuries, and the destruction of property and succeeded in delaying the counting of electoral votes for several hours.

Trump repeatedly used the power of the bully pulpit to smear women as liars, arguably with similar intent: to hold on to that power by putting down opposition. For example, on October 8, 2020, Trump tweeted the link to a headline from right-wing podcast, Blunt Force Truth, that read, "Kamala Harris Lied Repeatedly and Got Away with It" and was retweeted twenty-six thousand times. On June 19, 2020, he retweeted conservative syndicated talk show host Joe Pagliarula, who said "Susan Rice lied her ass off over and over about what caused the terrorist attack in #Benghazi." He retweeted his campaign staffer Erin Perrine, saying, "#BarelyThereBiden has some shady folks on his VP list Warren—lied about her heritage Rice—lied about Russian collusi . . . [sic]," on June 13, 2020. On February 12, 2020, he exhibited his propensity to double down on insults when, in a single tweet, he referred to Senator Elizabeth Warren (D-MA) as both a liar and "Pocahontas" (his nickname, disparaging her ultimately substantiated claim of distant Native American ancestry)[211]: "Every Democrat is running to raise taxes. She (Pocahontas) lied about her ethnicity, that was her problem."

The persisting belief that women routinely lie and are, therefore, untrustworthy also casts doubt on the veracity of their claims of sexual harassment and assault. More than two dozen women accused Trump of sexual harassment and assault since the 1970s. Of them, he said, during a rally in October 2016 in Gettysburg, Pennsylvania, "Every woman lied when they came forward to hurt my campaign. . . . Total fabrication. The events never happened. Never. All of these liars will be sued after the election is over."[212] Even after the revelation of the infamous Access Hollywood tapes just before the 2016 presidential election, in which Trump is heard to brag that you can do anything with women if you are "a star," including "grab 'em by the p—," he won the presidency over his female opponent, Hillary Clinton. In the face of his own admission, which he downplayed as mere "locker-room talk" and numerous credible accusations of sexual assault and harassment leveled against him, he gained the platform of the bully pulpit to perpetuate his sexist insults and lies, unleashing them to strengthen misogynist enforcement mechanisms that have long been used to constrain and silence women.

As president, Trump succeeded in installing three conservative justices on the Supreme Court, including Brett Kavanaugh, who himself was accused of having sexually assaulted Christine Blasey Ford, a professor of psychology at Palo Alto University, when the two were high school students. Trump mocked Dr. Ford after her testimony at a Senate Judiciary Committee hearing in September 2018. "'I don't know. I don't know,'" Trump said, pantomiming her testimony at a Mississippi rally on October 2, 2018. "'Upstairs? Downstairs? Where was it?' I don't know. But I had one beer. That's the only thing I remember'"[213] he said, ridiculing her inability to remember incidental details of the encounter that occurred thirty-six years earlier. After initially saying that Ford had been a "credible" witness, Trump subsequently said that the whole thing was a "hoax" cooked up by Democrats. "It was all made up, it was fabricated, and it's a disgrace" Trump declared, despite the fact that Ford was able to show therapist's notes and affidavits from friends and relatives substantiating that she had spoken of the incident long before Kavanaugh was being considered for the Supreme Court.[214]

Yet it was Kavanaugh for whom there was evidence of giving misleading statements to the Senate Judiciary Committee, as well as on other occasions.[215] MIT Professor Ezra Zuckerman Sivan explained the complacency of Kavanaugh's supporters in the face of his evident lies at the hearing, saying that such obvious "common knowledge" lies can serve the purpose of expressing what some hold as "deeper truths."[216] To "those who are primed to hear them" as with Trump and his followers, "the deeper truth held by that group is the belief that they are treated unfairly by the establishment."[217] Kavanaugh expressed this belief himself in his petulant, red-faced opening remarks, blaming left wing opposition for Ford's testimony.[218] If obvious lies can be framed as serving the larger belief of a group that feels it is being treated unfairly, then the liar can be embraced as that group's "authentic champion."[219] So, the word of men like Trump and Kavanaugh, who feel entitled to positions of power, can undercut and override the testimony of women who threaten their ascent. Male liars in such cases can evoke what Kate Manne calls "himpathy" from both women and men, as the Kavanaugh case makes clear.[220] And the word of women who speak out against them is most often discounted—leading to "herasure"—despite the fact that lying about sexual assault has been shown to be a relatively rare occurrence.[221]

Conclusion

Teddy Roosevelt called words "instruments" to be used for speaking of what is "elemental in civilization" and delighted in the excellent platform the presidency afforded him to extend his authority, inspire, and moralize.[222] Donald Trump used the tools of language and media, often weaponizing words, to advance his worldview through constant repetition, which, like advertising jingles, get into people's heads and influence how they think.[223] As for the bully pulpit, the antiquated meaning of *bully* as first rate here could be said to have transformed during his presidency to the more modern understanding of the word as a "blustering, browbeating person"[224] "who habitually seeks to harm or intimidate those whom they perceive as vulnerable."[225] Any high-minded allusions to a pulpit were also dispatched by the continuous, cacophonous stream of insults repeated at rallies, in interviews, and his omnipresent twitter feed.

In considering the gendered implications of Trump's command of the bully pulpit, we identified six categories of insults that have historically been used to keep women silent and sidelined. These words, that question women's stamina and stature, intelligence, looks, emotional state, necessary qualifications, and trustworthiness, do the work of evoking stereotypes and prejudices that can disqualify women, despite their credentials, and support structural impediments to their advancement to positions of power in the public sphere. As Lakoff and Duran[226] describe, language activates "frame circuits" in the brain that influence how people understand the world, and these frame circuits are strengthened by repetition and reference to prior belief systems.

We also note some patterns in Trump's use of language in disparaging his opponents and detractors, with particular interest in their implications for women. For a start, the vast preponderance of his rhetorical attacks was aimed at critics, following directly on the heels of their specific criticisms of him for some action or statement on his part, often opposing a policy position of his, for instance. His retaliatory responses typically took the form of personal, eviscerating attacks, largely devoid of substantive policy response, and often rudely mocking in tone. We found that the president's excoriating diatribes against others made regular headline news, but it often took some digging to discover what the precipitating critique of the president had been. And so, it seems, that the blustering, browbeating attacks against so-called dummies, liars, losers, and morons succeeded in diverting attention from the issues at hand, debasing public discourse, and scuttling opportunities for meaningful dialogue.

It can be argued that Hillary Clinton's loss of the presidency was due, in part, to the impressions voters formed of her, some of which were promulgated by Trump on Twitter and amplified in other media. The unrelenting portrayal of Clinton as crooked and incompetent, lacking stamina and spouting lies—all playing on time-honored gendered stereotypes—were both personally excoriating and professionally disqualifying. Stoking fear of national security and economic risk, Trump played on implicit biases that cast women us unfit to lead as commander in chief or to run anything so important as the national economy.

The power differential between President Trump and those who piqued his fury is also worth noting. When he attacked state or local government officials or journalists of modest repute, he brought the full power of the presidency to bear against relatively powerless people, precipitating further bullying and threats aimed at them in the wake of his tweets. As president, he could be said to have enjoyed outsize status and ability to command attention relative to almost anyone, and he exhibited little respect even for others whose credentials, whether academic, economic, moral, or in public service chops, demonstrably surpassed his own, including Pulitzer Prize–winning journalists, Supreme Court justices, and heads of state, to name just a few. He often bragged about himself in the course of dissing his targets, noting his own magnificent brilliance, stamina, or deserving to win. Yet his tweets often contained grammatical or spelling errors, belying his self-professed mastery in just about every sphere, and his tweets often contained lies and misleading innuendo in addition to being laced with repetitive insults.

Trump's attacks on women and people of color were noted by many, and illustrated here, to have been particularly virulent. He regularly played upon sexist and racist stereotypes to insult and undercut those who questioned or criticized him. Another tactic he employed at times was to erase or disregard women by failing to refer to them by name, such as identifying them only as someone's wife. And he regularly labeled others as possessing negative attributes or engaging in disreputable actions that could seem more applicable to himself, such as being corrupt, lying, or perpetrating a hoax. In any case, such slights served to call the credibility of his critics into question, undercutting their authority by appealing to time-honored stereotypes and smears. Beyond setbacks to advancements of thought about the leadership capacity of women in the public sphere, this treatment by the commander in chief from the bully pulpit also put the safety and well-being of individual women at risk, subjecting them to threats ranging from verbal abuse, to sexual violence and kidnapping and assassination plots, thus considerably raising the costs of, and creating structural barriers to, women's participation in the public sphere.

Notes

1. Katherine Shaw, "Beyond the Bully Pulpit: Presidential Speech in the Courts," *Texas Law Review* 96, no. 1 (2017): 71–140.

2. H. Paul Jeffers, *The Bully Pulpit: A Theodore Roosevelt Book of Quotations* (Lanham, MD: Taylor Trade Publishing, 2002).

3. Ron Elving, "Trump Puts a Twist on the Meaning of 'Bully Pulpit,'" *NPR*, July 4, 2017, https://www.npr.org/2017/07/04/535429508/trump-s-weekend-gives-twist-to-meaning-of-bully-pulpit.

4. Merriam-Webster, "Bully," accessed February 19, 2021, https://www.merriam-webster.com/dictionary/bully.

5. Elving, "Meaning of 'Bully Pulpit.'"

6. Katherine Shaw, "Beyond the Bully Pulpit: Presidential Speech in the Courts," *Texas Law Review* 96, no. 1 (2017): 71–140.

7. Neal Gabler, "Donald Trump, the Emperor of Social Media," *Moyers* (blog), April 29, 2016, quoted in Brian L. Ott, "The Age of Twitter: Donald J. Trump and the Politics of Debasement," *Critical Studies in Media Communication* 34, no. 1 (2017): 62, https://doi.org/10.1080/15295036.2016.1266686.

8. Gabriel Michael and Colin Agur, "The Bully Pulpit, Social Media, and Public Opinion: A Big Data Approach," *Journal of Information Technology and Politics* 15, no. 3 (2018): 263, https://doi.org/10.1080/19331681.2018.1485604.

9. Michael Patrick Cullinane and Clare Frances Elliott, *Perspectives on Presidential Leadership: An International View of the White House* (New York: Routledge, 2014).

10. Michael and Agur, "The Bully Pulpit," 273.

11. Michael and Agur, "The Bully Pulpit," 273–274.

12. Kara Alaimo, "Why Trump Keeps Calling Women 'Nasty,'" *CNN*, August 21, 2019, https://www.cnn.com/2019/06/01/opinions/trumps-meghan -markle-nasty-proves-her-point-alaimo/index.html.

13. Kate Conger and Mike Isaac, "Twitter Permanently Bans Trump, Capping Online Revolt," *The New York Times*, January 8, 2021, sec. Technology, https://www.nytimes.com/2021/01/08/technology/twitter-trump-suspended .html.

14. Andrew Solender, "Biden Blames Trump 'Liberate Michigan' Tweet for Whitmer Kidnapping Attempt," *Forbes*, October 8, 2020, https://www.forbes .com/sites/andrewsolender/2020/10/08/biden-blames-trump-liberate-michigan -tweet-for-whitmer-kidnapping-attempt/.

15. Solender, "Biden Blames Trump."

16. Nikki Schwab and Jennifer Smith, "Joe Biden Says Donald Trump Encouraged Militia's Foiled Plot to Kidnap Gretchen Whitmer and Said: 'Why Won't the President Say Stop, Stop, Stop, Stop?'" Daily Mail, October 8, 2020, https://www.dailymail.co.uk/news/article-8820993/Joe-Biden-says-Donald -Trump-encouraged-militias-foiled-plot-kidnap-Gretchen-Whitmer.html.

17. Jenna Goudreau, "The 10 Worst Stereotypes about Powerful Women," *Forbes*, October 24, 2011, https://www.forbes.com/sites/jennagoudreau/2011 /10/24/worst-stereotypes-powerful-women-christine-lagarde-hillary-clinton /#5935c00d61ca.

18. Naomi Ellemers, "Gender Stereotypes," *Annual Review of Psychology* 69 (2018): 275–298.

19. Ritu Prasad, "How Trump Talks about Women—And Does It Matter?" *BBC News*, November 29, 2019, https://www.bbc.com/news/world-us-canad -50563106.

20. Prasad, "How Trump Talks about Women—And Does It Matter?"

21. Kate Manne, *Down Girl: The Logic of Misogyny* (Oxford: Oxford University Press, 2018).

22. Manne, *Down Girl*, xxiii.

23. Avery Hartmans, "Donald Trump's First-Ever Tweet Was a Plug for 'Late Night with David Letterman,'" *Business Insider*, May 12, 2017, https://www .businessinsider.com/donald-trump-first-tweet-2017-5.

24. Evie Liu, "Yes, Trump's Tweets Move the Stock Market. But Not for Long," *Barron's*, September 7, 2019, sec. Daily, https://www.barrons.com/articles /donald-trump-twitter-stock-market-51567803655.

25. Megan Brown and Zeve Sanderson, "How Trump Impacts Harmful Twitter Speech: A Case Study in Three Tweets," *Brookings Institute* (blog), October 22, 2020,

https://www.brookings.edu/techstream/how-trump-impacts-harmful-twitter
-speech-a-case-study-in-three-tweets/.

26. Brown and Sanderson, "Trump Impacts Harmful."

27. Aaron Mak, "Trump Was Losing Twitter Followers until He Incited a Riot," *Slate*, January 12, 2021, https://slate.com/technology/2021/01/trump
-twitter-ban-followers-capitol-riot.html.

28. Philip Bump, "The Expansive, Repetitive Universe of Trump's Twitter Insults," *The Washington Post*, August 20, 2019, https://www.washingtonpos
t.com/politics/2019/08/20/expansive-repetitive-universe-trumps-twitter-insults
/; Liu, "Trump's Tweets Move the Stock Market."

29. Ott, "The Age of Twitter," 60.

30. Jayeon Lee and Young-shin Lim, "Gendered Campaign Tweets: The Cases of Hillary Clinton and Donald Trump," *Public Relations Review* 42, no. 5 (2016): 849–855.

31. Ott, "The Age of Twitter," 60.

32. Ott, "The Age of Twitter," 62.

33. Leanna Garfield, "3 Things an MIT Scientist Learned about How Donald Trump Speaks by Studying His Debates," *Business Insider*, September 27, 2016, https://www.businessinsider.com/how-donald-trump-talks-2016-9, quoted in Ott, "The Age of Twitter," 63.

34. Garfield, "How Donald Trump Speaks."

35. Ott, "The Age of Twitter," 60–62.

36. Zachary Crockett, "What I Learned Analyzing 7 Months of Donald Trump's Tweets," *Vox Media*, May 16, 2016, https://www.vox.com/2016/5/16
/11603854/donald-trump-twitter.

37. Carole McGranahan, "A Presidential Archive of Lies: Racism, Twitter, and a History of the Present," *International Journal of Communication* 13 (July 2019): 3164–3182.

38. McGranahan, "A Presidential Archive," 3164.

39. McGranahan, "A Presidential Archive," 3167.

40. Ludovic Rheault, Erica Rayment, and Andreea Musulan, "Politicians in the Line of Fire: Incivility and the Treatment of Women on Social Media," *Research & Politics* 6, no. 1 (January 1, 2019), https://doi.org/10.1177/2053168018816228.

41. Mona Lena Krook and Juliana Restrepo Sanín, "Violence against Women in Politics. A Defense of the Concept," *Política y Gobierno* 23, no. 2 (December 2016): 466.

42. Alice H. Eagly, Wendy Wood, and Amanda B. Diekman, "Social Role Theory of Sex Differences and Similarities," in *The Developmental Social Psychology of Gender*, 1st ed., ed. Thomas Eckes and Hanns M. Trautner (Mahwah, NJ: Psychology Press, 2000), 123–174, quoted in J. Celeste Lay, Mirya R. Holman, Angela L. Bos, Jill S. Greenlee, Zoey M. Oxley, and Allison Buffett, "Time for Kids to Learn Gender Stereotypes: Analysis of Gender and Political Leadership in a Common Social Studies Resource for Children," *Politics & Gender*, September

27, 2019, 1–22, https://doi.org/10.1017/S1743923X19000540; Mary Beard, *Women & Power: A Manifesto*, First American Edition (New York: Liveright Publishing Corporation, 2017), 70.

43. Lay et al., "Time for Kids."

44. Lay et al., "Time for Kids."

45. Dina Gerdeman, "How Gender Stereotypes Kill a Woman's Self-Confidence," January 25, 2019, https://hbswk.hbs.edu/item/how-gender-stereotypes-less-than -br-greater-than-kill-a-woman-s-less-than-br-greater-than-self-confidence.

46. Joyce M. Roché and Alexander Kopelman, *The Empress Has No Clothes: Conquering Self-Doubt to Embrace Success*, 1st ed. (San Francisco: Berrett-Koehler Publishers, 2013).

47. Brian F. Schaffner, Matthew Macwilliams, and Tatishe Nteta, "Understanding White Polarization in the 2016 Vote for President: The Sobering Role of Racism and Sexism," *Political Science Quarterly* 133, no. 1 (March 2018): 9–34, https://doi.org/10.1002/polq.12737; Erin C. Cassese and Tiffany D. Barnes, "Reconciling Sexism and Women's Support for Republican Candidates: A Look at Gender, Class, and Whiteness in the 2012 and 2016 Presidential Races," *Political Behavior* 41, no. 3 (September 1, 2019): 677–700, https://do.org /10.1007/s11109-018-9468-2; Nicholas A. Valentino, Carly Wayne, and Marzia Oceno, "Mobilizing Sexism: The Interaction of Emotion and Gender Attitudes in the 2016 US Presidential Election," *Public Opinion Quarterly* 82, no. S1 (April 11, 2018): 799–821, https://doi.org/10.1093/poq/nfy003; Mark Setzler and Alixandra B. Yanus, "Why Did Women Vote for Donald Trump?," *PS: Political Science & Politics* 51, no. 3 (July 2018): 523–527, https://doi.org/10.1017 /S1049096518000355; Marianne C. Stewart, Harold D. Clarke, and Walter Borges, "Hillary's Hypothesis about Attitudes towards Women and Voting in the 2016 Presidential Election," *Electoral Studies* 61 (October 2019): 102034, https://doi.org/10.1016/j.electstud.2019.03.010.

48. Nancy Cohen, "Why Trump and His Supporters Love to Hate Nancy Pelosi," *Newsweek*, February 18, 2020, https://www.newsweek.com/why-trump-his -supporters-love-hate-nancy-pelosi-opinion-1487687.

49. Brendan Brown, "Trump Twitter Archive," https://www.thetrumparchive. com.

50. Brown, "Trump Twitter Archive."

51. Meghan Keneally, "Donald Trump Offends Some with Comment that Clinton Lacks 'Presidential Look,'" *ABC News*, accessed January 9, 2021, https://abcnews.go.com/Politics/donald-trump-offends-comment-clinton-lacks -presidential/story?id=41891411; Sophie Tatum, "Trump: Clinton 'Doesn't Have the Stamina' to Be President," *CNN*, September 27, 2016, https://www.cnn .com/2016/09/27/politics/donald-trump-hillary-clinton-stamina/index.html.

52. Sean Rossman, "Trump's Repetitive Rhetoric Is a Trick Used in Advertising," *USA Today*, February 16, 2017, https://www.usatoday.com/story/news/politics /onpolitics/2017/02/16/mess-fake-news-disaster-trumps-repetition-advertising

-tactic/98014444/; George P. Lakoff and Gil Duran, "Trump Has Turned Words into Weapons. And He's Winning the Linguistic War," *The Guardian*, June 13, 2018, sec. Opinion, https://www.theguardian.com/commentisfree/2018/jun/13/how -to-report-trump-media-manipulation-language.

53. Ben Strauss, "Is the President Fit?" *POLITICO Magazine*, July 18, 2017, https://www.politico.com/magazine/story/2017/07/18/is-the-president-fit -215385.

54. Plato, *Republic*, trans. G. M. A. Grube (Hackett Publishing, 1992).

55. Brent J. Hale and Maria Elizabeth Grabe, "Visual War: A Content Analysis of Clinton and Trump Subreddits During the 2016 Campaign," *Journalism & Mass Communication Quarterly* 95, no. 2 (June 1, 2018): 454–455.

56. Caroline Heldman, Meredith Conroy, and Alissa R. Ackerman, *Sex and Gender in the 2016 Presidential Election* (Westport, CT: Praeger, 2018), 119; Bonnie Stabile, Aubrey Grant, Hemant Purohit, and Kelsey Harris, "Sex, Lies, and Stereotypes: Gendered Implications of Fake News for Women in Politics," *Public Integrity* 21, no. 5 (2019): 494, https://doi.org/10.1080/10999922.2019 .1626695.

57. Heldman, Conroy, and Ackerman, *Sex and Gender*, 50; Stabile et al., "Sex, Lies, and Stereotypes."

58. Donald Trump Campaign, *Dangerous*, 2016, https://www.washingtonpost .com/video/politics/donald-trump-dangerous--campaign-2016/2016/10/11 /46c09464-8fc9-11e6-bc00-1a9756d4111b_video.html.

59. Ryan Neville-Shepard and Jaclyn Nolan, "'She Doesn't Have the Stamina': Hillary Clinton and the Hysteria Diagnosis in the 2016 Presidential Election," *Women's Studies in Communication* 42, no. 1 (2019): 60–79.

60. Katie Glueck, "Rove: Clinton Might Have Brain Injury," *Politico*, May 12, 2014, https://www.politico.com/story/2014/05/karl-rove-hillary-clinton-brain -injury-106613.

61. Gregory Krieg, "The New Birthers: Debunking the Hillary Clinton Health Conspiracy," *CNN*, August 22, 2016, https://www.cnn.com/2016/08/22 /politics/hillary-clinton-health-conspiracy-theory-explained/index.html; Stabile et al., "Sex, Lies, and Stereotypes."

62. Jonathan Swan, "Scoop: Trump Privately Predicts He Will Appoint Four Justices," *Axios*, October 15, 2017, https://www.axios.com/scoop-trump privately-predicts-he-will-appoint-four-justices-1513306203-6274d9b0-1824 -45ee-8556-fade9bdb2fd8.html.

63. Richard Gunther, Paul Beck, and Erik C. Nisbet, "Fake News May Have Contributed to Trump's 2016 Victory" (Ohio State University, March 8, 2018), https://www.documentcloud.org/documents/4429952-Fake-News-May-Have -Contributed-to-Trump-s-2016.html.

64. Rachel Dicker, "Donald Trump's #LittleMarco Is the Internet's New Favorite Thing," *US News & World Report*, March 4, 2016, https://www.usnews.com

/news/articles/2016-03-04/donald-trump-called-marco-rubio-little-marco-at
-the-gop-debate-and-twitter-went-crazy.

65. Danielle Kurtzleben, "Marco Rubio Defends His 'Small Hands' Criticism of Donald Trump," *NPR*, March 4, 2016, https://www.npr.org/2016/03/04/469170120/marco-rubio-defends-insulting-size-of-donald-trump-s-hands.

66. Kurtzleben, "Marco Rubio Defends."

67. Calvin Woodward, "AP Fact Check: Trump Gets Rise Out of 'Mini Mike' Bloomberg," *AP News*, February 13, 2020, sec. New York City, https://apnews.com/article/ac1ec9cba956c82550ca6e54528ab66d.

68. Woodward, "AP Fact Check."

69. Chris Cillizza, "Why Donald Trump Is So Obsessed with Michael Bloomberg," *CNN*, January 17, 2020, https://www.cnn.com/2020/01/17/politics/donald-trump-michael-bloomberg-2020/index.html.

70. Heather J. MacArthur, "Beliefs about Emotion Are Tied to Beliefs about Gender: The Case of Men's Crying in Competitive Sports," *Frontiers in Psychology* 10 (2019): 1–15, https://doi.org/10.3389/fpsyg.2019.02765.

71. MacArthur, "Beliefs about Emotion," 2.

72. Jordain Carney, "Schumer to Trump: Comey Firing a 'Big Mistake,'" *The Hill*, May 9, 2017, https://thehill.com/homenews/administration/332648-schumer-to-trump-comey-firing-a-big-mistake.

73. Jeffrey Martin, "Trump Reminds Louisiana Rally Attendees Why He Calls Schumer 'Cryin' Chuck'—Because 'I Saw Him Cry Once,'" *Newsweek*, November 14, 2019, https://www.newsweek.com/trump-reminds-louisana-rally-attendees-why-he-calls-schumer-cryin-chuck-because-i-saw-1471922.

74. Martin, "Trump Reminds Louisiana Rally."

75. MacArthur, "Beliefs about Emotion."

76. Suzanne Goldenberg, "Why Women Are Poor at Science, by Harvard President," *The Guardian*, January 18, 2005, sec. Science, https://www.theguardian.com/science/2005/jan/18/educationsgendergap.genderissues.

77. Lise Eliot, "Neurosexism: The Myth That Men and Women Have Different Brains," *Nature* 566, no. 7745 (February 27, 2019): 453–454, https://doi.org/10.1038/d41586-019-00677-x.

78. Jessica Guynn, "Google Employees Say the Company's Not Doing Enough to Protect Them from Harassment, Threats," *USA Today*, January 26, 2018, https://www.usatoday.com/story/tech/2018/01/26/google-diversity-culture-war/1071107001/.

79. Guynn, "Google Employees."

80. Lin Bian, Sarah-Jane Leslie, and Andrei Cimpian, "Evidence of Bias against Girls and Women in Contexts That Emphasize Intellectual Ability," *American Psychologist* 73, no. 9 (2018): 1139–1153; Kerri Anne Renzulli, "Research Finds Women Still Get Passed over for 'Intellectual' Jobs—but There's an Easy Way Companies Could Fix That," *CNBC*, January 8, 2019, sec. Make

It—Science of Success, https://www.cnbc.com/2019/01/07/study-men-still-seen-as-smarter-than-women-get-intellectual-jobs.html.

81. Alia E. Dastagir, "Women Are Now Seen as Equally Intelligent as Men, Study Finds," *USA Today*, July 18, 2019, https://www.usatoday.com/story/news/nation/2019/07/18/differences-between-men-and-women-most-now-say-intelligence-equal/1767610001/; Alice H. Eagly, Christa Nater, David Miller, Michèle Kaufmann, and Sabine Sczesny, "Gender Stereotypes Have Changed: A Cross-Temporal Meta-Analysis of U.S. Public Opinion Polls from 1946 to 2018," *American Psychologist* 75, no. 3 (April 2020): 301–315, https://doi.org/10.1037/amp0000494.

82. Michael Karson, "Why Do People Hate Smart Women?" *Psychology Today* (blog), November 6, 2017, https://www.psychologytoday.com/blog/feeling-our-way/201711/why-do-people-hate-smart-women.

83. Karson, "Hate Smart Women?"

84. Daniel Storage, Tessa E.S. Charlesworth, Mahzarin R. Banaji, and Andrei Cimpian, "Adults and Children Implicitly Associate Brilliance with Men More Than Women," *Journal of Experimental Social Psychology* 90 (September 1, 2020): 104020, https://doi.org/10.1016/j.jesp.2020.104020.

85. Jamie Ehrlich, "Maxine Waters Encourages Supporters to Harass Trump Administration Officials," *CNN Digital*, June 25, 2018, https://www.cnn.com/2018/06/25/politics/maxine-waters-trump-officials/index.html; John Walsh, "11 Insults Trump Has Hurled at Women," *Business Insider*, October 17, 2018, https://www.businessinsider.com/trumps-worst-insults-toward-women-2018-10.

86. Eliza Collins, "Donald Trump 2016: Calls Jennifer Rubin 'a Real Dummy,'" *Politico*, December 1, 2015, https://www.politico.com/story/2015/12/donald-trump-attacks-washington-post-jennifer-rubin-216322.

87. Ruth Marcus, "Rule of Trump vs. Rule of Law: His Ignorance and Reliance on His Gut over Any Guiding Principle Are Disturbing," *The Washington Post*, June 3, 2016, sec. EDITORIAL-OPINION, https://search.proquest.com/docview/1794348782/citation/854440FF99E4B45PQ/1.

88. Mark Moore, "Trump Slams Conservative Columnist for Urging Congress to Censure Him," *New York Post*, June 2, 2019, https://nypost.com/2019/06/02/trump-slams-conservative-columnist-for-urging-congress-to-censure-him/.

89. Aila Slisco, "Proud Boys Intended to Kill Mike Pence and Nancy Pelosi, FBI Witness Says," *Newsweek*, January 15, 2021, https://www.newsweek.com/proud-boys-intended-kill-mike-pence-nancy-pelosi-fbi-witness-says-1562062.

90. Charles M. Blow, "President Dumb and Dumber," *The New York Times*, August 5, 2018, sec. Opinion, https://www.nytimes.com/2018/08/05/opinion/donald-trump-lebron-james.html; David Smith, "Trump's Tactic to Attack Black People and Women: Insult Their Intelligence," *The Guardian*, August 10, 2018, sec. US news, https://www.theguardian.com/us-news/2018/aug/10/trump-attacks-twitter-black-people-women.

91. Molly Jong-Fast, "Why Trump Attacked Marie Yovanovitch," *The Atlantic*, November 16, 2019, https://www.theatlantic.com/ideas/archive/2019/11/why -trump-attacked-marie-yovanovitch/602134/.

92. Blow, "President Dumb and Dumber."

93. Smith, "Trump's Tactic."

94. Smith, "Trump's Tactic."

95. L. V. Anderson, "Clinton's Greatest Debate Accomplishment Was Ignoring Trump as He Lurked Behind Her," *Slate*, October 9, 2016, slate.com /human-interest/2016/10/clintons-greatest-debate-accomplishment-was -ignoring-trump-as-he-lurked-behind-her.html.

96. Leon Neyfakh, "Did Trump Just Say He 'Wasn't Impressed' by Clinton's Butt?," *Slate*, October 14, 2016, https://slate.com/human-interest/2016/10/did -trump-just-say-he-wasn-t-impressed-by-clinton-s-butt.html.

97. Stabile et al., "Sex, Lies, and Stereotypes," 494; Jennifer L. Lawless, "Sexism and Gender Bias in Election 2008: A More Complex Path for Women in Politics," *Politics & Gender* 5, no. 01 (March 2009): 71, https://doi.org/10.1017 /S1743923X09000051; Miki Caul Kittilson and Kim Fridkin, "Gender, Candidate Portrayals and Election Campaigns: A Comparative Perspective," *Politics & Gender* 4, no. 03 (September 2008): 373, https://doi.org/10.1017 /S1743923X08000330.

98. Walsh, "11 Insults."

99. Shakeil Mahjouri, "Heidi Klum Reflects on Donald Trump Saying She Is No Longer a '10': 'Why Am I Being Brought into This?,'" *ET Canada*, July 17, 2018, https://etcanada.com/news/348557/heidi-klum-reflects-on-donald -trump-saying-she-is-no-longer-a-10-why-am-i-being-brought-into-this/.

100. Walsh, "11 Insults."

101. Walsh, "11 Insults."

102. Nolan McCaskill, "Trump Suggests His Accusers Are Too Unattractive to Assault," *Politico*, October 14, 2016, https://www.politico.com/story/2016/10 /trump-jessica-leeds-accusations-229805.

103. Alia Dastagir, "Experts Explain Why the 'Too Ugly to Rape' Argument Doesn't Hold Up," *USA Today*, June 25, 2019, https://www.usatoday.com/story /news/nation/2019/06/25/trump-calls-accuser-e-jean-carroll-not-my-type-its -rape-myth-too-ugly/1554488001/.

104. Dastagir, "Too Ugly to Rape."

105. Eric Lutz, "Donald Trump Is Still Feuding with the Wind," *Vanity Fair*, December 23, 2019, https://www.vanityfair.com/news/2019/12/donald-trump -still-feuding-with-wind-energy; Tina Nguyen, "Donald Trump Loses Fight against Windmills," *Vanity Fair*, December 16, 2015, https://www.vanityfair .com/news/2015/12/donald-trump-lawsuit-golf.

106. Adam Shaw, "Trump Mocks 'Staged' Greeting for Ilhan Omar, Accuses Media of 'Sick Partnership' with Squad," *Fox News*, July 19, 2019, https://www

.foxnews.com/politics/trump-mocks-staged-greeting-for-ilhan-omar-accuses
-media-and-squad-of-sick-partnership; Sabrina Siddiqui, "'Welcome Home!'
Ilhan Omar Returns to Minnesota Amid Trump Smears," *The Guardian*, July 19,
2019, sec. US news, https://www.theguardian.com/us-news/2019/jul/19/ilhan
-omar-trump-attacks-minnesota-support.

107. Rachel Frazin, "Trump Renews Attacks on Omarosa, Slamming Her as
'Disgusting and Foul Mouthed,'" *The Hill*, August 31, 2019, https://thehill.com
/homenews/administration/459522-trump-slams-omarosa-as-disgusting-and
-foul-mouthed.

108. Annie Hill, "Nondisclosure Agreements: Sexual Harassment and the
Contract of Silence," *Gender Policy Report* (blog), November 14, 2017, https://
genderpolicyreport.umn.edu/nondisclosure-agreements-sexual-harassment-and
-the-contract-of-silence/.

109. "Chrissy Teigen 'Filthy Mouthed,' Says President Trump," *BBC News*,
September 9, 2019, https://www.bbc.com/news/newsbeat-49633346.

110. Manne, *Down Girl*, 63.

111. Julie Keller, "The Martha Show," *Chicago Tribune*, September 29, 2002,
https://www.chicagotribune.com/news/ct-xpm-2002-09-29-0209290310-story
.html.

112. Martha C. Nussbaum, *Hiding from Humanity: Disgust, Shame, and the
Law* (Princeton, NJ: Princeton University Press, 2004), 114.

113. "Nasty," in *Dictionary.com*, accessed February 19, 2021, https://www
.dictionary.com/browse/-nasty.

114. Alaimo, "Calling Women 'Nasty.'"

115. Ryan Teague Beckwith, "Trump: Moderator Had 'Blood Coming Out
of Her Wherever,'" *Time*, August 7, 2015, https://time.com/3989652/donald
-trump-megyn-kelly-blood-wherever/.

116. Beckwith, "Blood Coming Out of Her Wherever"; Walsh, "11 Insults."

117. Alaimo, "Calling Women 'Nasty.'"

118. Mark Hensch, "Report: Trump Called Breastfeeding Mom 'Disgusting,'"
The Hill, July 29, 2015, https://thehill.com/blogs/ballot-box/presidential-races
/249584-report-trump-called-breastfeeding-mom-disgusting.

119. Hensch, "Breastfeeding Mom 'Disgusting.'"

120. Sonja Haller, "Finally! In 2018 It's Legal to Breastfeed in Public in All 50
States," *USA TODAY*, accessed May 18, 2022, https://www.usatoday.com
/story/life/allthemoms/2018/07/25/public-breastfeeding-now-legal-all-50
-states/835372002/.

121. Amanda Barnes Cook, "Breastfeeding in Public: Disgust and Discomfort
in the Bodiless Public Sphere," *Politics & Gender* 12 (2016): 678.

122. Andrew Jacobs, "Opposition to Breast-Feeding Resolution by U.S. Stuns
World Health Officials," *The New York Times*, July 8, 2018, https://www.nytimes
.com/2018/07/08/health/world-health-breastfeeding-ecuador-trump.html.

123. Nussbaum, *Hiding from Humanity*, 111–112.

124. Nussbaum, *Hiding from Humanity*, 111–112.

125. "Period Shame, Misinformation Linked to Serious Human Rights Concerns," *United Nations Population Fund* (blog), June 7, 2018, https://www.unfpa.org/news/period-shame-misinformation-linked-serious-human-rights-concerns.

126. Danielle Preiss, "Why It's Hard to Ban the Menstrual Shed," *NPR*, May 13, 2019, https://www.npr.org/sections/goatsandsoda/2019/05/13/721450261/why-its-so-hard-to-stop-women-from-sleeping-in-a-menstrual-shed.

127. David Brand, "When Periods Are Political: 5 Laws That Stigmatize Menstruation," *Global Citizen* (blog), March 16, 2018, https://www.globalcitizen.org/en/content/period-stigma-5-laws-us-taboos/.

128. Nussbaum, *Hiding from Humanity*, 83.

129. Chris Cillizza, "Who Exactly Is 'the Squad'?" *The Point* (CNN, July 23, 2019), https://www.cnn.com/videos/politics/2019/07/23/the-point-chris-cillizza-the-squad.cnn.

130. Cillizza, "'the Squad'?"

131. Tom McCarthy, "Trump Rally Crowd Chants 'Send Her Back' after President Attacks Ilhan Omar," *The Guardian*, July 18, 2019, https://www.theguardian.com/us-news/2019/jul/17/trump-rally-send-her-back-ilhan-omar.

132. Mary Ann Georgantopoulos, "Trump Referred to Immigrants as Vermin, Saying They Will 'Infest Our Country,'" *BuzzfeedNews*, June 19, 2018, https://www.buzzfeednews.com/article/maryanngeorgantopoulos/trump-immigrants-vermin-infest.

133. McCarthy, "Trump Rally Crowd."

134. Tom Porter, "House Democrats Want Extra Security for Ilhan Omar after the 'Send Her Back' Chants," *Business Insider*, July 19, 2019, https://www.businessinsider.com/ilhan-omar-house-democrats-extra-security-send-her-back-chants-2019-7.

135. Sarah Elbeshbishi, "Texas Man Charged after Storming US Capitol, Making Death Threats against Rep. Ocasio-Cortez and Police Officer," *USA Today*, January 23, 2021, https://www.usatoday.com/story/news/politics/2021/01/23/fbi-charges-capitol-rioter-threat-kill-alexandria-ocasio-cortez/6687691002/.

136. Baltimore Sun Editorial Board, "Better to Have a Few Rats than to Be One," *The Baltimore Sun*, July 27, 2019, https://www.baltimoresun.com/opinion/editorial/bs-ed-0728-trump-baltimore-20190727-k6ac4yvnpvcczlaexdfglifada-story.html.

137. David Smith, "Trump Condemned for Trivializing Homeless Crisis in Attack on Pelosi," *The Guardian*, December 26, 2019, https://www.theguardian.com/us-news/2019/dec/26/donald-trump-trivializing-homeless-crisis-nancy-pelosi.

138. Kate Manne, "In Ferguson and Beyond, Punishing Humanity," *New York Times*, October 12, 2014, sec. Opinion, https://opinionator.blogs.nytimes.com/2014/10/12/.

139. Manne, "Punishing Humanity."

140. Walsh, "11 Insults."

141. David Smith, "Omarosa Says Trump Is a Racist Who Uses N-Word—and Claims There Is Tape to Prove It," *The Guardian*, August 11, 2018, sec. US news, https://www.theguardian.com/us-news/2018/aug/10/omarosa-trump-book -the-apprentice-memoir.

142. Victoria L. Brescoll, "Leading with Their Hearts? How Gender Stereotypes of Emotion Lead to Biased Evaluations of Female Leaders," *The Leadership Quarterly* 27, no. 3 (2016): 415, https://doi.org/10.1016/j.leaqua.2016.02.005.

143. Brescoll, "Leading with Their Hearts?" 423.

144. Victoria L. Brescoll and Eric Luis Uhlmann, "Can an Angry Woman Get Ahead?: Status Conferral, Gender, and Expression of Emotion in the Workplace," *Psychological Science* 19, no. 3 (March 1, 2008): 268–275, https://doi.org /10.1111/j.1467-9280.2008.02079.x.

145. Harper Neidig, "Trump Blasts 'Neurotic' New York Times Columnist," *The Hill*, September 17, 2016, https://thehill.com/blogs/ballot-box/presidential-races /296471-trump-blasts-neurotic-new-york-times-columnist.

146. Neidig, "Trump Blasts 'Neurotic.'"

147. "Meltdown," in *Merriam-Webster* (Merriam-Webster, 2021), https://www .merriam-webster.com/dictionary/meltdown.

148. "Democrats Walked Out of Syria Meeting After Trump Had 'Meltdown', Pelosi Says," *The Guardian*, October 17, 2019, sec. US news, https://www .theguardian.com/us-news/2019/oct/16/democrats-pelosi-meltdown-trump -meeting.

149. "Democrats Walked Out," *The Guardian*.

150. Nina Burleigh, "Trump's Nancy Pelosi 'Meltdown' Tweet Was the Perfect Self One. Here's Why," *NBC News*, October 17, 2019, https://www.nbcnews .com/think/opinion/trump-s-nancy-pelosi-meltdown-tweet-was-perfect-self -own-ncna1068301?cid=sm_npd_nn_tw_ma.

151. Dan Mangan, "Trump Has 'Legal Responsibility' to Wear Coronavirus Mask during Ford Factory Visit, Michigan Attorney General Says," *CNBC*, May 20, 2020, sec. Politics, https://www.cnbc.com/2020/05/20/coronavirus-trump -required-to-wear-mask-for-ford-visit-michigan-ag-says.html.

152. Meredith Spelbring, "Nessel Calls Trump 'Petulant Child,' Says He Would Not Be Welcomed Back to Michigan," *Detroit Free Press*, May 21, 2020, https://www.freep.com/story/news/local/michigan/2020/05/21/dana-nessel -donald-trump-face-mask-ford-tour/5240604002/.

153. Spelbring, "'Petulant Child.'"

154. Nicole Lyn Pesce, "Trump Calls Dana Nessel the 'Wacky Do Nothing Attorney General of Michigan'—Here's How She Is Responding," *MarketWatch*, May 23, 2020, sec. Economy & Politics, https://www.marketwatch.com/story/ trump-slams-the-wacky-do-nothing-attorney-general-of-michigan-heres-how -dana-nessel-is-responding-2020-05-22; Jamie Ross, "Michigan's AG Called Trump a 'Petulant Child' Then He Proved Her Point with a Twitter Tantrum," *The Daily Beast*, May 22, 2020, https://www.thedailybeast.com/dana-nessel-called -trump-a-petulant-child-then-he-proved-her-point-with-a-twitter-tantrum.

155. Pesce, "'Wacky Do Nothing.'"

156. Spelbring, "'Petulant Child.'"

157. Pesce, "'Wacky Do Nothing.'"

158. Smith, "Trump Is a Racist."

159. Brown, "Trump Twitter Archive."

160. Yamiche Alcindor and Julie Hirschfeld Davis, "Soldier's Widow Says Trump Struggled to Remember Sgt. La David Johnson's Name," *The New York Times*, October 23, 2017, sec. U.S., https://www.nytimes.com/2017/10/23 /us/politics/soldiers-widow-says-trump-struggled-to-remember-sgt-la-david -johnsons-name.html.

161. Quint Forgey, "Trump Promotes Conspiracy Theory Accusing MSNBC's Joe Scarborough of Murder," *Politico*, May 12, 2020, https://www.politico.com /news/2020/05/12/trump-conspiracy-theory-msnbc-251108.

162. Harris O'Malley, "Men Really Need to Stop Calling Women Crazy," *Washington Post*, July 9, 2014, sec. Post everything, https://www.washingtonpost .com/posteverything/wp/2014/07/09/men-really-need-to-stop-calling-women -crazy/; Shannon Ashley, "Women Aren't Crazy So Let's Quit Telling Them that They Are," *Medium* (blog), January 29, 2019, https://medium.com/awkwardly -honest/women-arent-crazy-5e59fb0e8e6d; Jennifer Wright, "Women Aren't Crazy," *Harper's Bazaar*, December 28, 2017, https://www.harpersbazaar.com /culture/politics/a14504503/women-arent-crazy/.

163. Lexico.com, "Competence," in *Lexico Dictionaries*, accessed May 17, 2022, https://www.lexico.com/en/definition/competence.

164. Robin Devroe and Bram Wauters, "Political Gender Stereotypes in a List-PR System with a High Share of Women MPs: Competent Men versus Leftist Women?" *Political Research Quarterly* 71, no. 4 (December 1, 2018): 788–800, https://doi.org/10.1177/1065912918761009; Jeffrey W. Koch, "Candidate Gender and Assessments of Senate Candidates," *Social Science Quarterly* 80, no. 1 (1999): 84–96; Jennifer L. Lawless, "Women, War, and Winning Elections: Gender Stereotyping in the Post-September 11th Era," *Political Research Quarterly* 57, no. 3 (September 1, 2004): 479–490, https://doi.org/10.1177/106591290405700312.

165. Eli Watkins, "Donald Trump Hits Back at 'Goofy' Elizabeth Warren," *CNN*, May 6, 2016, https://www.cnn.com/2016/05/06/politics/donald-trump -elizabeth-warren/index.html.

166. Nolan D. McCaskill, "Trump Vows to Swamp Ginsburg with 'Real Judges, Legal Opinions,'" *Politico*, July 13, 2016, https://www.politico.com/story/2016 /07/trump-ginsburg-justices-225509.

167. Judy Woodruff, "Sally Yates on Trump's Travel Ban and Protecting the Rule of Law," *PBS NewsHour*, April 25, 2018, https://www.pbs.org/newshour/show /sally-yates-on-trumps-travel-ban-and-protecting-the-rule-of-law.

168. Saliqa Khan, and Khalida Volou, "DC Mayor Unveils Black Lives Matter Plaza, Mural Painted on 16th Street," *WUSA 9*, June 5, 2020, https://www.wusa9 .com/article/news/local/dc/black-lives-matter-mural-painted-on-dc-street/65 -970aeb55-caed-4188-8dd0-3fea4abe2b98.

169. "In Tweet, Pres. Trump Says Michigan Gov. Whitmer 'Must Work Harder,' and 'Be More Proactive' on Coronavirus," *Click On Detroit*, March 17, 2020, sec. Local News, https://www.clickondetroit.com/news/local/2020/03/17/in-tweet-pres-trump-says-michigan-gov-whitmer-must-work-harder-and-be-more-proactive-on-coronavirus/.

170. Garrett H. Graff, "An Oral History of the Pandemic Warnings Trump Ignored," *Wired*, April 17, 2020, https://www.wired.com/story/an-oral-history-of-the-pandemic-warnings-trump-ignored/; Jason Karlawish, "A Pandemic Plan Was in Place. Trump Abandoned It—And Science—In the Face of Covid-19," *STAT* (blog), May 17, 2020, https://www.statnews.com/2020/05/17/the-art-of-the-pandemic-how-donald-trump-walked-the-u-s-into-the-covid-19-era/; German Lopez, "The Trump Administration's Botched Coronavirus Response, Explained," *Vox Media*, April 2, 2020, https://www.vox.com/policy-and-politics/2020/3/14/21177509/coronavirus-trump-covid-19-pandemic-response.

171. Allan Smith, "'That Woman from Michigan': Gov. Whitmer Stands Out in the Pandemic. Just Ask Trump," *NBC News*, April 8, 2020, https://www.nbcnews.com/politics/donald-trump/woman-michigan-gov-whitmer-stands-out-pandemic-just-ask-trump-n1170506.

172. Brie Stimson, "Trump Says Michigan's Whitmer 'Doesn't Have a Clue' after She Calls Him 'Biggest Threat' to US," *Fox News*, September 10, 2020, https://www.foxnews.com/politics/trump-says-michigans-whitmer-doesnt-have-a-clue-after-she-calls-him-biggest-threat-to-us.

173. Steven H. Woolf, Derek A. Chapman, and Jong Hyung Lee, "COVID-19 as the Leading Cause of Death in the United States," *JAMA* 325, no. 2 (December 17, 2020): 123–124, https://doi.org/10.1001/jama.2020.24865.

174. Stimson, "'Doesn't Have a Clue.'"

175. Tamara Keith, "Fact Check: 'Puerto Rico Was an Incredible, Unsung Success'?" *NPR*, September 12, 2018, https://www.npr.org/2018/09/12/646997771/fact-check-puerto-rico-was-an-incredible-unsung-success.

176. Rishika Dugyala, "Trump Slams 'Corrupt' Puerto Rican Officials as Protesters Call for Governor's Resignation," *Politico*, July 18, 2019, https://politi.co/2M0NSOL.

177. Tal Axelrod, "Trump Lashes Out at NYT Reporter Over Dayton, El Paso Coverage," *The Hill*, August 10, 2019, https://thehill.com/homenews/administration/456944-trump-lashes-out-at-nyt-reporter-over-dayton-el-paso-coverage.

178. Kathryn Watson, "Trump Lashes Out at New York Times Reporter in Latest Attack on Press," *CBS News*, April 21, 2018, https://www.cbsnews.com/news/trump-new-york-times-reporter-maggie-haberman-michael-cohen-coverage-attack-on-press/.

179. Hadas Gold, "Donald Trump to NBC's Katy Tur: 'Be Quiet,'" *Politico*, July 26, 2016, https://www.politico.com/blogs/on-media/2016/07/donald-trump-to-katy-tur-be-quiet-226286.

180. Ruben Navarrette Jr., "Trump Has a Particular Ire for Minority Commentators," *Visalia Times-Delta*, January 22, 2016, https://www.visaliatimesdelta.com/story/opinion/2016/01/22/trump-particular-ire-minority-commentators/79126392/.

181. Navarrette, "Ire for Minority Commentators."

182. Lindsey Ellefson, "Trump Calls Upon MSNBC to Fire Joy Reid After She Compares His Supporters to 'Muslims,'" September 2, 2020, https://www.yahoo.com/entertainment/trump-calls-upon-msnbc-fire-145319071.html.

183. Ariel Zilber and Keith Griffith, "'Such Xenophobia and Racism': Trump Demands MSNBC Fire 'Very Untalented' Joy Reid after Cable Host Likened President's 'Radicalized' Supporters to 'the Way Muslims Act,'" *Daily Mail Online*, September 2, 2020, https://www.dailymail.co.uk/news/article-8690681/Trump-demands-MSNBC-fire-untalented-Joy-Reid-cable-hosts-Islamophobic-comments.html.

184. Rachel Frazin, "Trump Lashes Out at MSNBC's Joy Reid, Claims She Has 'No Talent,'" *The Hill*, September 14, 2019, https://thehill.com/homenews/administration/461408-trump-attacks-joy-reid-claims-she-has-no-talent.

185. Jesse Byrnes, "Trump: Katie Couric 'Should Be Ashamed,'" *The Hill*, May 31, 2016, https://thehill.com/blogs/ballot-box/281801-trump-katie-couric-should-be-ashamed.

186. Mark Memmott, "Let's Put 'Truth Sandwiches' on Our Menu," *NPR*, June 20, 2018, https://www.npr.org/sections/memmos/2018/06/20/621753252/lets-put-truth-sandwiches-on-our-menu.

187. Byrnes, "Katie Couric."

188. Mary Beard, *Women & Power: A Manifesto*, First American Edition (New York: Liveright Publishing Corporation, 2017).

189. Jessica Valenti, "Hillary Clinton's Problem? We Just Don't Trust Women," *The Guardian*, September 22, 2016, sec. Opinion, https://www.theguardian.com/commentisfree/2016/sep/22/hillary-clinton-women-trust.

190. Valenti, "Hillary Clinton's Problem?"

191. Katie M. Edwards, Jessica A. Turchik, Christina M. Dardis, Nicole Reynolds, and Christine A. Gidycz, "Rape Myths: History, Individual and Institutional-Level Presence, and Implications for Change," *Sex Roles* 65, no. 11–12 (December 1, 2011): 761–773, https://doi.org/10.1007/s11199-011-9943-2; Bonnie Stabile, Aubrey Grant, Hemant Purohit, and Mohammad Rama, "'She Lied': Social Construction, Rape Myth Prevalence in Social Media, and Sexual Assault Policy," *Sexuality, Gender & Policy* 2, no. 2 (2019): 84, https://doi.org/10.1002/sgp2.12011.

192. Glenn Kessler, Salvador Rizzo, and Meg Kelly, "President Trump Made 16,241 False or Misleading Claims in His First Three Years," *Washington Post*, January 20, 2020, https://www.washingtonpost.com/politics/2020/01/20/president-trump-made-16241-false-or-misleading-claims-his-first-three-years/.

193. Timothy Egan, "Lord of the Lies," *The New York Times*, June 10, 2016, https://go-gale-com.mutex.gmu.edu/ps/i.do?p=GIC&u=viva_gmu&v=2.1&it

=r&id=GALE%7CA454692675&inPS=true&linkSource=interlink&sid=GIC; Michael Gerson, "Trump Is the King of Lies," *The Washington Post*, July 23, 2020; Glenn Kessler, *Donald Trump and His Assault on Truth: The President's Falsehoods, Misleading Claims and Flat-Out Lies*, Illustrated Edition (New York: Scribner, 2020).

194. Carole McGranahan, "An Anthropology of Lying: Trump and the Political Sociality of Moral Outrage," *American Ethnologist* 44, no. 2 (2017): 243–248, https://doi.org/10.1111/amet.12475.

195. McGranahan, "Anthropology of Lying."

196. Kessler, *Assault on Truth*.

197. Valenti, "Hillary Clinton's Problem?"

198. Veronica Stracqualursi, "Poll: 'Liar' Most Frequently Associated Word with Hillary Clinton," *ABC News*, August 27, 2015, https://abcnews.go.com /Politics/poll-liar-frequently-word-hillary-clinton/story?id=33361629.

199. Stracqualursi, "Poll: 'Liar' Most Frequently Associated Word with Hillary Clinton."

200. Stabile et al., "'She Lied.'"

201. Stabile et al., "Sex, Lies, and Stereotypes."

202. Tim Hains, "Clinton: ISIS Is Literally Using Videos of Donald Trump to Recruit Jihadists," *RealClear Politics*, December 19, 2015, https://www .realclearpolitics.com/video/2015/12/19/clinton_isis_is_literally_using_videos _of_donald_trump_to_recruit_jihadists.html.

203. C. Eugene Emery, "Politifact—Donald Trump Now Being Used in Terrorist Propaganda Videos, Hillary Clinton Says," *Politifact* (blog), May 20, 2016, https://www.politifact.com/factchecks/2016/may/20/hillary-clinton/donald -trump-now-being-used-terrorist-propaganda-v/.

204. Louis Jacobson and Amy Sherman, "Donald Trump's Pants on Fire Claim that Barack Obama 'Founded' ISIS, Hillary Clinton Was 'Cofounder,'" Politifact, August 11, 2016, https://www.politifact.com/factchecks/2016/aug/11 /donald-trump/donald-trump-pants-fire-claim-obama-founded-isis-c/.

205. Angie Holan, "The Principles of the Truth-O-Meter: PolitiFact's Methodology for Independent Fact-Checking," PolitiFact, February 12, 2018, https://www.politifact.com/article/2018/feb/12/principles-truth-o-meter -politifacts-methodology-i/.

206. Politifact, "Donald Trump Scorecard," accessed February 20, 2021, https://www.politifact.com/personalities/donald-trump/.

207. Politifact, "Barack Obama Scorecard," accessed February 20, 2021, https://www.politifact.com/personalities/barack-obama/.

208. Politifact, "Hillary Clinton Scorecard," accessed February 20, 2021, https:// www.politifact.com/personalities/hillary-clinton/.

209. Melissa Block, "Can the Forces Unleashed by Trump's Big Election Lie Be Undone?" *NPR*, January 16, 2021, https://www.npr.org/2021/01/16/957291939 /can-the-forces-unleashed-by-trumps-big-election-lie-be-undone.

210. McGranahan, "A Presidential Archive."

211. D'Angelo Gore, "Elizabeth Warren's 'Pocahontas' Controversy," *FactCheck. Org* (blog), December 1, 2017, https://www.factcheck.org/2017/12/elizabeth -warrens-pocahontas-controversy/.

212. Eliza Relman, "The 26 Women Who Have Accused Trump of Sexual Misconduct," *Business Insider*, September 17, 2016, https://www.businessinsider .com/women-accused-trump-sexual-misconduct-list-2017-12.

213. Walsh, "11 Insults."

214. Jack Holmes, "The President Just Turned Around and Called Dr. Christine Blasey Ford's Story a Democratic 'Hoax,'" *Esquire*, October 8, 2018, sec. News, https://www.esquire.com/news-politics/a23645073/president-trump-brett -kavanaugh-hoax-democrats/.

215. Jack Holmes, "Jeff Flake Says Brett Kavanaugh's Nomination Is 'Over' if He Lied to the Senate. So What Are We Still Doing Here?" *Esquire*, October 1, 2018, https://www.esquire.com/news-politics/a23545277/jeff-flake-brett-kavanaugh -lies-committee-fbi-investigation/.

216. Ezra Zuckerman Sivan, September 29, 2018, Twitter post, https://twitter .com/ewzucker/status/1046219645546614784.

217. Sivan, September 29, 2018.

218. Kate Manne, *Entitled: How Male Privilege Hurts Women* (New York: Crown, 2020).

219. Oliver Hahl, Minjae Kim, and Ezra W. Zuckerman Sivan, "The Authentic Appeal of the Lying Demagogue: Proclaiming the Deeper Truth about Political Illegitimacy," *American Sociological Review* 83, no. 1 (2018): 1–33, https://doi .org/10.1177/0003122417749632.

220. Manne, *Down Girl*.

221. Bonnie Stabile, Aubrey Grant, Hemant Purohit, and Sai Sharan Bonala, "Take Back the Tweet: Social Media Use by Anti-Gender-Based Violence Organizations," *Sexuality, Gender & Policy* 4, no. 1 (2021): 38–56, https://doi .org/10.1002/sgp2.12029.

222. Jeffers, *The Bully Pulpit*.

223. Lakoff and Duran, "Words into Weapons."

224. Merriam-Webster, "Bully," accessed February 19, 2021, https://www .merriam-webster.com/dictionary/bully.

225. Oxford English Dictionary, "Bully," https://languages.oup.com/google -dictionary-en/.

226. Lakoff and Duran, "Words into Weapons."

3

The Campus Context:
Proving Ground for Power

It was clear that their stories are not often told, and there are lives that have been ruined and lives that have been lost in the process.—(Betsy DeVos, Secretary, United States Department of Education July 13, 2017,[1] speaking of men accused of campus rape)

This is not your fight alone. . . . You are not alone, and we have your back.—(President Barack Obama, September 2014,[2] speaking to survivors of campus rape)

Introduction

At a summit held in July 2017, President Trump's secretary of education, Betsy DeVos, deliberated over the fate of protections for student survivors of rape, sexual assault, and sexual harassment under Title IX of the Education Amendments Act of 1972 (Title IX).[3] In this process, she gave prominent audience to "men's rights" groups,[4] who promoted the idea that the true crisis on campuses was not the pervasive problem of sexual violence but, rather, what they purported to be the lies and mischaracterizations of those reporting such incidents. For context, the Rape, Abuse & Incest National Network (RAINN) estimates that 26 percent of female and 7 percent of male undergraduate students[5] experience rape or sexual assault. The Department of Justice has found that 80 percent of rapes and sexual assaults of college women are not reported to law enforcement at all,[6] and false reports have been found to be rare.[7] Yet when lamenting the lives "ruined" and "lost" in relation to campus sexual assault, Secretary DeVos referred not to the lives of survivors of sexual assault but to those who claimed they were falsely accused of perpetrating it. DeVos's sympathies on this point are perhaps not surprising, given that she was appointed by a president who himself had been accused of sexual misconduct by more than two dozen women in incidents dating back to the 1970s,[8] accusations he fervently denies. The administration's marked departure from Obama-era support for survivors was further underscored by remarks from acting director of the Department of Education (ED)'s Office of Civil Rights, Candice Jackson, who called Trump's accusers "fake victims" and opined that the majority of Title IX investigations were predicated on false pretenses.[9] "The accusations—90 percent of them—" she said, "fall into the category of 'we were both drunk,' 'we broke up, and six months later I found myself under a Title IX investigation because she just decided that our last sleeping together was not quite right.'"[10]

Jackson's flippant statement and DeVos's tangible and rhetorical support for the position of men's rights groups in the orchestration of the July 2017 Title IX summit, together typified the Trump administration's downplaying of the problem of sexual violence on campuses. Despite its epidemic proportions, as described in diverse outlets,[11,12,13,14,15] DeVos claimed in a 2018 interview for *60 Minutes* that "she didn't know which was greater—the number of false accusations of sexual assault on campus or the number of campus rapes."[16] Though an ED spokeswoman later said that the Secretary agreed "that false reports are a fraction of the overall complaints," under DeVos's stewardship, the Trump administration's Department of Education rolled back Obama era advances to the interpretation of Title IX that had made it less onerous for survivors of rape, sexual assault, or harassment to come forward and seek redress. Taking the position that "one sexual assault is one too many and one falsely accused student is one too many"[17] the Trump administration misleadingly equated the incidence of false reporting with the far more pervasive problem of sexual assault itself. With Trump in the White House, men's rights groups had found not only a sympathetic ear, but also an administration that would take policy action based on their apparent belief that "as women and minority groups gain rights, men—primarily white men—begin to lose theirs."[18]

In this chapter, we propose a social construction policy frame infused with the concept of testimonial injustice as a basis for understanding the policy landscape of campus sexual assault (see table 3.1). The proposed frame depicts both the social construction of reporters of sexual assault

Table 3.1   Social Construction of Reporters and Respondents in Cases of
Campus Sexual Assault with a Testimonial Injustice Lens

		Social Construction	
		Positive	**Negative**
	High	Athletes, fraternity brothers Seen as promising, at top of credibility hierarchy [i]*	
Power		**Favor "clear and convincing evidence" and "severe, pervasive, and objectively offensive" standard**	**Favor preponderance-of-evidence standard**
		POLICY BENEFIT **For the accused**	**POLICY BURDEN** **For those reporting**
	Low	"Legitimate rape victim" Seen as not culpable	Sexually active or drinking women Seen as culpable, not trustworthy* or competent*

*Terms from the concept of testimonial injustice.
[i] Concept of "credibility hierarchy" from: José Medina, "The Relevance of Credibility Excess in a Proportional View of Epistemic Injustice: Differential Epistemic Authority and the Social Imaginary," *Social Epistemology* 25, no. 1 (2011), as referenced in Manne, Kate. *Down Girl: The Logic of Misogyny* (Oxford: Oxford University Press, 2018).

and that of their respondents—the accused—and the policy instruments preferred and achieved by each in accord with their social construction and testimonial injustice status. Placement of elements on the frame, including policy actors and policy instruments, is informed by literature review and interviews with leaders of organizations focused on mitigating the problem of campus sexual assault from the point of view of survivors (see table 3.1).

We hold that rape culture and the threat and experience of sexual harassment or assault on campus represent structural barriers to women's advancement in the public sphere, and that these barriers can have long term implications, both for the health and well-being of individual women, and for women's wider representation in positions of power across society through degree completion and career attainment. We conceive of the campus context as a proving ground for power, where young people form foundational relationships and experiences from which to continue their personal and professional lives. While some sizable portion of that population—disproportionately women—experiences rape or sexual assault during their undergraduate careers, few access justice—with women of color even less likely to report or be believed—and many face setbacks to their education completion (and, thus, professional advancement) and internalize long-term trauma as a result.

The American Association of Universities and the National Institute of Justice have estimated that between one-fifth and one-quarter of undergraduate students experience rape or sexual assault.[19] Given that the undergraduate student population in the United States numbered an estimated seventeen million in 2018 (up from thirteen million since 2000),[20] a conservative estimate—one-fifth of thirteen million students—would represent 2.6 million campus rapes occurring annually. Since over three quarters, or 80 percent, of campus rapes are never reported,[21] the number of unreported campus rapes annually could be estimated to be over two million (2,080,000), while a conservative estimate of the number of reported campus rapes is just over four hundred thousand (416,000). According to clinical psychologist David Lisak's widely cited studies on the topic, about 6 percent of rapes reported to campus police could be false, with a lower bound of 2 percent,[22] meaning that false reports might be estimated to be in the range of between eight and twenty-five thousand annually.

Policies confer benefits for some while imposing burdens on others, often in accord with the degree of political power such groups possess and whether they are viewed positively or negatively in the public sphere. In the case of the DeVos ruling on Title IX, the benefit of the doubt was shifted more firmly in favor of young men on campus, who are most often the perpetrators of sexual harassment and assault, and the burden of proof was placed more squarely on young women, who are more often the victims. As members of a historically socially subordinate social group, women have been afforded less credibility than men and are generally seen as less competent.[23] This status can be exacerbated by intersecting identities, including race, ability, socioeconomic status, and gender expression. Policies that create hurdles to reporting sexual harassment and assault and that fail to provide redress in their aftermath can be seen as especially burdensome for members of historically socially subordinate groups and can contribute to perpetuating their continued subordinate status by imposing structural barriers to equitable treatment and outcomes.

For the purposes of this investigation, we sought the reflections and insights of current leaders of organizations aimed at mitigating the problem of campus sexual assault, eliciting their views on related policy and campus climate. We asked each of them about activism and politics around the issue of campus sexual assault and harassment, giving attention to predominant policy mechanisms and emerging interventions and approaches of promise.

Social Construction and Testimonial Injustice

Schneider and Ingram's foundational article "Social Construction of Target Populations" examines "who benefits or loses from policy."[24] Public officials, they note, are likely "to provide beneficial policy to powerful, positively constructed target populations, and to devise punitive, punishment-oriented policy for negatively constructed groups."[25] In cases of sexual violence, legal responses for protecting women have been limited, as women have historically held less power and property rights than men.[26] Since those in positions of power determine and enforce rules about "sexual access," according to the sexual stratification hypothesis in conflict theory, punishment for sexual crimes is not widely or evenly established or imposed and is also influenced importantly by both race and class of offenders and victims.[27] Individuals and groups are accorded varying degrees of social recognition and worth, according to the social construction of violence in the sociology literature, and this status influences whether they are seen as blameworthy or deserving of remediation when victimized.[28] In an earlier study of social construction, rape myth prevalence in social media, and sexual assault policy, we found that nearly half of all social media messages about rape are accusational, meaning that they express doubts about or undermine accusers and/ or perpetuate the idea that women lie about rape.[29] Social construction in policy design takes into account the values, context, and content of policy, examining its instrumental components that can benefit advantaged groups and burden those with lesser power or political resources.[30,31] It also provides a frame for examining policy design as both reflecting prevailing social constructions and beliefs about its target population as rationale for policy and contributing to perpetuating such construction and beliefs through the codification of benefits and burdens in policy.

"Testimonial injustice arises due to systemic biases in the 'economy of credibility,' afflicting members of social groups that have historically been 'unjustly socially subordinate.'"[32] It consists of such social groups being seen as less credible when they make statements against certain others. According to philosopher Kate Manne, those subjected to testimonial injustice experience it in two distinct forms, as originally outlined by philosopher Miranda Fricker: by being seen as less competent and/or by being seen as less trustworthy.[33] Further, says Manne, they are often dismissed as not credible without any conscious thought on the part of those disbelieving them due to the "surplus credibility enjoyed by dominant group members."[34] Manne wants us to consider the "plausible political basis" for the stereotypes that help sustain testimonial injustice, which include maintaining the status quo balance of power between the sexes and the advantages accrued to men.[35] It can be argued that in typical "'he said"/"she said," "her word against his" scenarios, "there are obvious reasons to give him testimonial priority, from the point of view of upholding patriarchal order."[36] It is the contention of the present analysis that this dynamic is evident in the case of campus sexual assault and that policy is the mechanism of affording that testimonial priority.

Fricker offers two literary examples to illustrate the concept of testimonial injustice. The first is from Harper Lee's famous book *To Kill a Mockingbird*, in which a Black man's claim of innocence is disbelieved and he is wrongly convicted, despite exculpatory evidence; in the second, from Anthony Minghella's screenplay of *The Talented Mr. Ripley*, a woman's suggestion that her missing fiancé could have been murdered is summarily dismissed with the sexist line, "Marge, there's female intuition, and then there are facts."[37]

Philosopher Jeremy Wanderer distinguishes between two types of testimonial injustice: that which occurs when a testifier's claims are ignored, and another that occurs when a testifier's claims are inappropriately rejected.[38] Both are relevant to those, mostly women, reporting campus sexual assault, and both are exacerbated by race, which can often play a role in dissuading women from reporting at all or being even less likely to be believed in the rare instances when they do report.[39,40] Further, philosopher José Medina explains, "The hierarchy of credibility assumptions at play" when "epistemic authority is implicitly given" to those whose historically dominant gender, race and social status contribute to their perception as being the more credible party in any contested case.[41]

Importantly, testimonial injustice is defined as one of two forms of epistemic injustice; the other is hermeneutical injustice, which entails an injustice that is structural rather than perpetrated by an individual.[42] Testimonial injustice—not being believed—"can have bad effects on the individual who suffers it," including an undermining of their confidence in their own beliefs, and thus their own knowledge.[43] Hermeneutical injustices—like sexual harassment—are structural; exacted upon groups that are systematically disadvantaged; and attributable, in part, to a collective gap in knowledge, understanding, or awareness as to how to conceptualize the problem. This ignorance can advantage some—usually those from historically privileged groups who enjoy positive social construction, and cause marginalization for others—usually those from historically subjugated groups that endure negative social construction. In either case, Fricker argues, hermeneutical injustice causes damage for all who live under its holes in understanding, just as all people who live under holes in the ozone are subject to risk.[44] Such systemic, structural threats and inequalities are precisely the type of problems that public policy is designed to ameliorate.

Consulting the Experts: Methods

We identified ten national organizations with the primary purpose of mitigating the problem of campus sexual assault and invited the leaders of each organization to participate in an unstructured interview of about one hour in length. Interviews were conducted using Zoom as a platform and were recorded. Participants were provided in advance with a description of the project, the questions to be asked, and a consent form, and were asked for their verbal consent at the start of each recorded interview. All correspondence was conducted via email. Of the organizations we identified, two were found to be no longer active. Eight organizational leaders were invited to participate, two of whom did not reply. Leaders who were interviewed were each asked for the names of others whose position and expertise would make them appropriate for us to interview for the project, according to respondent-driven sampling methodology. During our interviews, several respondents identified an additional organization, Every Voice Coalition, which was not included in our initial outreach list, so we invited the coexecutive directors, Nora Gallo and Lily James, to participate in the study. The seven organizational leaders representing six organizations that agreed to participate in our interviews are identified in table 3.2.

Title IX and Its Contested Interpretations

Currently, Title IX is the primary legislation governing sexual assault and harassment allegations stemming from universities.[45]

"When I train lawyers—even lawyers," related victim's rights attorney and Founder of SurvJustice, Laura Dunn, "I go out of my way to remind people that when a sexual assault occurs, there are three different

Table 3.2   Leaders of Organizations Focused on Mitigating Campus Sexual Assault

Leader and Title	Organization	@Twitter	# Followers	Year Founded	Type
Sage Carson, Manager	Know Your IX	@knowyourIX	22,700	2013	501(c)(3)
Laura Dunn	LL Dunn Law Firm, PLLCSurv Justice*	@LauraL- DunnEsq@ SurvJustice	3,683	2020	Professional limited- liability corporation
Nora Gallo, Lily James, Coexecutive Directors	Every Voice Coalition	@everyvoiceco- alition (national chapter plus individual state chapters)	1,082	2015	501(c)(3)
Allison Tombros Korman, Senior Director	Culture of Respect NASPA	@CofRespect	1,934	2013; 2016 became part of NASPA	501(c)(3)
Kenyora Parham, Executive Director	End Rape on Campus	@endrapeon- campus	3,069	2013	501(c)(3)
Tracey Vitchers, Executive Director	It's On Us	@ItsOnUs	1,193	2014	501(c)(3)

*SurvJustice ceased operations in March 2020.

legal systems that come into play"—criminal, civil and administrative. Equating the campus context to the workplace, Dunn explained that in either case, these three options apply. When someone is sexually assaulted in the workplace, they can "go criminal, sue, or go after that person [the assailant] in the workplace and get them kicked out due to Title VII" or, if on campus, through Title IX. These latter administrative means—Title VII and Title IX, involve hearings, which, in the campus context, are a major point of contention for those who claim that such hearings deprive the accused of due process rights. This claim, oft repeated by DeVos's ED and men's rights groups, is misleading, Dunn said, because due process in the criminal system has a constitutional basis and is "extreme, because imprisonment and potential death penalties are at stake, and that is not the analogy for campus hearings" where the stakes might involve school suspension or expulsion, though even students found responsible for sexual assaults "often face little or no consequence for their acts."[46]

Title IX of the Education Amendments Act of 1972 prohibits schools that receive federal funds from discriminating on the basis of sex and has come to provide the legal underpinning for addressing campus sexual assault.[47] The Education Department's Office for Civil Rights issued guidance in 2001 "that sexual harassment constituted a threat to students' ability to pursue educational opportunities."[48] A 1992 Supreme Court case, *Franklin v. Gwinnet County Public Schools*, established that victims of sexual harassment had the right to monetary damages under Title IX from schools receiving federal funds, based on the case of a high school student who sought damages after her teacher repeatedly subjected her to "harassment," including "coercive intercourse."[49,50] While the Bush administration had opposed this broadened interpretation of Title IX, citing concern for exposing schools to "potentially massive financial liability," women's rights advocates cheered the ruling for its potential to incentivize schools to address sexual misconduct to which they had previously, for the most part, turned a blind eye.[51] According to Tracey Vitchers, executive director of It's On Us, the definition of "misconduct," includes harassment, intimate partner violence (IPV), rape, and sexual assault. Dunn noted that during the Bush era, Title IX was not really enforced, and "most people didn't know how to use it."[52]

Dunn herself had become "one of the very few who had ever used Title IX" in the pursuit of justice after a campus sexual assault. Two fellow students on the crew team at the University of Wisconsin, Madison, raped Dunn during a night of drinking in 2004 when she was a freshman.[53] Like many survivors, Dunn did not immediately speak of the incident; she reported to campus authorities (the university's dean of students and the UW–Madison police) and her parents almost a year later, in July 2005.[54] When, ultimately, neither assailant was charged by the police or disciplined by the school, Dunn, unlike most survivors, spoke out publicly about what had happened to her, which is how Daniel Carter of the *Clery Center for Security on Campus* saw her name, reached out, and told her that Title IX could be used in this context.[55,56] When she filed on her own in 2008, the case "got dismissed because the incident did not take place on the physical campus, even though it involved rowers in a house owned by someone who worked for the crew team and only rented to rowers." Since "this obviously impacted" her "access to the rowing team thereafter," Carter and Security on Campus helped Dunn appeal, making it "the first case of an off-campus incident being covered under Title IX for purposes of investigation."[57,58]

"My story," Dunn said, "came out in 2010 on National Public Radio and really featured Title IX in a way that helped the public begin to understand that it actually covered sexual harassment and assault, and that coverage helped lead to the Dear Colleague letter of 2011, which was already in discussions, but really helped bring it to the forefront."[59] In fact, Dunn was present, at the invitation of then vice president Joe Biden, for the unveiling of the Dear Colleague letter on April 4, 2011, at an event at the University of New Hampshire.[60] One provision of the new guidance being announced then said that Title IX investigations should take no more than sixty days to avoid the agonizingly long waits that students often endured before having any sense of resolution. Dunn herself waited nine months for the university to tell her that it was dropping her case.[61] The 2011 Dear Colleague letter also "told schools they couldn't simply hand cases over to cops or ignore assaults because they had happened off campus."[62]

The Obama administration's focus on the issue of campus sexual assault and the explicit use of Title IX as a mechanism to address it resulted from its assembling a team to study and make recommendations regarding the broader problem of violence against women in the United States. At the request of Vice President Biden, the first ever senior advisor to the White House on Violence Against Women (VAW) was appointed in June 2009: Lynn Rosenthal, whose credentials included serving as executive director and president of the National Network to End Domestic Violence (NNEDV) from 2000 to 2006 and, subsequently, as executive director of the New Mexico Coalition Against Domestic Violence. Her charge was to pull together various thought leaders from ED OCR and the Department of Justice (DOJ)'s Office on Violence Against Women as part of a team tasked with assessing the progress made in the United States on the issue of violence against women, with the intent to use the power of the presidency to contribute to progress in that realm.[63] The team came to the conclusion that, though much progress had been made in reducing some forms of sexual violence like child sexual abuse and domestic violence, things had either gotten worse or no progress had been made at all among sixteen- to twenty-four-year-olds, depending on socioeconomic status and sexual identity. Further investigation revealed that college campuses were a locus of the problem, with as many as one in four young women reporting that they had experienced some form of sexual violence during their time on campus. It was also found that repeat perpetrators were responsible for 90 percent of the incidents of such violence, constituting just 6 percent of the men on campus.[64]

In response to these findings, the Obama administration undertook two categories of initiatives with a campus focus: culture change and policy/legal change. It's On Us was created by the administration to address the former category by engaging the majority of young men on campus, who were not committing sexual offenses, to contribute positively to the campus climate, largely through bystander awareness and prevention and education efforts, and addressing toxic masculinity, according to executive director Tracey Vitchers.[65] Where policy is concerned, change was achieved through the "Dear Colleague" letter of 2011, and follow-up "Dear Colleague" letter of 2014, which provided guidelines on interpreting Title IX for the purposes of addressing campus sexual assault. The first of these letters asserted that campus sexual assault "interferes with a student's right to receive an education free from discrimination and . . . is a crime."[66] This guidance from the Department of Education's Office of Civil Rights stated that a "'preponderance of evidence' standard should be applied by campuses in making determinations about administering student discipline in response to rape allegations by students against other students."[67] The practical effect of this change was to make the reporting of sexual assault on college campuses less onerous than it had been under the previous "clear and convincing evidence" standard.

Centering Men's Rights

The Trump administration Education Department, under the direction of Secretary Betsy DeVos, made one of its first official acts in 2017 to revoke the 2011 and 2014 Dear Colleague letters.[68] The move was made after the secretary consulted extensively with men's rights activists, including the National Coalition for Men (NCFM), Families Advocating for Campus Equality (FACE), and Stop Abusive and Violent Environments (SAVE), who held that the predominant problem in the campus context was that men were being wrongfully accused.[69,70] Men's rights groups have been shown to embrace the trope that women lie about rape and that men are actually the ones experiencing disempowerment in the current political climate. These views were also espoused by President Trump, who frequently described himself as being the victim of various "witch-hunts" and declared this to be "a very scary time for young men in America when you can be guilty of something that you may not be guilty of."[71] According to reporting by *The Nation* based on information obtained by the Freedom of

Information Act, members of NCSM, FACE, and SAVE exchanged nearly three thousand emails with ED over the changes, met with high-level officials, offered legal advice, and helped to draft the new regulations.[72]

For the members and views of men's rights groups, DeVos expressed her sympathies, saying "their stories are not often told, and there are lives that have been ruined and lives that have been lost in the process."[73] Yet extensive evidence attests that false rape accusations of sexual assault are no more common than false allegations of other criminal offenses, at around 5 percent,[74] and reports of lawsuits by young men complaining of having been treated unfairly in the course of Title IX investigations of sexual assault allegations since 2011 have been relatively rare, numbering just 150, according to a 2017 *Washington Post* article on the topic.[75] The evidence suggests that the vast number of untold stories and lives ruined in the case of reports of campus sexual assault were those of the women whose attacks were never reported or, even when they were, only rarely resulted in offenders being held responsible for their crimes.

The backlash against the measures taken by the Obama administration to address sexual violence on campuses was, at times, vitriolic and could be said to be overblown when considering their practical effect. Though symbolically important, the advances made by the Dear Colleague guidance of 2011 and 2014 might be regarded as modest, or perhaps even represent a policy failure. Even once in effect and campuses had responded by establishing Title IX infrastructure with more explicit mechanisms for student services and accountability, most cases remained unreported. And many, if not most, cases that were reported were either dismissed or resulted in "slap on the wrist" measures for the accused, leaving unaddressed many costly burdens borne by survivors.[76] Nonetheless, critics described measures aimed at facilitating reporting as resulting from "hysteria" over "rape culture" that "breeds chaos and mob justice . . . claims innocent victims, undermines social trust, and distracts from genuine cases of abuse"[77] in the words of Christina Hoff Sommers. Sommers, a resident scholar at the American Enterprise Institute, was also the author of the 2000 book *The War against Boys: How Misguided Feminism Is Harming Our Young Men.* "The frenzy will die down" Sommers said in 2015 "when the stories of the falsely accused become too much for the public to bear."[78]

Such overweening concern for the plight of the relatively few falsely accused given the actual proportionality of the problem—with over one hundred times as many students subject to sexual harassment and assault annually than those likely to face actionable false allegations—can be explained, in part, by what Kate Manne calls "exonerating narratives" and their connection to the concept of testimonial injustice set forth by Miranda Fricker and José Medina.[79] These narratives reflect and perpetuate "a strenuous collective effort . . . to uphold certain men's innocence, to defend their honor, and to grant them a pardon prematurely . . . extending the benefit of the doubt to the alleged perpetrator over his accuser-cum-victim."[80] These "certain" men include the traditionally privileged—usually white men, often financially well-off or from families of some social stature—and, in the context of campus hierarchy, can include athletes and fraternity brothers who are lionized as "golden boys" or "good guys" who may be more likely to be exonerated or excused.[81]

Raising policy concerns that elevate the suffering of the falsely accused above the suffering of victims—who number in the millions and whose access to education and quality of life are impeded by the pervasive problem of sexual harassment broadly defined—is a form of erasure of women from the story. In the DeVos Title IX regulation revision, the public is asked to pay attention to and have sympathy for the falsely accused as undeserving victims in a way that eclipses the enormity of the larger problem of sexual assault on campuses, of which the problem of falsely accused men is a mere fraction. The accused and their apologists often inflate the incidence of false reporting, employ hyperbolic rhetoric, seek the mantle of victimhood, and characterize accusers as being untrustworthy, thereby exhibiting a form of gaslighting wherein they employ the very tactics of which they accuse women and those who would give women greater testimonial authority. As Manne explains, in "'her word against his' scenarios, we move from the premise that he's an 'honorable man' or 'good guy' to the conclusion that she must be lying or hysterical, instead of responding to the stronger evidence that *she's* the one telling the truth."[82]

Why Don't We Believe Women?

"Drawing attention to one's moral injuries in a public forum," Manne explains, "is liable to provoke hostility" toward members of subordinate groups.[83] She outlines structural barriers (a few of which we elaborate on below) that those from subordinate groups are likely to face if they seek justice, recognition, or sympathy, such as in the case of a woman pressing charges against a dominant man or activists advancing policy that facilitates women coming forward to do so. Both risk:

- Not being believed, and being called crazy, duplicitous, or hysterical
- Being blamed for what happened, by, for instance, being questioned about what she was wearing at the time of a sexual assault (as Dunn was asked by her own father when she told him of her rape by fellow students[84])

- "Having the crime held to be random and inexplicable, rather than admitted to be part of a larger pattern," such as when campus authorities chalk up campus rape to the careless socializing of individual students (lapses of judgment while drinking, for instance) rather than admitting that campus administrators have long had language to describe a particular pattern of campus rape and when it occurs—the Red Zone—when undergraduate women, mostly freshmen or sophomores, often novice drinkers, are at high risk for being raped by upperclassmen hosting parties where a lot of alcohol is served, and victims find themselves in unfamiliar surroundings, unsuspecting of the circumstances, and trusting of college acquaintances, while perpetrators knowingly rely on this playbook with the cooperation, both explicit and implicit, of their male classmates.[85] Sommers objects to Lisak's characterization of campus rapists as predatory,[86] but the systematic similarity of circumstances suggests some premeditation in the perpetration of this crime[87]

- Being subject to counteraccusations, including "mendacity and manipulativeness (often mooted as grounds for particular concern about false rape allegations, despite there being little evidence of a particular actual, as opposed to hypothetical, problem here)"[88]

- Being harassed and threatened; Sage Carson, Manager of Know Your IX, spoke of anticipating "massive backlash" in the renewed fight to address gender violence in the wake of Trump's presidency. Because, she explained, "we can't put a single thing out without facing death threats and if folks are going to attack our team of 15- to 25-year-olds—if people are going to see folks our age as this threat, I can't imagine what's going to come with an Administration that sides with us and takes this on" (assuming that the incoming Biden administration would do so). There are groups and articles out there "that are like, 'Know Your IX is the Death Star that has come to destroy men's rights' . . . meanwhile, we're on an 8pm Zoom call in our pajamas being like, 'ok does anyone have any ideas about how to handle this policy?'"[89] (Carson was referencing the remarks of Justin Dillon, a defense attorney for accused students, who said of Know Your IX, "They are not the underdogs, they are the Death Star. And we are Luke and his scrappy band of freedom fighters."[90]) This narrative typifies a tactic of dominant group actors—to claim the status of the dispossessed in fights with less powerful members of subordinate groups who are less positively socially constructed. (Dillon is a Harvard Law School–educated partner in a Washington, D.C. white-collar defense firm who has defended Ivy League students accused of sexual assault.[91] He lauded the Trump administration's process in revamping and rolling back Title IX protections for victims, which was advanced by "well-funded conservative think tanks," as "honest" and "thorough."[92])

Mobilizing to #Stop Betsy

The Obama administration's Dear Colleague letter provisions were fully revoked in 2017. Vitchers noted during our interview that the proposed rule changes were posted just before Thanksgiving, on November 16, 2018, seemingly with the intent of garnering the fewest possible responses during the mandatory public comment period, given that it was the beginning of the holiday season.[93] To bring attention to the proposed changes, which would disadvantage women reporting sexual misconduct in the campus context, It's On Us partnered with Mekanism, an advertising agency that had designed the original campaign for It's On Us and whose clients also included Coca-Cola, Uber, HBO, and Amazon.[94] Mekanism CEO Jason Harris took part in a brainstorming session of It's On Us that included Vitchers, who, in a moment of frustration, described the administration's actions as "shitty." Her offhand comment led to the development of an online mass mobilization campaign with the hashtag "OneShIXttyGift" to educate the target population about the rule change and to provoke action that might disrupt it.

Actress and activist Alyssa Milano partnered with *Cosmopolitan* and It's On Us to create a video portraying DeVos as a cartoon version of Dr. Seuss's Grinch. Playing on the holiday theme, in the video, Milano sits in a fireside chair next to a Christmas tree and says sarcastically, "This Holiday Season Betsy DeVos sent a lovely gift to the students of America—new Title IX guidelines. Here's a little story about it," while brandishing a book whose cover reads, "One ShIXtty Gift by Betsy DeVos."[95] "Late one evening at the Department of Ed., thoughts were bouncing round Betsy DeVos's head. She needed a gift, she started to think—a present for the people that would really stink," the story begins. During the sing-song, faux-Seuss tale, Milano reads, "Title IX protects women, that much she knew. And something so good simply won't do." Going on, the parody contains some specific references to the guidelines, including

> No more investigations for off campus rape. . . . The meaning of harassment she would remove, squeeze and twist, until it was hard to prove; live hearings where attackers defend their own violence sounded like a good way to keep victims silenced; sweep assault under the rug; walk back student rights; protect predators when they put up a fight, after all, when all was said and done, rape stats would go down, not because things got better, but because fewer would count.

The story ends with a call to action as the video cuts to an image of the Regulations.gov website, whose tagline is "Your voice in federal decision making," with directions to go to the notice and comments section. "Submit a comment, and she is required to legally review every comment before changing the policy," says Milano. "Tell Betsy no way," she continues before giving directions for accessing the website via itsonus.org.

Vitchers related that the campaign succeeded in garnering one hundred and twenty-five thousand public comments, five thousand of which can be attributed to the efforts of *End Rape on Campus* (EROC) according to Executive Director Kenyora Parham, who described the new regulations as "blowing up the Title IX landscape" and constituting a wholesale "dismantling of protections and rights" for students. The "OneShIXttyGift" and related "Stop Betsy" and "Hands Off IX" campaigns can be said to serve as examples of how "women have found a ready medium, or least another form of speech, that can be used to promote solidarity with one another in speaking out and speaking truth to power" through the vehicle of social media.[96] And, while anti–gender-based violence organizations demonstrated that they could effectively mobilize and galvanize students, survivors, parents, and administrators in this way, Parham said, "despite all of the effort, we are essentially back at square one where we started." A couple of tweaks were made and a few supportive measures added to it, but ultimately, the new regulation saw the "definition of sexual harassment overall very narrowed," with student survivors having to "endure repeated levels of abuse in order to be seen or heard or taken seriously."[97]

Severe, Pervasive, and Objectively Offensive

Indeed, the new standard for what constituted sexual harassment said that violations must be "severe, pervasive and objectively offensive" before schools would be required to formally investigate a complaint.[98] The "severe, pervasive and objectively offensive" language originated in the 1999 Supreme Court Case *Davis v. Monroe County Board of Education*, which held that in cases of student-on-student harassment, "private Title IX damages action may lie against a school board . . . but only where the funding recipient is deliberately indifferent to sexual harassment, of which the recipient has actual knowledge, and that harassment is so severe, pervasive, and objectively offensive that it can be said to deprive the victims of access to the educational opportunities or benefits provided by the school."[99] Verna Williams, lead counsel for the plaintiff in the Davis case, declared the decision a victory, since this was the first case where a student had won the right to seek damages against an educational institution based on sexual harassment from a fellow classmate (the right to seek damages against a teacher was already established).[100] But, due to the stringency of the standard, it has been called a hollow victory that, in practice, could lead schools to ignore the problem[101] or courts to dismiss many students' Title IX claims even when they are, in fact, "subjected to what should amount to actionable sexual harassment."[102] It was this precedent that the DeVos regulation sought to further codify through regulation, a stronger tool than mere guidance, as had been offered by the Obama administration's Dear Colleague letters. Guidance is enforceable, but rule changes, Tracey Vitchers pointed out during our interview, change the actual language of the law and are harder to undo.

In both the Davis decision and the DeVos regulation, the standard for sexual harassment in the school setting under Title IX is "less expansive than the workplace standard for sexual harassment under Title VII and related state anti-discrimination laws."[103] "So policymakers thought that what adults [in the workplace setting] couldn't tolerate, somehow kids [in the school setting] could," noted Dunn with chagrin. The changes were "vigorously opposed" by the National Education Association (NEA), which outlined its opposition to the then-proposed changes in a 12-page letter to Secretary DeVos in 2018.[104] "Let me be clear," said Senator Patty Murray (D-WA) of the rule change, this "is not about 'restoring balance,' this is about silencing survivors. . . . This rule will make it that much harder for a student to report an incident of sexual assault or harassment—and that much easier for a school to sweep it under the rug."[105]

On March 27, 2020, the Office of Management and Budget (OMB) finally completed its review of the rule changes posted in November 2018. Attorneys General from seventeen states and the District of Columbia, several Senate Democrats, and "hundreds of education and victims advocacy groups" urged ED to postpone overhauling Title IX rule changes until after the resolution of the COVID-19 pandemic, calling it "wholly unacceptable" for "the Department to finalize a rule that fundamentally will change the landscape of how schools are required to respond to incidents of sexual harassment and assault" during a time when they were "grappling with how to maintain basic services for and supports to their students" (per a letter to DeVos signed by Senators Murray, Gillibrand, and Warner on March 31, 2020).[106] Kenyora Parham, who said she can't help but see things through the lens of her social work degree when considering the "tumultuous" pandemic year and the attendant public health crisis, relayed that mental health and other resources for students were stymied as campus doors closed in response to public health guidance; not all students had a home to go back to, and some who did go home faced an increased risk of domestic violence, which became a pandemic in its own right alongside COVID-19.[107]

The policy change and its added complexity caused confusion for student survivors and campus administrators as to what Title IX would look like on their campuses, said Parham, speculating that creating chaos and confusion may have been part of the administration's agenda. Brett Sokolow, an attorney and Title IX consultant, predicted "systemic failure" within a few years of the rule change as both colleges and K–12 schools struggle to put the federal requirements in place. "I think the system potentially collapses under the weight of the litigation that comes from this," he said.[108]

One aspect of the confusion of the policy change was the rescission of the Clery handbook by the Trump administration in October 2020. "Clery is a support beam for Title IX," said Parham, noting that, even before the proposed changes, Clery wasn't well understood by students as a tool for their protection or for the rights of the school. "The Clery Act requires colleges and universities to provide annual reports of sexual assault and other campus crimes, and there are stiff financial penalties for not reporting. But the numbers are self-reported, and there are also strong financial incentives for colleges *not* to report. No college wants to tell the government—let alone parents of prospective students—that it has a high rate of sexual assault."[109] Allison Korman, senior director of Culture of Respect, a NASPA initiative aimed at ending campus sexual violence said, "Clery is, in essence, a consumer protection law, meant to inform a consumer [in this case, a prospective student] with an understanding of the realities of campus sexual violence at the institution." The handbook had been meant to offer guidance for higher education and K–12 administrators to understand how to go about the annual reporting process, what constitutes geography with regard to sexual assault, what to do in terms of retaliatory measures and how to generally carry out those things underpinning Title IX.[110] The rescission of the handbook was not immediately made widely known, though, said Korman, so it was unclear to campus administrators or others in the campus community as to whether the guidelines it offered should continue to be used or not.

Various political observers have speculated that the Trump administration used the tactic of creating chaos strategically to shrink and discredit government, rolling back Obama-era rules in a plethora of policy areas.[111] In the case of Title IX, survivor advocates contend that a rushed timeline for the rule change (going into effect on August 14, 2020, just three months after its release), followed this recipe for chaos, including a complete restructuring of Title IX across academia during the pandemic, outlined in a 2,033-page document that allowed for the obfuscation of provisions that would "make Title IX cases all but impossible for survivors to win."[112]

Korman spoke movingly about the burden of sexual violence on campus from the point of view of student affairs practitioners. (NASPA is an association of student affairs administrators in higher education with a membership of fifteen thousand.[113]) For the "folks who live, eat and breathe this work" of supporting primary prevention and response, she said, the work is inherently exhausting and emotional, and this is only exacerbated by "policy driven whiplash" brought on by conflicting interpretations of Title IX. Student affairs administrators will "just make it work" she said, referring to "whatever is handed down to them from ED," but noted that "it would be better if they were brought into the conversation more," as their firsthand experience could usefully inform improved response mechanisms. As it is, their voices are often overlooked, said Korman, who shared that there is as an extremely high turnover among those in Title IX and prevention student affairs cohorts due to burnout. "There is so much about this work that is heart wrenching and difficult," Korman added, pointing to an April 2021 report by *Know Your IX* that chronicles the pervasiveness of the problem of campus sexual violence, and the ramifications students face in terms of costs, including educational, financial, career, and health impacts.[114] "Survivors have been forced out of school, been punished for being raped or speaking out, lost thousands of dollars, died by suicide, and been killed by intimate partners after their schools refused to take action to keep them safe," the report concludes. "Heartache upon heartache" is how Korman described the findings, which are based on survey responses of over one hundred student survivors who formally reported sexual violence to their schools.

The problem of sexual violence on campus can indeed be characterized as "severe, pervasive and objectively offensive" based on ample empirical evidence, even if legal standards create hurdles to demonstrating that fact when individual student survivors seek recourse in the campus context (or are dissuaded from trying to do so). Schools are obligated by Title IX to ensure that students' access to education is not impeded or disrupted due to sexual violence. In the absence of fuller accountability for perpetrators or adequate accessibility of accommodations and justice for those subjected to sexual violence, it can be said to have fallen short of achieving that goal in any iteration.

Intersectional Concerns and Male Entitlement

"I thought Title IX was about sports, not as anything to do with sexual assault or sexual harassment," said Kenyora Parham, when recounting her own experience of sexual assault at Simmons University, a predominantly white private institution in Boston where she was a student from 2006 to 2010. Like so many students, she said she lacked even a baseline understanding of what her rights and resources were in the aftermath of assault. Compounding that general lack of knowledge are the issues associated with the intersecting identities that Parham focuses on through End Rape on Campus's "Center the Margins" campaign. Not much of what has been happening on campus, said Parham, has sought to center the voices of the underserved and the marginalized, such as those in communities of color. Parham cites the work of activist Tarana Burke, who is credited with founding the MeToo movement and whose hashtag has been used over nineteen million times on Twitter alone,[115] as inspiration for her vision for End Rape on Campus, which is to "galvanize and speak to the experiences of women at the intersection of their identities."[116] In Parham's view, campus efforts "have been focused on cis gendered white women," who have been first to receive support, an observation shared by Tracey Vitchers of It's On Us. Parham wondered, "how do we bring in the voices of other students?" and shift the narrative to include "hidden survivors of the movement" who are not "uplifted in the media as they should be."[117] Expressing the desire to embody a bit of Sojourner Truth in the effort, Parham said, "All of us can be represented and uplifted simultaneously." It's not about excluding anyone, she explained, but making sure that those with intersecting identities—including LGBTQIA people, immigrants, those with disabilities—are seen and heard. Not only are those who are marginalized in multiple ways less likely to access campus services in the aftermath of an assault, they may be more likely to be assaulted in the first place. As Manne notes, the proportion of men who may rape those who are multiply marginalized with impunity is large. Such victims may even find that their rape kits are more likely to go untested, liable to languish along with their basic entitlement to moral concern or justice.[118]

Despite what is known in general in the sexual violence space, which includes domestic violence, stalking, intimate partner violence, and harassment, Parham said we do not know enough about the rate of victim-ization or subsequent experience of people of color or those of multiple intersecting identities on campuses. As D'Ignazio and Klein note in their book *Data Feminism*, the numbers don't necessarily speak for themselves, as often those from underrepresented or historically marginalized groups are literally not counted, making it difficult to substantiate or address their needs. A complaint filed against Columbia University in 2014 alleging that the university had systematically mishandled "cases of rape and sexual violence reported by LGBTQ students" underscores just such a lack of knowledge and failure to address student needs based on identity.[119]

One thing we have learned, though, said Parham, "is that whether you attend a historically Black college or university (HBCU) or a predomi-nantly white college as a person of color, the rate of sexual assault is essen-tially the same, so it doesn't matter which institution you attend from that perspective." In either case, victims are likely, more often than not, to remain silent about the sexual assaults they experience. What differs are the factors contributing to their silence in either locale. At HBCUs, Parham explained, the Black community may live by a code of silence, honoring a cultural norm to "protect your fellow student," even if they are your attacker, "because they already have these other pressures placed upon them, so how dare you disrupt their educational access" considering the other hurdles that they've had to endure in life.[120] As a person of color experiencing sexual assault at a predominantly white institution, said Par-ham, "you don't even know where to go because you don't have the same rights and opportunities as your white counterparts," who themselves are unlikely to be able to successfully navigate the system or report due to the plethora of burdens associated with doing so.

In any case, men are treated as being more entitled to concern in instances of campus sexual assault; even when they are the perpetrators, people tend to express explicit concern for their disrupted education or lost earning potential should they suffer any consequences for their actions, while such concerns are rarely mentioned regarding women who are the victims. Chanel Miller's memoir *Know My Name* describes in detail her experience as a victim of Stanford swimmer Brock Turner, who was seen assaulting her next to a dumpster on campus when she was unconscious during a party. Even with witnesses, who had happened upon the crime scene and held Turner until the authorities arrived, testifying, Turner was accorded much concern due to his status as the student with "the high-est GPA of all freshman on the swim team" who had been awarded a 60 percent scholarship to a university with a 4 percent acceptance rate.[121]

Miller, on the other hand, was subjected to years of shaming and blame for having been drinking and had her sexual history and motives put on trial in court and in the media. Kate Manne describes this phenomenon as "himpathy"—"the disproportionate or inappropriate sympathy extended to a male perpetrator over his similarly or less privileged female targets or victims, in cases of sexual assault, harassment, and other misogynistic behavior."[122]

Educational Setbacks and Career Costs

The educational and financial setbacks experienced by those who have been subjected to sexual violence and harassment during their college education can have related implications for their career trajectories.[123] A 2017 article in the *Journal of American College Health* found that for women experiencing assault in college, "the human capital benefits of a college degree are often negated by detrimental effects of the assault including mental and physical health conditions and missed educational opportunities."[124] Human capital investments include "education, career training, and health," and, for the estimated 20 percent of women who are sexually assaulted during their undergraduate education, these benefits "can be undermined or lost as survivors struggle to cope with the trauma of having been assaulted."[125] These findings were substantiated by the National Academies of Sciences, Engineering and Medicine, which reported in 2018 that sexual harassment of undergraduates has been found to have significant consequences for students' educational paths, noting that "sexually harassed students have reported dropping classes, changing advisors, changing majors, and even dropping out of school altogether just to avoid hostile environments."[126]

"We know that higher ed has insane rates of sexual violence," said Laura Dunn during our interview, "and while it is less in graduate school, the impact when it does happen is astronomical on people's careers—so many women trying to get PhDs just have their careers exploded because their assailant is either in the lab that they are trying to work in or is the person running the lab, more often than not."[127] The 2021 documentary *Picture a Scientist* chronicles the costs of sexual harassment and discrimination, beginning in graduate school, on women in the fields of science, technology, engineering, and math (STEM), where they make up only one quarter of professionals (far fewer for women of color).[128]

Setbacks suffered in educational and professional development can contribute to women's underrepresentation in leaderships ranks across professions. A 2017 study on the "Economic and Career Effects of Sexual Harassment on Working Women" found that sexual harassment played a role in shaping women's early career trajectories, knocking many women off-course in the formative years of their careers during their twenties and early thirties.[129] Catharine MacKinnon's groundbreaking work published in 1979, *Sexual Harassment of Working Women*, argued that sexual harassment "undercuts women's autonomy outside the home" and "reinforces economic dependence on men."[130] The threat and experience of sexual harassment and assault in educational and workplace environments still raises the cost of women's participation and can be understood as illustrations of how misogyny acts as an enforcement strategy (per Manne and Nussbaum), favoring women's traditional roles in giving "support, service and care" and encumbering their ascent to leadership roles, especially in traditionally male-dominated venues.[131]

Data and Doubt

Though there is substantial evidence, both empirical and movingly anecdotal, attesting to the pervasive problem of campus sexual assault, there seems to be "a refusal to acknowledge what is revealed by the evidence" by many in the public sphere; such refusal, says Manne, can be explained by the relationship between social hierarchies and testimonial injustice.[132] In numerous news articles, authors claim to have presented "both sides of the explosive Title IX debate," without any substantive reference to the proportionality of the problem at hand. The DeVos "both sides approach" similarly reflected her disproportionate concern for the accused, whom she described as "victims of a lack of due process" that the revised regulations were intended to protect.[133] Some who had been unmoved by the victimhood of campus sexual assault survivors were inclined to exhibit concern when the "victims" in the narrative were said to be young men, such as Dillon's client, "who he says was expelled just months before graduating from an Ivy League school with a 3.9 GPA"[134] and, of course, professed his own innocence.

When the Obama administration placed focus on addressing sexual misconduct on campus and warned of imposing consequences for perpetrators, critics balked at what they described as pressure "to side with accusers without extending sufficient rights to the accused,"[135] and emphatically cast doubt on the existence or extent of the problem. Ironically, the history of societal response to the problem of sexual harassment and assault can be said to exhibit just the opposite playbook: a tendency to doubt accusers and deny their rights while siding with the accused. The record shows that few accused perpetrators are ever held accountable. Yet Emily Yoffe, a contributing writer for *The Atlantic*, wrote a piece concluding that though "victims do not always receive justice when they come forward," the Obama guidance had heralded a time when "the definition of sexual misconduct on many campuses . . . expanded beyond reason."[136] Stuart Taylor, a fellow at the Brookings Institution, assailed the Association of American Universities (AAU) latest survey, calling it "more hype than science" and claiming, in a critique lacking scholarly rigor, that it "was itself deliberately designed to exaggerate the number of sexual assaults on campus."[137]

What might explain this "'systemic and coordinated misinterpretation of the world' and ignorance of the *willful* variety"? asks Manne of an analogous circumstance.[138] For a start, holding the accused accountable en masse would require first believing the accounts of the accusers, which "would run counter to existing social hierarchies." Men's historical and cultural sense of entitlement to women sexually—including catcalling, uninvited touching, and the expectation of sexual attention and access they feel is owed to them by women—contribute to a sense of incredulity that their advances could so often be unwanted or coercive. Manne's melding of the concept of testimonial injustice with her own "logic of misogyny" helps explain the sympathy and credibility afforded to men relative to the hostility that women face when making claims for consideration (not to mention plays for power, which can result in even more vitriolic pushback). Misogyny, as Manne describes it, enforces gendered norms[139] and involves "patriarchal virtue-signaling," such as slut shaming and victim blaming, and a "disposition to sympathize with men's pain over women's" and "forgive privileged men."[140] Related credibility deficits are experienced by historically subordinate group members, while credibility surpluses are enjoyed by those in traditionally dominant groups; this serves "the function of *buttressing dominant group members' current social position*, and protecting them from downfall in the existing social hierarchy."[141] The revisionist regulation of Title IX can be argued to set the record straight according to this account, by reducing the ability of those over whom men have historically been dominant—women—to accuse, impugn, convict, correct, or diminish men who have subjected them to some form of sexual violence.[142]

"Misogyny directed toward one woman in public life may serve as a warning to others not to follow her lead," says Manne.[143] And misogyny visited upon women and girls by dominant social actors on campuses, in legal systems, and beyond encumbers their path toward positions of power from which they might advocate for more just policies. Moving toward proportional representation of women across professional realms—those who cull data, write journalistic accounts, craft or implement policy, formulate research questions, and produce scholarly research—will be needed to transform the systemic structures that benefit those already advantaged in the social construction of target populations and continue to burden those who deviate from historical gendered norms, thus perpetuating testimonial injustice. Though the evidentiary record is strong, more consistently accrued data and ongoing rigorous research could better inform the policy process and demonstrate for doubters the preponderant problematic features of sexual violence, even in the face of distorting narratives.

As an addendum, it is acknowledged that those who act in the service of enforcing patriarchal norms are often women themselves, as evidenced by Betsy DeVos leading the charge for reactionary reform of Title IX. Women sometimes zealously police and promote adherence to traditional feminine roles; a 2016 study even found that women were more likely than men to use misogynistic language on Twitter.[144] Manne explains that women as well as men internalize and enforce gendered norms and can exhibit excessive moralism toward those who violate such norms; women can even experience guilt or shame for violating those norms themselves. Women can be rewarded and advance to relatively powerful positions by working to uphold existing hierarchies, so merely having a few women in power is not sufficient for transformational change. Only the proportional representation of women, encompassing the full spectrum of identities and life experiences, arguably has that potential.

State Initiatives and Transformative Change

Every Voice Coalition (EVC) is a student- and survivor-led initiative begun in 2016 by eight students in a basement in western Massachusetts that became active in twelve states and succeeded in passing bills into law in five (New Hampshire, Massachusetts, Illinois, Nevada, and Connecticut) by June 2021. These bills had two main objectives: to provide support for survivors of campus sexual assault and to lay the groundwork for prevention. In the 2021 legislative cycle alone, "EVC organizers introduced student-written legislation in six states: Connecticut, Hawaii, Illinois, Maine, Nevada, and New Mexico."[145] Acknowledging that only 10 percent of survivors or fewer ever make any report through official channels, coexecutive directors of The Every Voice Coalition, Nora Gallo and

Lily James, expressed their belief in the need for mechanisms outside of the federal Title IX (and/or criminal justice?) reporting process "to meet the needs of one hundred percent of survivors."[146] In the wake of sexual assault, survivors may need counseling and academic or other campus accommodations in order to mitigate any disruptions to their education attendant to the traumatic event.

The coalition promotes a set of five core components of state policy in its two main categories: (1) support for survivors and (2) preventive measures. The first three components of the "core five" are aimed at survivor support, and the remaining two target prevention. In the survivor support category, the first component calls for memorandums of understanding (MOUs) between local rape crisis centers and universities that would give all students and employees access to local legal, medical, and support services that often are not available otherwise. "Fewer than 50% [of survivors] access any support post incident," said James, "so we want to make sure they are widely available and accessible." The second is an amnesty policy for students who might otherwise worry about getting in trouble for alcohol or drug use or other honor-code violations at the time of the incident, to remove a common barrier for reporting or coming forward to seek support. The third is the establishment of a confidential resource advisor with whom survivors could talk over their rights and options about reporting or accessing support services without worry of inadvertently triggering an investigation unless they chose to do so. A confidential resource advisor could inform survivors of available accommodations, such as a housing or class schedule change to avoid having to interact with their attackers.

The last two elements of the "core five" point toward prevention, with provisions made for biennial campus climate surveys and annual evidence-based prevention and response training for all students and employees. The campus climate survey requirement is aimed at getting a true sense of the scope of the problem, to increase transparency through statistics on campus and within the state to measure progress and have better data to improve policy. As it stands, in spite of what is known about the prevalence of sexual misconduct on campuses, the data often fails to reflect this fact; for instance, 89 percent of campuses reported zero incidents of rape in 2016 according to Clery data, which "lets institutions sweep the issue under the rug," said Gallo. Indeed, the silence around sexual assault continues, D'Ignazio and Klein point out, in part because the data itself, is silent.[147] Clery report data from Boston University and Emerson College in 2014, for instance, showed only a .04 and .15 percent incidence of sexual assault, while campus surveys conducted in 2015 reported that 18 and 9 percent of students, respectively, had experienced some type of sexual harassment, assault, or nonconsensual sexual contact during their time on campus.[148]

The biggest lapse for those entering college for the first time, said Gallo, is understanding of consent and healthy relationships. Required training could help students navigate college upon their arrival on campus and make them aware of resources that are available to them, as well as interventions such as active bystanders and other ways to keep the community safe. Several organization leaders that we interviewed echoed the need for prevention. "We are so late to the game" if we only begin to address issues of prevention and consent in higher ed, said Korman, who expressed the view that there is not as much focus on prevention in Clery or Title IX as there should be.[149] Prevention must be meaningful from the earliest days, said Korman, but it is a struggle. And not just for would-be victims, but would-be assailants, as well. Notes Dunn, "We have people thinking that sexual harassment and assault is ok because they did it all through K–12, in high school . . . no one stopped them then, so why would all of a sudden the light bulb switch on" because they are a student in higher ed or, later, an adult with a career? "You learn that behavior in elementary school through high school at a minimum," says Dunn.

James and Gallo stress that Every Voice Coalition's approach to policy at the state level is noncarceral. Women's studies scholar and journalist Nicole Froio explains that such an approach focuses on listening to survivors more so than fixating on punishment for abusers, as it is felt that "current laws and policies place too much emphasis on punitive approaches and policing, and not enough emphasis on changing culture, keeping survivors mentally and physically safe and independent from their aggressors, and supporting survivors after the assault"[150] Not only do current measures often fail to help, they can actually do further harm. As Froio notes, "The current criminal justice systems routinely disbelieves survivors, re-traumatize them, do[es] not deliver justice and do[es] not protect them."[151]

James and Gallo evoked this sentiment in our discussion when they pointed out that the focus in federal policy on reporting, adjudication, and investigation in Title IX still leaves a big gap for survivors to be able to access support "post incident" and continues to give power to the perpetrators. Those who have experienced trauma, "something I have heard a lot about and personally experienced," Gallo said, would prefer a focus on getting survivors the support they need. From their perspective, Title

IX reform is needed, but it is a separate, federal issue, said James, who pointed out that Title IX was originally "not designed to handle sexual violence or support survivors."[152]

"In my dream world, states would enforce a similar vein of Title IX," said Sage Carson, "and when students' rights are violated, there would be a place students could file a complaint in their state and that state would have an enforcement piece of it." Because, she continued, "filing a complaint with the U.S. Department of Education after you've experienced sexual violence is a tough order to give students." The process could potentially be made somewhat less onerous and effective if it were handled by more local authorities such as the state Education Department, Department of Justice, or Attorney General. State governments have a lot more interaction with and control over the schools in their state than the federal government does, and that could also increase enforcement, Carson explained.[153]

The state level, noncarceral model Every Voice Coalition envisions reflects a model centering community accountability. Its dual goals of promoting survivor support and prevention measures work toward enhancing self-determination of survivors and promoting values and practices that support safety and accountability in the wider campus community (see figure 3.1).

A direct, explicit mechanism of accountability for perpetrators is missing from this model, though an element aimed at "addressing community member's abusive behavior" appears in the framework from which it is drawn. The practice of restorative justice (RJ) is one such mechanism. It involves "a facilitated conference between affected parties" and resolution that "takes place through a collaborative process wherein the parties attempt to arrive at a consensus about what happened and then agree on a plan to repair the harm."[154] As Korman related during our interview, new Title IX rules issued in August 2020 "made space for informal resolution" (as distinct from mediation), which can mean RJ on campuses and in K–12 settings, as DeVos had made clear in earlier interim guidance.[155] Korman said that there has been growing discussion of RJ as an option for survivors, given the paucity of meaningful and effective measures available. One of its purported benefits is that "RJ can represent a way to disrupt the school to prison pipeline when dealing with misconduct in K–12 education" said Korman. This is an important consideration from the point of view of those advocating a noncarceral approach, and when taking intersectional concerns into consideration. (Though the criminal justice system rarely penalizes perpetrators of campus sexual assault, men of color are less likely to be treated fairly in the criminal justice system.)

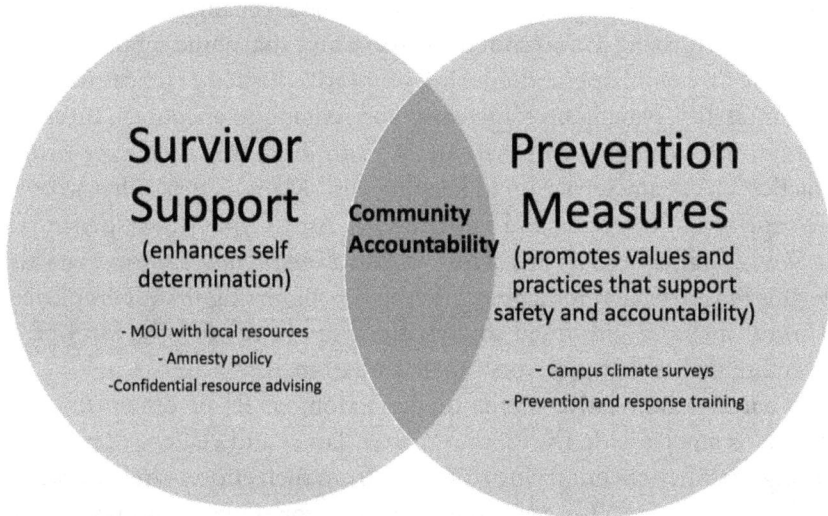

Figure 3.1 Community Accountability Model of Transformational Change in Campus Sexual Assault Policy. (Source: Figure based on INCITE's framework on community accountability featured in Nicole Froio, "Non-Carceral Approaches to #MeToo," Medium [blog], June 1, 2019, https://medium.com/academica-feminista /non-carceral-approaches-to-metoo-12a4479e0406, and the "core five" goals of Every Voice Coalition, as described by Lily James Nora Gallo [Nora Gallo and Lily James, interview by Bonnie Stabile and Aubrey Grant, video recording, April 1, 2021]).

Some believe that another benefit of RJ, said Korman, who was studying for a certificate in the practice at the time of our interview, is that it may result in the person who did the harm having more accountability and understanding through RJ than other available tools.

Others are less sanguine about the suggestion that survivors should be encouraged to sit down and talk it out with those who have violated them. "Unless accountability is the core and we are actually trying to hold someone accountable and do that in a way that the community is invested and restoring, then it is just another way for schools not to do their job," said Laura Dunn. "To be blunt," Dunn said, the reason some think that RJ is "the new thing" is because of the systemic failure to "fix the old thing." Turning substantially to RJ as an alternative justice option, she said, leaves behind an unreformed criminal justice system rife with gender bias, state violence and racism. "When the other system works—when there is accountability, of course, choose mercy and justice, but if there is not accountability then it is not really a choice."[156] As it stands, said Sage Carson, RJ probably should not "live in a school," though, as Dunn notes, schools may well prefer such relatively informal mechanisms and steer students toward them. Concerningly, Carson says that some schools, in her view, are "weaponizing and diluting restorative justice practices to avoid accountability, playing on forgiveness and religion to encourage survivors to enter into dialogue with their attackers through this alternative justice practice." (A characterization in keeping with Manne's thesis that women are expected to be giving and forgiving.)[157] Amy Cyphert, lecturer in law at West Virginia University, wrote in the *Denver Law Review* that "the devil is in the details" for a program like RJ, suggesting that, if employed, RJ must include, "informed consent from survivors" and "be just one of several remedies that survivors can choose from."[158]

Whatever the relative merits or detractions of RJ or other efforts to reform or amend Title IX, for that matter, James and Gallo—respectfully noting that they are not trying to detract from such efforts—remain steadfastly focused on EVC's main pillars of survivor support and prevention measures. While their main focus is on passing laws on the state level, they are also actively working on federal Title IX reform. In any case, centering survivors is inherent to the mission of EVC. "Our goal is to create avenues of choice for survivors," said Nora Gallo, to "offer choice and voice" to those who have had choice stripped from them in navigating college post-assault. "Those closest to the pain should be closest to the power," is the motivating mantra of EVC, as articulated by Congresswoman Ayanna Pressley (D-MA), said Gallo. "Empowering students with the knowledge and skills and tools to be not only at the table, but at the forefront of leading the conversations" is the self-defined theory of change impelling their efforts.[159, 160]

Lily James encourages other young activists to get involved in the process. "You were probably not supposed to get involved in policy in the first place for whatever reason—because of your identity, race, gender, age, class status, etc. or because you don't have an expensive law degree." She adds, "You are worthy of being taken seriously and of being respected. So don't shy away from demanding it."[161]

All EVC policy measures are developed, advanced, and sourced by and from survivors and students after conversations about what they needed or saw as lacking in their own experiences. In the process, students testify, share their stories, and find hope in the legislation, said James. To encourage awareness, teach, and knowledge share, EVC runs a ten-week fellowship program on core skills, advocacy, and policy writing called The Next Generation Leaders Fellowship. These efforts are undertaken intentionally to break down barriers to young people's participation in the

Table 3.3   Campus Sexual Assault Policy Options and Goals

	Purpose/Goals	Target Population	Mechanism
	Preventative	Future Victims/Survivors/ Perpetrators	Data Culture Change Information Provision Training
Campus Sexual Assault Policy Options	Restorative	Victims/Survivors (Those Harmed)	Services (Accommodations, Counseling)
	Retributive (Accountability)	Perpetrators of Sexual Harassment/Assault	Expulsion Payment of Damages Incarceration

policy process, inculcating a sense of agency—competence, confidence, and assertiveness—often discouraged in women[162] and denied to survivors. Legislation is the codification of power; training and involving those normally excluded from the process of creating it offers a potential path forward for both individuals and communities to be better served by law and policy and more fully exercise their own citizenship.

When considering the goals of any policy aimed at addressing the problem of campus sexual assault, it seems clear that the primary purpose of policies favored by EVC are preventative and restorative rather than retributive (see table 3.3). Such policy, designed by survivors themselves, primarily targets the needs of current and future survivors, through the provision of services, including accommodations and counseling, lays the groundwork for prevention through data collection, and aims at culture change through information provision and training. Elements aimed at accountability with a retributive edge are omitted, in keeping with the principles of noncarceral feminism and EVC's own theory of change aimed at training and empowering the next generation of change agents.

Controversy regarding changing interpretations of Title IX largely centered on the adjudication of "he said, she said" scenarios, which the tenets of social construction and testimonial injustice predict, based on long historic precedent, that survivors are bound to lose. Related proceedings, even before the DeVos debacle, not only failed to serve the needs of most survivors; they also often served to either ostracize or retraumatize them, generally worsening their plight. Given the opportunity costs of policy, it seems reasonable, in accord with EVC's model, to focus on what survivors themselves articulate as their most compelling needs and preferred course of policy action. In the EVC model, survivors are at the center of efforts in the immediate aftermath of incidents of sexual assault, with provisions made for prevention over the course of time.

Feminist values articulated by D'Ignazio and Klein in the conduct of research for their book *Data Feminism* are identifiable in aspects of EVC's operations: insisting on intersectionality, keeping in mind issues of social power; advocating for equity, giving priority to voices from marginalized perspectives; and prioritizing proximity, raising up the voices of those with direct experience of injustice and seeking answers in more localized community.[163] Adherence to these criteria, along with an acknowledgment of the importance of data to shaping solutions, are hallmarks of forward-looking, potentially transformative change mechanisms in addressing the pernicious social problem and long-standing societal ill of campus sexual assault.

Conclusion

> The criminal system is too broken to pretend that it is an effective mechanism—I think it is like under 1% of cases get prosecuted—why would anyone bother with that? Until we fix it then let's stop pretending it's a solution—people can choose it—I think we need to put pressure on the system to be fixed, don't get me wrong, but to stop the campus from being effective in the interim isn't an option.[164] (Laura Dunn)

We began with a social construction policy frame infused with the concept of testimonial injustice to inform an analysis of the policy landscape of campus sexual assault. In our interviews with leaders of organizations focused on mitigating the problem of campus sexual assault, we heard of their efforts to reform existing policies and tools that have been used, with quite limited success, in addressing the problem thus far. Such policies and tools emerged from a system in which women and other underrepresented groups have been historically socially subordinate. Therefore, these tools can be seen as having the implicit intent to protect the powerful actors in the system that created them and provide minimal or nominal succor to aggrieved survivors. Title IX, as Lily James of Every Voice Coalition rightly noted, was never designed to address sexual violence or provide support for survivors. It was a makeshift tool, ill fitted for its new purpose and, not surprisingly, didn't do that job very well, particularly as it is situated in a system that devalues and discourages the voices of victims. Even the Clery Act, which arose in response to the murder and rape of a young woman in her college dorm room in 1986, can be said to have failed to meaningfully aid in prevention and protection, given that the numbers reported by colleges and universities under its auspices are incongruously low. If, as Allison Korman noted, Clery is a consumer protection law meant to inform a consumer of the incidence of sexual violence on campuses, then institutions can be understood to have an implicit bias against giving reports of statistics that could damage their brand and depreciate their product in the competitive education market.

Situated in the system as they are, it seems reasonable to consider that these tools might never meaningfully address the problem at hand. Though Obama-era reforms improved the chances for survivors to be heard, they were still navigating a system that burdened them with reporting hurdles and in which they were cast as blameworthy, as the concepts of social construction and testimonial injustice make plain. Even in that circumstance of relative policy advantage, most survivors made the reasonable calculation that they were better off not to report at all. And those limited advances achieved by the 2011 and 2014 Dear Colleague letters proved tenuous as the system lurched backward during Trump's tenure, when those who perceived their historic power advantage eroding sought to take on the mantle of victimhood themselves and impose standards, in the form of regulatory rules with some staying power, to ensure that their voices would prevail over those of survivors who might seek to speak up.

So, in addition to reform, the organizational leaders we interviewed spoke of transformational change, most notably embodied in the aspirations of Every Voice Coalition. By asserting that their approach to addressing campus sexual violence must be noncarceral, these organizational leaders promoted a community- and survivor-focused approach that would stop centering perpetrators. The choice to sidestep responses born of carceral feminism, which "restricts feminist horizons to the individual and the punitive, rather than the collective and redistributive"[165] also avoids "safety strategies protecting survivors of violence" that can entrap "them into set options violating the right to self-determination."[166] By turning away from a focus on federal rules that have failed and focusing on state-, local-, and campus-based responses aimed at support and prevention, rather than retribution, Every Voice Coalition offers a paradigm-shifting model that has begun to take on legislative life. Rather than operate within the confines of the social construction frame of power and representation (see table 3.1), it invites an alternative framework of community accountability that spotlights safety and support, encourages practices that promote safety and accountability (see figure 3.1), and ultimately seeks to transform political conditions that can perpetuate violence.[167] The efforts of college administration, local law enforcement, and federal lawmakers have yet to stem the tide of sexual violence on campuses and have also either neglected or insufficiently addressed the attendant trauma and challenges experienced by survivors. These burdens borne by survivors can constitute setbacks to their educational attainment, professional development, and personal well-being, and thus threaten to hamper their representation in positions of power in the public sphere. Paradigm-shifting, transformational change, then, seems to be just what is called for if policy solutions are to hold meaningful sway. Yet it will arguably and paradoxically require many more women in positions of power to affect the type of transformational change that is needed to meaningfully address the pernicious problem of sexual violence on campuses and beyond.

Notes

1. Erin Dooley, Janet Weinstein, and Meredith McGraw, "Betsy Devos' Meetings with 'Men's Rights' Groups over Campus Sex Assault Policies Spark Controversy," *ABC News*, July 14, 2017, https://abcnews.go.com/Politics/betsy-devos-meetings-mens-rights-groups-sex-assault/story?id=48611688.

2. Tyler Kingkade, "Campus Rape's Toughest Young Attorney Is Ready for Trump and DeVos," *BuzzFeed News*, February 9, 2017, https://www.buzzfeednews.com/article/tylerkingkade/laura-dunns-campus-rape-fight.

3. Dooley, Weinstein, and McGraw, "Betsy Devos' Meetings."

4. Hélène Barthélemy, "How Men's Rights Groups Helped Rewrite Regulations on Campus Rape," *The Nation*, August 14, 2020, https://www.thenation.com/article/politics/betsy-devos-title-ix-mens-rights/.

5. RAINN, "Campus Sexual Violence: Statistics," RAINN, accessed April 3, 2021, https://www.rainn.org/statistics/campus-sexual-violence.

6. Ben Kamisar, "DOJ: 80 Percent of Campus Rapes Unreported," *The Hill*, December 11, 2014, https://thehill.com/blogs/blog-briefing-room/news/226822-doj-80-percent-of-campus-rapes-unreported.

7. Jeremy Bauer-Wolf, "Education Dept. Clarifies DeVos Comments on Sexual Assault," *Inside Higher Ed*, March 14, 2018, https://www.insidehighered.com/news/2018/03/14/education-department-devos-says-false-reports-sexual-assault-are-rare.

8. Eliza Relman, "The 26 Women Who Have Accused Trump of Sexual Misconduct," *Business Insider*, September 17, 2020, https://www.businessinsider.com/women-accused-trump-sexual-misconduct-list-2017-12.

9. Jenavieve Hatch, "What Happened When a Lesbian Sexual Assault Survivor Went to Work for Donald Trump," *Huffington Post*, June 25, 2018, https://www.huffpost.com/entry/candice-jackson-lesbian-survivor-donald-trump-education-department_n_5b27c816e4b0783ae12b993d.

10. Barthélemy, "Men's Rights Groups."

11. Michael Dolce, "How Trump Officials' Fixation on False Rape Accusations Hurts the Real Victims," *NBC News*, February 27, 2020, https://www.nbcnews.com/think/opinion/epidemic-rape-campus-gettingworse-under-betsy-devos-ncna1143806.

12. John Gabrieli, "Amid Sexual Assault Epidemic, Students Are Writing Their Own Civil Rights into Law," *Concord Monitor*, July 29, 2020, sec. Opinion/Columns, https://www.concordmonitor.com/Students-writing-their-own-civil-rights-laws-35441983.

13. Abby Olheiser, "Study Finds 'Epidemic' of Sexual Assault among First-Year Women at One U.S. College," *Washington Post*, May 20, 2015, https://www.washingtonpost.com/news/grade-point/wp/2015/05/20/study-finds-epidemic-of-sexual-assault-among-first-year-women-at-one-u-s-college/.

14. Tina Tchen and Valerie Jarrett, "Civic Nation BrandVoice: We Cannot Turn Our Back On this Epidemic: Sexual Assault on Colleges Campuses," *Forbes*, September 21, 2017, https://www.forbes.com/sites/civicnation/2017/09/21/we-cannot-turn-our-back-on-this-epidemic-sexual-assault-on-colleges-campuses/.

15. Jennifer Gerson Uffalussy, "Campus Sexual Assault Is an Epidemic—But What Are We Doing about It?" *Teen Vogue*, April 20, 2016, https://www.teenvogue.com/story/campus-sexual-assault-cases-epidemic-universities-response-title-ix.

16. Bauer-Wolf, "Education Dept. Clarifies DeVos Comments on Sexual Assault."

17. Bauer-Wolf, "Education Dept. Clarifies DeVos Comments on Sexual Assault."

18. Joshua Bote, "Shooting Suspect Roy Den Hollander Was a Men's Rights Activist. What Does That Mean?" *USA TODAY*, July 21, 2020, https://www.usatoday.com/story/news/nation/2020/07/21/roy-den-hollander-what-mens-rights-activism-how-did-start/5481054002/.

19. Kamisar, "80 Percent of Campus Rapes Unreported."

20. National Center for Education Statistics, "Undergraduate Enrollment," May 2020, https://nces.ed.gov/programs/coe/indicator_cha.asp.

21. Kamisar, "80 Percent of Campus Rapes Unreported."

22. Bauer-Wolf, "Education Dept. Clarifies DeVos Comments on Sexual Assault."

23. Kate Manne, *Down Girl: The Logic of Misogyny* (Oxford: Oxford University Press, 2018), 186.

24. Anne Schneider and Helen Ingram, "Social Construction of Target Populations: Implications for Politics and Policy," *American Political Science Review* 87, no. 2 (June 1993): 334, https://doi.org/10.2307/2939044.

25. Schneider and Ingram, "Social Construction of Target Populations," 334.

26. Bonnie Stabile, Aubrey Grant, Hemant Purohit, and Mohammad Rama, "'She Lied': Social Construction, Rape Myth Prevalence in Social Media, and Sexual Assault Policy," *Sexuality, Gender & Policy* 2, no. 2 (2019): 80–96, https://doi.org/10.1002/sgp2.12011.

27. Katharine M. Tellis and Cassia C. Spohn, "The Sexual Stratification Hypothesis Revisited: Testing Assumptions about Simple Versus Aggravated Rape," *Journal of Criminal Justice* 36, no. 3 (July 2008): 252, https://www.sciencedirect.com/science/article/abs/pii/S0047235208000470?via%3Dihub.

28. Diane Richardson and Hazel May, "Deserving Victims?: Sexual Status and the Social Construction of Violence," *The Sociological Review* 47, no. 2 (May 1999): 309, https://doi.org/10.1111/1467-954X.00174.

29. Stabile et al., "'She Lied.'"

30. Schneider and Ingram, "Social Construction of Target Populations," 334–347.

31. Anne Schneider and Mara Sidney, "What Is Next for Policy Design and Social Construction Theory?" *Policy Studies Journal* 37, no. 1 (February 1, 2009): 103–119, https://doi.org/10.1111/j.1541-0072.2008.00298.x.

32. Manne, *Down Girl*, 185.

33. Manne, *Down Girl*, 188.

34. Manne, *Down Girl*, 190.

35. Manne, *Down Girl*, 189.

36. Manne, *Down Girl*, 185.

37. Federico Luzzi, "Testimonial Injustice Without Credibility Deficit (or Excess)," *Thought: A Journal of Philosophy* 5, no. 3 (2016): 204, https://doi.org/10.1002/tht3.212.

38. Jeremy Wanderer, "Addressing Testimonial Injustice: Being Ignored and Being Rejected," *The Philosophical Quarterly* 62, no. 246 (2012): 148, https://doi.org/10.1111/j.1467-9213.2011.712.x.

39. Colleen Murphy, "Another Challenge on Campus Sexual Assault: Getting Minority Students to Report It," The Chronicle of Higher Education, June 18, 2015, https://www.chronicle.com/article/another-challenge-on-campus-sexual-assault-getting-minority-students-to-report-it/.

40. Lauren Rosenblatt, "Q&A: Why It's Harder for African American Women to Report Campus Sexual Assaults, Even at Mostly Black Schools," *Los Angeles Times*, August 28, 2017, sec. Politics, https://www.latimes.com/politics/la-na-pol-black-women-sexual-assault-20170828-story.html.

41. Manne, *Down Girl*, 190.

42. Rae Langton, "Epistemic Injustice: Power and the Ethics of Knowing. By Miranda Fricker," *Hypatia* 25, no. 2 (2010): 459–464.

43. Langton, "Epistemic Injustice," 459–464.

44. Langton, "Epistemic Injustice," 459–464.

45. Rachael A. Goldman, "When Is Due Process Due?: The Impact of Title IX Sexual Assault Adjudication on the Rights of University Students Notes & Comments," *Pepperdine Law Review* 47, no. 1 (2019–2020): 185–228.

46. Kristen Lombardi, "A Lack of Consequences for Sexual Assault," Center for Public Integrity, February 24, 2010, https://publicintegrity.org/education/a-lack-of-consequences-for-sexual-assault/.

47. Ruth Marcus, "Harassment Damages Approved," *Washington Post*, February 27, 1992, https://www.washingtonpost.com/archive/politics/1992/02/27/harassment -damages-approved/9e277d14-1896-4203-b8ff-68015d845d9e/.

48. Juliet Eilperin, "Biden and Obama Rewrite the Rulebook on College Sexual Assaults," *Washington Post*, July 3, 2016, sec. Politics, https://www.washingtonpost .com/politics/biden-and-obama-rewrite-the-rulebook-on-college-sexual-assaults /2016/07/03/0773302e-3654-11e6-a254-2b336e293a3c_story.html.

49. Eilperin, "Biden and Obama Rewrite the Rulebook."

50. Marcus, "Harassment Damages Approved."

51. Marcus, "Harassment Damages Approved."

52. Laura Dunn, Interview by Bonnie Stabile and Aubrey Grant. Video recording, March 24, 2021.

53. Kingkade, "Campus Rape's Toughest Young Attorney."

54. Kingkade, "Campus Rape's Toughest Young Attorney."

55. Kingkade, "Campus Rape's Toughest Young Attorney."

56. Kristin Jones, "Lax Enforcement of Title IX in Campus Sexual Assault Cases," *Center for Public Integrity*, February 25, 2010, https://publicintegrity.org /education/lax-enforcement-of-title-ix-in-campus-sexual-assault-cases/.

57. Dunn, Interview by Stabile and Grant.

58. Jones, "Lax Enforcement of Title IX."

59. Dunn, Interview by Stabile and Grant.

60. Eilperin, "Biden and Obama Rewrite the Rulebook."

61. Kingkade, "Campus Rape's Toughest Young Attorney."

62. Kingkade, "Campus Rape's Toughest Young Attorney."

63. Tracey Vitchers, Interview by Bonnie Stabile and Aubrey Grant, video recording, March 24, 2021.

64. Vitchers, Interview by Stabile and Grant.

65. Vitchers, Interview by Stabile and Grant.

66. United States Department of Education, Office of Civil Rights, "Dear Colleague Letter from Assistant Secretary for Civil Rights," Policy Guidance, U.S. Department of Education (ED), April 4, 2011, https://www2.ed.gov/about /offices/list/ocr/letters/colleague-201104.html.

67. Stabile et al., "'She Lied.'"

68. Vitchers, Interview by Stabile and Grant.

69. Dooley et al., "Betsy DeVos' Meetings."

70. Vitchers, Interview by Stabile and Grant.

71. Sarah Banet-Weiser, "'Ruined' Lives: Mediated White Male Victimhood," *European Journal of Cultural Studies* 24, no. 1 (February 1, 2021): 60–80, https:// doi.org/10.1177/1367549420985840.

72. Barthélemy, "Men's Rights Groups."

73. Dooley et al., "Betsy Devos' Meetings."

74. Claire E. Ferguson and John M. Malouff, "Assessing Police Classifications of Sexual Assault Reports: A Meta-Analysis of False Reporting Rates," *Archives*

of Sexual Behavior 45, no. 5 (July 2016): 1185–1193, https://doi.org/10.1007/s10508-015-0666-2.

75. T. Rees Shapiro, "Expelled for Sex Assault, Young Men Are Filing More Lawsuits to Clear Their Names," *Washington Post*, April 28, 2017, https://www.washingtonpost.com/local/education/expelled-for-sex-assault-young-men-are-filing-more-lawsuits-to-clear-their-names/2017/04/27/c2cfb1d2-0d89-11e7-9b0d-d27c98455440_story.html.

76. Sarah Nesbitt and Sage Carson, "The Cost of Reporting: Perpetrator Retaliation, Institutional Betrayal, and Student Survivor Pushout," Know Your IX, 2021, https://www.knowyourix.org/thecostofreporting/.

77. Christina Hoff Sommers, "The Media Is Making College Rape Culture Worse," *The Daily Beast*, January 23, 2015, sec. politics, https://www.thedailybeast.com/articles/2015/01/23/the-media-is-making-college-rape-culture-worse.

78. Sommers, "The Media Is Making College Rape Culture Worse."

79. Manne, *Down Girl*, 179.

80. Manne, *Down Girl*, 178.

81. Manne, *Down Girl*, 180.

82. Manne, *Down Girl*, 180.

83. Manne, *Down Girl*, 236.

84. Kingkade, "Campus Rape's Toughest Young Attorney."

85. Angela Hattery and Earl Smith, *Gender, Power, and Violence: Responding to Sexual and Intimate Partner Violence in Society Today* (Lanham: Rowman & Littlefield Publishers, 2019).

86. Sommers, "The Media Is Making College Rape Culture Worse."

87. Hattery and Smith, *Gender, Power, and Violence*.

88. Manne, *Down Girl*, 238.

89. Sage Carson, Interview by Bonnie Stabile and Aubrey Grant, video recording, March 25, 2021.

90. Tyler Kingkade, "Can They Get Along?" *BuzzFeed News*, September 22, 2017, https://www.buzzfeednews.com/article/tylerkingkade/title-ix-changes-are-coming-can-the-sides-find-common-ground.

91. Tovias Smith, "Push Grows for a 'Scarlet Letter' on Transcript of Campus Sexual Offenders," *National Public Radio*, May 11, 2016, https://www.npr.org/2016/05/11/477656378/push-grows-for-a-scarlet-letter-on-transcripts-of-campus-sexual-offenders.

92. Erica L. Green, "DeVos's Rules Bolster Rights of Students Accused of Sexual Misconduct," *The New York Times*, May 6, 2020, sec. U.S., https://www.nytimes.com/2020/05/06/us/politics/campus-sexual-misconduct-betsy-devos.html.

93. Vitchers, Interview by Stabile and Grant.

94. Mekanism, "About Us," accessed April 4, 2021, https://mekanism.com/.

95. Kenneth Nelson, "Alyssa Milano Channels Dr. Seuss in Video Mocking Betsy DeVos," Campus Reform, December 6, 2018, https://www.campusreform.org/?ID=11609.

96. Michael A. Peters and Tina Besley, "Weinstein, Sexual Predation, and 'Rape Culture': Public Pedagogies and Hashtag Internet Activism," *Educational Philosophy and Theory* 51, no. 5 (April 16, 2019): 463, https://doi.org/10.1080/00131857.2018.1427850.

97. Kenyora Parham, Interview by Bonnie Stabile and Aubrey Grant, video recording, March 25, 2021.

98. Editorial Board, "Title IX Fails the Very Group It Exists to Protect: Survivors of Campus Sexual Violence," *The Georgetown Voice*, April 16, 2021, https://georgetownvoice.com/2021/04/16/title-ix-fails-survivors/.

99. Justia Law, Davis v. Monroe County Board of Education, No. 526 U.S. 629 (U.S. Supreme Court 1999).

100. Gigi Rollini, "Davis v. Monroe County Board of Education: A Hollow Victory for Student Victims of Peer Sexual Harassment Notes & Comments," *Florida State University Law Review* 30, no. 4 (2002–2003): 987–1016.

101. Beth Grube and Vicki Lens, "Student-to-Student Harassment: The Impact of Davis v. Monroe," *Children & Schools* 25, no. 3 (July 1, 2003): 173–185, https://doi.org/10.1093/cs/25.3.173.

102. Rollini, "Davis v. Monroe County Board of Education."

103. Monica Shah, "What Is the Impact of the Narrowed Definition of 'Sexual Harassment' Under the New Title IX Regulations?" *Boston Lawyer Blog* (blog), May 12, 2020, https://www.bostonlawyerblog.com/what-is-the-impact-of-the-narrowed-definition-of-sexual-harassment-under-the-new-title-ix-regulations/.

104. Mary Ellen Flannery, "New Title IX Regulations Needed to Protect Survivors of Sexual Assault," NEA.org, April 14, 2021, https://www.nea.org/advocating-for-change/new-from-nea/new-title-ix-regulations-needed-protect-survivors-sexual-assault.

105. Greta Anderson, "U.S. Publishes New Regulations on Campus Sexual Assault," Inside Higher Ed, May 7, 2020, https://www.insidehighered.com/news/2020/05/07/education-department-releases-final-title-ix-regulations.

106. Nicole Gaudiano, "New Title IX Rule Ready to Drop, Despite Pleas for Delay," *POLITICO*, April 1, 2020, https://politi.co/39FOiCJ.

107. Jia Xue, Junxiang Chen, Chen Chen, Ran Hu, and Tingshao Zhu, "The Hidden Pandemic of Family Violence During COVID-19: Unsupervised Learning of Tweets," *Journal of Medical Internet Research* 22, no. 11 (November 6, 2020): e24361, https://doi.org/10.2196/24361.

108. Juan Perez Jr. and Bianca Quilantan, "How the New DeVos Rules on Sexual Assault Will Shock Schools—And Students," *POLITICO*, March 6, 2020, https://www.politico.com/news/2020/03/06/betsy-devos-school-sexual-assault-rules-122401.

109. Catherine D'Ignazio and Lauren F. Klein, *Data Feminism* (Cambridge, MA: MIT Press, 2020), 157, https://data-feminism.mitpress.mit.edu/.

110. Parham, Interview by Stabile and Grant.

111. Alexander Nazaryan, "What If the Chaos Is Strategic?" *The Atlantic*, June 18, 2019, https://www.theatlantic.com/ideas/archive/2019/06/chaos-works/591688/.

112. Nicole Bedera, Seth Galanter, and Sage Carson, "A New Title IX Rule Essentially Allows Accused Sexual Assailants to Hide Evidence against Them," *Time*, August 14, 2020, https://time.com/5879262/devos-title-ix-rule/.

113. "NASPA," accessed May 19, 2021, https://www.naspa.org/home.

114. Nesbitt and Carson, "The Cost of Reporting."

115. Kerri Lee Alexander, "Tarana Burke Biography," National Women's History Museum, 2020, https://www.womenshistory.org/education-resources/biographies/tarana-burke.

116. Parham, Interview by Stabile and Grant.

117. Parham, Interview by Stabile and Grant.

118. Kate Manne, *Entitled: How Male Privilege Hurts Women* (New York: Crown, 2020), 48.

119. D'Ignazio and Klein, *Data Feminism*, 159.

120. Parham, Interview by Stabile and Grant.

121. Chanel Miller, *Know My Name: A Memoir* (New York: Viking, 2019), 231.

122. Manne, *Entitled*.

123. Nesbitt and Carson, "The Cost of Reporting."

124. Sharyn Potter, Rebecca Howard, Sharon Murphy, and Mary M. Moynihan, "Long-Term Impacts of College Sexual Assaults on Women Survivors' Educational and Career Attainments," *Journal of American College Health* 66, no. 6 (August 18, 2018): 496–507, https://doi.org/10.1080/07448481.2018.1440574.

125. Potter, Howard, Murphy, and Moynihan, "Long-Term Impacts of College Sexual Assaults."

126. Paula A. Johnson, Sheila E. Widnall, and Frazier F. Benya, "Sexual Harassment of Women: Climate, Culture, and Consequences in Academic Sciences, Engineering, and Medicine at NAP.Edu," A Consensus Study Report (Washington, D.C.: National Academies of Science, Engineering and Medicine, 2018), https://doi.org/10.17226/24994.

127. Dunn, Interview by Stabile and Grant.

128. *Picture a Scientist*, directed and produced by Sharon Shattuck and Ian Cheney (The Uprising LLC, 2020), accessed May 31, 2022, https://www.pbs.org/wgbh/nova/video/picture-a-scientist/.

129. Heather McLaughlin, Christopher Uggen, and Amy Blackstone, "The Economic and Career Effects of Sexual Harassment on Working Women," *Gender & Society: Official Publication of Sociologists for Women in Society* 31, no. 3 (June 2017): 333–358, https://doi.org/10.1177/0891243217704631.

130. McLaughlin, Uggen, and Blackstone, "The Economic and Career Effects of Sexual Harassment."

131. Martha C. Nussbaum, "Foreword," in *Down Girl: The Logic of Misogyny*, ed. Kate Manne (Oxford: Oxford University Press, 2018), xi.

132. Manne, *Down Girl*, 190.

133. Abby Leonard and Mia Arias Tsang, "A Tale of 'Both Sides': Betsy DeVos vs. Title IX," October 9, 2017, https://www.broadsatyale.com/a-tale-of-both-sides-betsy-devos-vs-title-ix/.

134. Smith, "Push Grows for a 'Scarlet Letter.'"

135. Green, "DeVos's Rules Bolster Rights of Students Accused of Sexual Misconduct."

136. Emily Yoffe, "The Uncomfortable Truth about Campus Rape Policy," *The Atlantic*, September 6, 2017, https://www.theatlantic.com/education/archive/2017/09/the-uncomfortable-truth-about-campus-rape-policy/538974/.

137. Stuart S. Taylor, "The Latest Big Sexual Assault Survey Is (like Others) More Hype Than Science," *Washington Post*, September 23, 2015, https://www.washingtonpost.com/news/grade-point/wp/2015/09/23/the-latest-big-sexual-assault-survey-is-like-others-more-hype-than-science/.

138. Manne, *Down Girl*, 190–191.

139. Manne, *Down Girl*, 256.

140. Manne, *Down Girl*, 192–193.

141. Manne, *Down Girl*, 193–194.

142. Manne, *Down Girl*, 194.

143. Manne, *Down Girl*, 111.

144. Berit Brogaard, "12 Ways to Spot a Female Misogynist," *Psychology Today*, August 12, 2019, https://www.psychologytoday.com/us/blog/the-mysteries-love/201908/12-ways-spot-female-misogynist.

145. Amanda Nguyen, "How Students Are Making Change with Campus Sexual Assault Laws," *Forbes*, April 13, 2021, https://www.forbes.com/sites/amandanguyen/2021/04/13/how-students-are-making-change-with-campus-sexual-assault-laws/.

146. Nora Gallo and Lily James, Interview by Bonnie Stabile and Aubrey Grant, video recording, April 1, 2021.

147. D'Ignazio and Klein, *Data Feminism*.

148. D'Ignazio and Klein, *Data Feminism*.

149. Allison Tombros Korman, Interview by Bonnie Stabile and Aubrey Grant, video recording, March 18, 2021.

150. Nicole Froio, "Non-Carceral Approaches to #MeToo," *Medium* (blog), September 5, 2018, https://medium.com/academica-feminista/non-carceral-approaches-to-metoo-12a4479e0406.

151. Froio, "Non-Carceral Approaches to #MeToo."

152. Gallo and James, interview with Stabile and Grant.

153. Carson, Interview by Stabile and Grant.

154. Alletta Brenner, "Transforming Campus Culture to Prevent Rape: The Possibility and Promise of Restorative Justice as a Response to Campus Sexual Violence," *Harvard Journal of Law and Gender* (2013), https://harvardjlg.com/2013/10/transforming-campus-culture-to-prevent-rape-the-possibility-and-promise-of-restorative-justice-as-a-response-to-campus-sexual-violence/#_ftn1.

155. Amy B. Cyphert, "The Devil Is in the Details: Exploring Restorative Justice as an Option for Campus Sexual Assault Responses under Title IX," *Denver Law Review* 96, no. 1 (2018–2019): 51–86.

156. Dunn, Interview by Stabile and Grant.

157. Manne, *Down Girl*, 279.

158. Cyphert, "The Devil Is in the Details," 51–86.

159. Gallo and James, Interview by Stabile and Grant.

160. Nguyen, "How Students Are Making Change."

161. Nguyen, "How Students Are Making Change."

162. Manne, *Down Girl*, 254.

163. D'Ignazio and Klein, *Data Feminism*, 215–216.

164. Dunn, Interview by Stabile and Grant.

165. Alex Press, "#MeToo Must Avoid 'Carceral Feminism,'" *Vox*, February 1, 2018, https://www.vox.com/the-big-idea/2018/2/1/16952744/me-too-larry -nassar-judge-aquilina-feminism.

166. Mimi E. Kim, "Anti-Carceral Feminism: The Contradictions of Progress and the Possibilities of Counter-Hegemonic Struggle," *Affilia* 35, no. 3 (August 1, 2020): 309, https://doi.org/10.1177/0886109919878276.

167. Froio, "Non-Carceral Approaches to #MeToo."

4

Who's Holding Court?
A Tale of Two Justices

It is as important today as it was in 1991 that I feel free to speak. If I let my fears silence me now, I will have betrayed all of those who supported me in 1991and those who have come forward since. More than anything else, the Hill-Thomas hearing of October 1991 was about finding our voices and breaking the silence forever.—(Anita Hill, in *Speaking Truth to Power*, 1998 on her testimony against Supreme Court nominee Judge Clarence Thomas)[1]

Why suffer through the annihilation if it's not going to matter?—(Christine Blasey Ford, speaking of her decision in August 2018 not to come forward with allegations of sexual assault by Supreme Court nominee Brett Kavanaugh back when they were both in high school)[2]

Now I feel like my civic responsibility is outweighing my anguish and terror about retaliation [for testifying].—(Christine Blasey Ford, after her request to have her allegations remain confidential was violated, explaining her decision to come forward in September 2018)[3]

I think you look to judges to be the arbiters of right and wrong. . . . If they don't have a moral code of their own to determine right from wrong, then that's a problem. So I think it's relevant. Supreme Court nominees should be held to a higher standard.—(Russell Ford, Christine Blasey Ford's husband, speaking of her testimony in 2018)[4]

Harassment is more about upholding gendered status and identity than it is about expressing sexual desire or sexuality. Harassment provides a way for some men to monopolize prized work roles and to maintain a superior masculine position and sense of self.—(Vicki Schultz in an Open Statement on Sexual Harassment from Employment Discrimination Law Scholars in Stanford Law Review, 2018)[5]

Introduction

At the end of 2017, just after the MeToo movement had been declared *Time* magazine's "Person of the Year," Supreme Court Chief Justice Roberts wrote that the judicial branch was also "not immune" to the "problem of sexual harassment in the workplace."[6] The remark came in the context of his annual State of the Judiciary report, where he announced plans to evaluate standards of conduct and procedures for addressing "inappropriate behavior . . . to ensure an exemplary workplace for every judge and every court employee."[7] By mid-December 2017, Judge Alex Kozinski, of the U.S. Court of Appeals for the Ninth Circuit, had joined the ranks of powerful men accused of sexual harassment, after a total of fifteen of his former clerks and externs came forward to report incidents they had experienced while in his employ.[8] During his thirty-two years on the Ninth Circuit, where he had for many years presided as chief judge, his accusers alleged that he had shown them pornography, subjected them to offensive comments, and touched them inappropriately. Kozinski, who retired following the allegations, admitted only to having "a broad sense of humor and a candid way of speaking," and apologized only for perhaps not having "been mindful enough of the special challenges and pressures that women face in the workplace."[9]

Supreme Court Justices Clarence Thomas and Brett Kavanaugh had also each been publicly accused of sexual harassment or assault but survived their confirmation hearings nonetheless and succeeded in securing lifetime appointments on the nation's highest court. Both were nominated to the Supreme Court by Republican presidents, George H. W. Bush and Donald J. Trump, respectively, and each consistently votes with the conservative side of the court. In this chapter, we consider the implications of their presence on the court for women as citizens whose lives will be impacted by their judicial decisions and for the individual women who came forward to testify as character witnesses. We also consider whether and to what extent the personal experiences of these justices with regard to the sexual harassment and assault allegations, as well as their ideological persuasions, might influence or be reflected in their judicial decision-making. Champions of women's rights have seen the ascension of these candidates to the Supreme Court as a significant setback for women's autonomy. We further suggest that such setbacks can constrain women's ability to participate and gain positions of power in the public sphere, exacerbating their overall underrepresentation. The conservative credentials of Justices Thomas and Kavanaugh contribute to the tangible effect of constraining rather than advancing women's rights in cases covering sexual harassment, reproductive rights, and sex discrimination cases. We consider that their status as men accused of sexual harassment and assault, whose accusers were ultimately dismissed in the process of their confirmation hearings, may also influence their judicial decision-making.

Despite the prominent examples of Kozinksi, Kavanaugh, and Thomas, there are very few instances of judges being accused of sexual harassment or assault on public record, making the question of how judicial decisions might be influenced with regard to the experience of committing or being accused of such behaviors impossible to investigate systematically. What is known about sexual misconduct across populations, though, suggests that harassment and assault are likely underreported in the judiciary, as elsewhere. Chief Justice Roberts's call for investigation and policy to prevent sexual harassment in the federal judiciary resulted in the establishment of a working group, which recommended "expanding the definition of workplace misconduct and streamlining reporting procedures by broadening protections for accusers, ensuring that there are fewer obstacles for reporting misconduct and barring retaliation against victims."[10] These measures could serve to enhance accountability in the judiciary and might mitigate the burdens imposed on women by workplace misconduct, lessening the attendant detrimental effects on women's job retention and career advancement often associated with reporting such misconduct. But the measures may prove to be more symbolic than tangibly effectual. Speaking of the incidence of workplace sexual harassment in the decades since employers started routinely providing anti-harassment training, U.S. Equal Employment Opportunity Commissioner Victoria Lipnic said in 2019 that she "was appalled at the number of sexual harassment cases the EEOC continued to see. . . . Everything that people have been doing for the last 30 years is not working."[11] In fact, *Harvard Business Review* reported in 2017 that harassment numbers "haven't budged" since the 1980s, with about 25 percent of women recounting having been sexually harassed at work.[12]

We propose a model for considering the role of judges in women's underrepresentation, based on both their ideology and their status as potential perpetrators of sexual harassment or assault, or as purveyors of sexist attitudes (see figure 4.1). Any judge who engages in sexually harassing behavior, commits sexual assault, or exhibits sexist attitudes in the course of their work can be seen as imposing costs on the women in

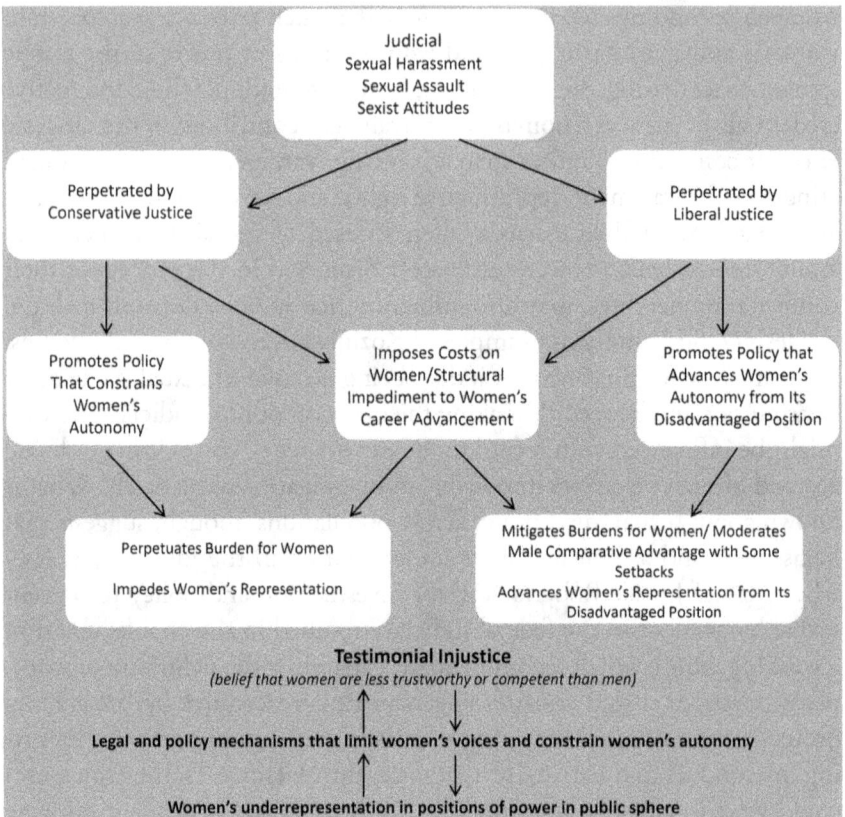

Figure 4.1 Modeling a Role of Judges in Women's Underrepresentation

their employ and collectively creating structural impediments to women's career advancement. These behaviors can affect women's well-being and the course of their career trajectories due to the attendant burdens they impose. Conservative judges can also be expected to promote policy that constrain women's autonomy by supporting measures that, for instance, limit reproductive choice, narrow reporting mechanisms for workplace harassment or violence against women, or limit recourse to establish fair pay. The net effect of the personal behaviors and judicial decisions of conservative judges, then, is expected to perpetuate burdens for women and thus impede women's representation in positions of power overall.

Liberal judges may be no less likely to sexually harass women, commit sexual assault, or perpetuate sexist attitudes than conservative judges, and the same burdens imposed by these noxious behaviors hold true regardless of who perpetrates them. But liberal judges can be relied upon to more likely favor legal judgments that promote policy that advances women's autonomy from its disadvantaged position by strengthening reproductive rights, supporting mechanisms for reporting harassment or violence against women, or advancing measures for workplace equity with regard to pay and treatment. Therefore, despite setbacks attributable to their own sexist or offending behaviors, if they do exhibit them, liberal judges may, nonetheless, contribute to mitigating burdens for women and moderating male comparative advantage, thus having the net effect of facilitating advances in women's representation in the public sphere.

In addition to modeling a role of judges in women's underrepresentation, we suggest extending the use of the theoretical frame of testimonial injustice, which we also applied explicitly in the campus context, for understanding the larger context in which judges' actions—their rulings and workplace or personal behavior—exist. Testimonial injustice is defined as a systemic bias consisting of the belief that women are less trustworthy or competent than men.[13] This bias can be seen as both leading to and resulting from legal and policy mechanisms that limit women's voices and constrain women's autonomy. Ultimately, these structural impediments can be understood as contributing to women's underrepresentation in positions of power and authority. Paradoxically, as we noted in the campus setting and as applies across contexts, it is just such representation that could arguably contribute to legal and policy mechanisms that would make women's testimonial priority more commensurate with that of men.

With this model and framework in mind, we conduct an analysis of cases in several categories related to women's autonomy, examining the rulings of Justices Thomas and Kavanaugh with consideration of both their ideological perspectives and their status as judges plausibly accused of sexual harassment and assault. Further, we consider the confirmation hearings for each of their appointments to the Supreme Court, examining the proceedings and behaviors of the primary actors involved from the perspective of testimonial injustice. As the hearings ostensibly play a gatekeeping role as to who might ascend to lifetime appointments on the nation's highest court, with the power to decide cases with lasting impact through precedent, we believe it is important to examine the construct and conduct of those hearings with regard to who is accorded testimonial priority and to what effect.

Expected Influences on Judicial Decision-Making: Ideological Persuasion and Individual Experience

Since the mid-twentieth century, scholars have investigated the question of whether and to what extent ideology influences judicial behavior.

The majority of social scientists agree that "individual experience . . . informs judicial decision making."[14] These individual experiences have been shown to have a pronounced impact on how justices rule on gender-related cases. Research has found, for instance, that "judges who parent daughters as opposed to sons are more likely to reach liberal decisions—possibly because having daughters causes judges to learn about women's issues."[15] Other scholars find "that ideology—usually measured via partisanship—is among the most important factors shaping judicial decision making."[16] The extent to which ideology influences judicial decisions is contested, though. One study, based on experiments conducted with over two thousand judges suggested that "the political ideology of the judge matters, but only very little."[17] Other scholars suggest that the extent to which a judge's ideology influences their behavior differs across levels of the judiciary.[18] Through the hierarchy postulate, political scientists Christopher Zorn and Jennifer Barnes Bowie argue that the influence of ideology increases as one moves up the judicial hierarchy.[19] They find that "the justices of the U.S. Supreme Court—commanding the 'top' of the pyramid—are widely understood to focus primarily, if not exclusively, on policy-related considerations in their decision making."[20] Other studies find that the politics surrounding judicial appointments influences judicial decision-making; one found that Republican-appointed judges sentenced Black defendants to more time in prison than non-Black defendants and women to less time (at three and two months, respectively) than judges appointed by Democrats.[21] It has been suggested that judicial polarization has grown in recent years and is most visible on the Supreme Court, where justices are sorted in voting blocs; indeed "the notion that a president would nominate a justice who would align with the opposing ideological camp, something that had been relatively common in the past, is now unthinkable."[22]

Representation and Testimonial Injustice

As discussed in the campus context, dominant group members—and here we are referring to men, mostly white—enjoy a surplus of credibility in the wider economy of credibility, while members of historically socially subordinate groups, including women and people of color, are prone to experiencing testimonial injustice due to systemic bias.[23] As evidence of that dominance, it has been noted that of the 114 justices who served on the Supreme Court between when it was established in 1789 and 2020, all but six were white men.[24] When law professor Anita Hill, an African

American woman, testified during Clarence Thomas's Supreme Court confirmation hearing before the Senate Judiciary Committee in 1991, the committee consisted of fourteen white men, and just two women were serving in the Senate at the time.[25] Only one woman had ever served on the Supreme Court: Justice Sandra Day O'Connor, who had been nominated by President Ronald Reagan in his first year in office a decade earlier.[26]

When Christine Blasey Ford testified before the Senate Judiciary Committee in 2018, it consisted of twenty-one members, four of whom were women and three were people of color; all eleven of the Republicans were white men.[27] By then, the Supreme Court, for which Brett Kavanaugh was being vetted at the time, included three women among the nine justices—Ruth Bader Ginsburg, Sonia Sotomayor, and Elena Kagan, who had all been appointed by Democratic presidents (Ginsburg by Bill Clinton in 1993 and Sotomayor and Kagan by Obama, in 2009 and 2010).[28] Supreme Court justices are appointed for life, and though senators must face election every six years, the entrenchment of power achieved by many incumbent office holders is illustrated by the fact that three of the senators on the Judiciary Committee when Hill testified were still on it twenty-seven years later when Blasey Ford appeared before them: Senators Chuck Grassley (R-IA), Orrin Hatch (R-UT), and Patrick Leahy (D-VT). During this period, incumbent senators were reelected between 79 and 96 percent of the time and consistently raised ten times as much or more in campaign funds than the million dollars or so typically raised by their challengers.[29]

Senator Joe Biden (D-DE), in his third term in office at the time, was the chair of the Senate Judiciary Committee in 1991 and served in either that capacity or as ranking member for sixteen of his thirty-six years in the Senate, after which he served as vice president of the United States under Barack Obama from 2009 until 2017, and president beginning in 2021. Reflecting on Hill's treatment during the Thomas hearings later, Biden said, "I did everything in my power to do what I thought was within the rules . . . I don't think I treated her badly."[30] But, as journalist and author Jane Mayer noted, Biden himself had determined the rules that guided the process in the following ways.[31] He agreed to expedite the proceedings, which favored Republican proponents of Thomas, allowing insufficient time to adequately investigate the charges against him. Biden also conceded to Thomas's team that the Judiciary Committee would consider Thomas's workplace behavior alone, which determined that corroborating testimony from witnesses about Thomas's proclivity for watching and talking about pornographic movies would be excluded from the hearing. And though Biden had said that any women who could corroborate Hill's accusations of sexual harassment would be allowed to testify, three such women were ultimately only allowed to submit written statements in the public record, ensuring that few senators would see them. This, as Mayer underscored, was Biden's call, damaging Hill's position and acceding to the favor of traditional power brokers. The rules, as established, meant that the committee would see Senator Orrin Hatch brandishing a copy of *The Exorcist* as he speculated that Hill had cribbed her accusation of Thomas's conduct in part from a passage in that book,[32] but that they would not hear from Angela Wright, Rose Jourdain, or Sukari Hardnett, each of whom could corroborate Hill's accusations and wanted to testify.[33]

Women were seldom seen and heard even less often in any capacity in the Senate environs except in secretarial or other support roles, when Anita Hill, at age thirty-five, raised her right hand to testify before the Senate Judiciary Committee.[34] Wearing a bright blue suit, she stood in sharp contrast to the monochromatic bank of white men in dark suits, many greying or balding, arrayed along the table of questioners before her. As a graduate of Yale Law School and then current professor with experience working at two federal agencies (the Department of Education and Equal Employment Opportunity Commission), Hill's credentials matched those of the committee members, but, as a woman, and a Black woman in particular, younger than most of her interrogators that day, she was an anomaly in their midst.

Biden, for his part, ultimately voted against Thomas's confirmation but, nonetheless, supported a system that favored many of his ideological opponents, with whom he still shared the status of Senate brethren. The principle of homophily attests to the strength of ties between people of similar characteristics and experience.[35] The concept of testimonial injustice helps to explain why, as Hill was "speaking truth to power" (the title of her 1998 book chronicling the experience), her version of events would be considered less credible and her ability to be fully heard thus constrained. Hill's accusations and Thomas's categorical denial constituted the typical "he said, she said" scenario of testimonial injustice, in which men are more likely to be believed, to believe each other, and to favor leaving their collective comparative advantage intact. Senator Howard Metzenbaum (D-OH) quipped that that if Hill had been believed and the behavior she described being subjected to had been acknowledged as sexual harassment, half the Senate might also have been so charged.[36]

"Look at who has power and who is deemed entitled to have power. And what you tend to find is that men are considerably advantaged over their female counterparts," Kate Manne said in a *New Yorker* interview discussing her book *Entitled: How Male Privilege Hurts Women*.[37] This state of affairs is achieved and perpetuated, by a "systematic facet of social power relations"—"the law enforcement branch of the patriarchal order"—that defines misogyny.[38] Manne acknowledged that many men also face substantial disadvantages because of things like race, but said that "when they compare themselves to women in the same demographic, they are privileged under most dimensions."[39]

Based on the conduct and outcomes of the Thomas-Hill hearings and the Kavanaugh–Blasey Ford hearings nearly three decades later, women's ability to be heard in the Senate setting—a historical and persisting bastion of male power—did not seem to have appreciably advanced during that time period. Both episodes were beset by hallmarks of testimonial injustice, in two distinct forms, with women being seen as less competent and less trustworthy.[40] Comments by Senator Hatch, one of the trio of long-term veterans of the Senate Judiciary Committee who presided over both hearings, encapsulate how testimonial injustice continued to play out across the decades. Hatch, who had known Clarence Thomas personally and voted for his confirmation, suggested during the 1991 hearing that Hill had fabricated her testimony based on both the aforementioned horror novel and a court case involving sexual harassment that had recently been reported in Kansas.[41] Then, in 2018, after a phone call with Brett Kavanaugh, whom Hatch also voted to confirm, Hatch said that Blasey Ford, a fifty-one-year-old research psychologist, must have been "mixed up" when she identified Kavanaugh as the individual who had attempted to force himself on her, covering her mouth to suppress her screams, at a party when the two were teenagers.[42]

Various other actors also questioned the mental state and motives of each woman as she brought her story forward. Republican senators accused Professor Hill of being afflicted by "erotomania" and author David Brock called her "a little bit nutty and a little bit slutty"; rumors even circulated that she had returned papers to her University of Oklahoma law students that included pubic hairs.[43] In 2018, then president Trump mocked Blasey Ford's testimony at one of his infamous rallies, parodying her remarks and portraying her as ditzy and dithering: "How did you get home? I don't remember. How'd you get there? I don't remember. Where is the place? I don't remember. How many years ago was it? I don't know . . . I don't know," the president continued, egged on by laughter and applause. "What neighborhood was it in? I don't know. Where's the house? I don't know. Upstairs, downstairs—where was it? I don't know—but I had one beer. That's the only thing I remember."[44] Yet Blasey Ford, a professor of psychology herself, explained in response to questioning from Senator Diane Feinstein (D-CA) at the hearing that the neurotransmitter epinephrine "codes memories into the hippocampus, and so the trauma-related experience is locked there, whereas other details kind of drift."[45] "Indelible in the hippocampus is the laughter, the uproarious laughter between the two [men], and their having fun at my expense," Blasey Ford recounted to Senator Leahy when he asked what was her strongest memory from that night.[46]

Both Hill and Blasey Ford were accused of having been politically motivated or having plotted to bring down men of otherwise purportedly impeccable credentials by relating, in the most public of forums, their stories of harassment and assault. (President George H. W. Bush said of Thomas upon his nomination in July 1991 that he was "a model for all Americans" and that he had "earned the right to sit on this nation's highest court.")[47] Yet each woman had originally declined to testify and ultimately did so out of what they expressed as a sense of duty, after having first attempted to maintain confidentiality in sharing their stories with authorities.[48] After raising their voices, both received death threats.[49] And each comported herself with dignity and forbearance in the face of categorical denials and open expressions of anger on the part of the accused.[50] Hill's demeanor when testifying before the Senate Judiciary Committee in 1991 was described as poised[51] and reserved.[52] Ford, in 2018, was described as "respectful," "gracious, accommodating" and "soft-spoken."[53]

The behavior of the accused in this forum, on the other hand, "gave the lie to the idea that men are expected to be stoical and unemotional."[54] Kavanaugh, described by one observer as "incandescent with rage" was indignant, intractable, and thundering in his responses.[55] He claimed that the accusations amounted to "grotesque" and "coordinated character assassination."[56] Kavanaugh, like Thomas before him, declared the confirmation process "a national disgrace" and "a circus" and said the "advice and consent" role accorded to the Senate in the Constitution had been replaced by a "search and destroy" scenario for his confirmation.[57] Kavanaugh called the proceedings "a political hit fueled with pent up anger about President Trump," and even, without evidence or reason, "revenge on behalf of the Clintons."[58]

Thomas, for his part, had also been overtly outraged and agitated by the charges against him in 1991, calling the hearing "a high-tech lynching for uppity Blacks who in any way deign to think for themselves."[59] Though he was accused by a Black woman with a similar origin story to his, with roots in rural poverty,[60] a Yale Law pedigree, and high-level inside-the-beltway experience and he was championed for the role of Supreme Court Justice by most on the Committee before which he faced her allegations (he was ultimately confirmed by thirteen aye to one nay votes[61]), Thomas continued to portray himself as a victim of racial prejudice. "Unless you kowtow to an old order, this is what will happen to you," he said. "You will be lynched, destroyed, caricatured by a committee of the U.S. Senate, rather than hung from a tree."[62]

Kate Manne chose to open her book, *Entitled: How Male Privilege Hurts Women*, with a profile of Kavanaugh, "red-face, petulant" and shouting most of his answers at the 2018 proceedings,[63] because he was in that moment "the picture of entitlement."[64] What struck her, she said in a *New Yorker* interview, was his strong "sense of entitlement to be a Supreme Court Justice and to hold a position of the highest moral authority in the land, despite the very credible sexual-assault allegation against him."[65] The proceedings were a referendum not only on Kavanaugh's candidacy for the court but can be seen as symbolically important as an indicator of women's ability to be heard and heeded in the public sphere, to navigate halls of power traditionally and predominantly occupied by men, not just for Hill and Blasey Ford, but for all women watching and weighing the costs of entering such a fray.

Particularly when relating their experiences with sexual assault, women are often believed to be lying or mistaken and to see sympathy ceded to those who committed such acts rather than to their actual victims—a phenomenon Manne calls "himpathy."[66] Men accused of sexual assault are often described as having their lives "destroyed" or "ruined" or to be "going through hell," as Senator Lindsey Graham (R-SC) depicted Kavanaugh, while accusers are routinely doubted and denigrated, with "no comparable outpouring of feeling" for their suffering[67] either in the aftermath of the original experience of assault or in the punishing public spectacle of reporting.

A man's "life is in tatters" said Trump after mocking Ford's testimony. "A man's life is shattered."[68] Though he had earlier described her as "a very credible witness" and "a very fine woman,"[69] he ultimately doubled down on the narrative that men are under attack in America and considered "guilty until proven innocent," making no mention of survivors of sexual assault. "Think of your son. Think of your husband," Trump admonished the crowd at a rally, noting that he himself had what he claimed were "many false allegations" against him and calling it "a damn sad situation."[70] Ironically, this "discourse of victimhood" articulated by Thomas, Kavanaugh, and Trump, as described by Professor Sarah Banet-Weiser of the London School of Economics and Political Science, "is appropriated not by those who have historically suffered but by those in positions of patriarchal power," particularly those who are the object of her study of "highly visible, powerful men who have been accused of sexual violence."[71] One reporter described Judge Kozinski's three decades long career as having been "undone" over just ten days as women came forward with allegations against him in 2017,[72] rather than attributing its undoing to Kozinski's own actions over those many years.

Both Thomas and Kavanaugh were spoken of by some as victims, a mantle that they also took on themselves. But the system seems to have worked decisively in their favor during the proceedings, which, in both cases, moved rapidly to a vote on the confirmations, despite the revelations against the nominees, giving short shrift to the attendant FBI investigations of the allegations. In 1991, the FBI's investigation of Anita Hill's accusations was "a small and quiet affair, open and shut inside three days, with as few as three witnesses questioned about the nominee's behavior," that omitted four potential witnesses with prior knowledge of Hill's complaints and resulted in a report that misquoted Hill, according to *Wall Street Journal* reporters.[73] After the three-day-long FBI investigation, the White House declared Hill's allegations "unfounded" and the panel voted thirteen to one to forward Thomas's nomination to the Senate floor, where he was confirmed in a fifty-two to forty-eight vote.[74] Kavanaugh was confirmed by a fifty to forty-eight vote after an FBI investigation that was time-limited by the White House and addled by limits on subpoenas and evidence reached no conclusion and released no findings to the public.[75] Nearly three years after the fact, it was reported that forty-five hundred tips received by the FBI in the investigation (really a background check rather than a criminal investigation) were funneled to Trump White House lawyers "whose handling of them" was "unclear."[76]

Both the accusers and the accused in the Thomas and Kavanaugh cases endured public scrutiny and suffered reputational damage. But the testimony of the women who came forward to testify ultimately did not change the trajectory of the Supreme Court appointments of two men plausibly accused, respectively, of sexual harassment and assault. The result is that these men were granted the authority to adjudicate over many cases involving the well-being and autonomy of women for decades to come, including cases involving sexual harassment. Hill and Blasey

Ford, who served as character witnesses for these candidates, saw their credibility and competence questioned and their testimony constrained and disparaged. In the context of the confirmation hearings, presided over by men of privilege in a system of their own design, women's voices were significantly underrepresented and subject to two main manifestations of testimonial injustice: when a testifier's claims are ignored and when such claims are inappropriately rejected.[77]

We developed four primary categories of cases pertaining to women's autonomy for the purposes of this analysis: (1) sexual harassment, (2) violence against women, (3) reproductive rights, and (4) sex discrimination and workplace discrimination. We derived these classifications from a review of the American Civil Liberties Union (ACLU) Women's Rights Project timeline[78] of major Supreme Court decisions that have bearing on women's rights. In each category, we identified cases from 1992, Justice Thomas's first full year serving on the Supreme Court, through 2020, capturing Justice Kavanaugh's first two full years on the Supreme Court.

For cases coded as either advancing or constraining women's rights in these categories, we note each justice's votes, opinions, concurrences, and dissents, drawing from sources, including the Legal Information Institute of Cornell Law School and Oyez, a free law project from Cornell's Legal Information Institute (LII), Justia, and Chicago-Kent College of Law. As Justice Kavanaugh's track record on the court is still nascent at the time of this writing, additional sources are used in assessing his judicial record and propensities with regard to women's rights, including National Women's Law Center's report, "The Record of Brett M. Kavanaugh on Critical Legal Rights for Women."[79]

Further, we examine the court hearings and the circumstances surrounding them, prior to the confirmations of Justices Thomas and Kavanaugh, where testimony was given regarding the alleged misconduct of the nominees, informed by insights from the concept of testimonial injustice originated by Fricker.[80]

Justice Thomas's Decisions on Sexual Harassment Cases

We identified ten cases involving rulings with bearing on sexual harassment during Justice Thomas's tenure on the Supreme Court on which he weighed in through a vote, delivering an opinion, or registering concurrence or dissent. Of those ten cases decided between 1992 and 2013, eight can be construed as having advanced women's rights. In the eight cases that were decided in a way that can be seen as advancing women's rights, albeit with limitations, Justice Thomas dissented four times: once as the sole dissent (*PA State Police v. Suders*, 2004); twice joining Justice Scalia (*Faragher v. City of Boca Raton*, 1998 and *Burlington Industries, Inc. v. Ellerth*, 1998); and once joining the dissent, written by Justice Kennedy, with Chief Justice Rehnquist, and Justice Scalia also voting no (*Davis v. Monroe County Board of Education*, 1999). Of the two Supreme Court decisions involving harassment cases seen as constraining rather than advancing women's rights (both decided in a five to four vote), Justice Thomas wrote a concurring opinion for one, *Vance v. Ball State*, in 2013, and voted with the majority in the case of *Gebser v. Lago Vista Independent School District* in 1998.

In the *Vance v. Ball State* case, Maetta Vance, a Dining Services employee at Ball State University in Indiana, complained of having been slapped, blocked from exiting an elevator, and referred to by racial epithets, including "Sambo" and "Buckwheat" by Saundra Davis, a catering specialist. Davis was "responsible for supervising and providing leadership for kitchen assistants and substitutes," including Vance, who served as catering assistant.[81] Another employee, Connie McVickers, bragged at work about family ties to the Ku Klux Klan and also called Vance, the only African American in the department, by a racial slur.[82] Vance reported feeling unsafe at work and later sued the university in federal district court for being unjustly disciplined and having her work duties and ability to work overtime curtailed.[83] The district court held that "the University was not liable for the actions of individual coworkers," as it would be for those officially designated as supervisors under Title VII.[84] The Supreme Court decision announced in January 2013 similarly found that "for the purposes of liability for workplace harassment under Title VII, the definition of a 'supervisor' is limited to a person empowered to take tangible employment action against the victim."[85] Since Davis was not in a position to take "tangible employment actions" over Vance, such as hiring, firing, or changing work assignments, the court found that the employer, Ball State, could not be held liable for harassment. In his concurring opinion, Justice Thomas endorsed the majority's opinion establishing what he called the "'narrowest and most workable rule' for ruling on an employer's liability for harassment."[86]

According to Adaku Onyeka-Crawford, director of educational equity and senior counsel of the National Women's Law Center (NWLC), because of *Vance*, many who have suffered from workplace harassment, including sexual harassment, have been "denied their day in court, not because harassment didn't occur, but because of a legal technicality that leads to the conclusion the harassment wasn't the employer's fault."[87] The stricter definition of "supervisor" set forth by *Vance* means that some colloquially known as supervisors, like Davis, who do, in fact, exert authority over the daily work lives of others, are technically regarded as mere coworkers, and "the standard for coworker harassment is negligence, which is a much tougher standard to prove as a plaintiff."[88] According to the NWLC, by November 2014 alone, just short of two years after *Vance*, forty-three sexual harassment cases were dismissed because victims couldn't prove that the harasser was officially a supervisor. The five-to-four decision in *Vance* has been called a win for corporate America,[89] in keeping with the business-friendly nature of the Roberts court, the most pro-business court since at least World War II.[90]

In *Gebser v. Lago Vista Independent School District*, Justice Thomas had earlier voted with the majority in favor of a position that also narrowed institutional liability, setting a "highly restrictive standard . . . for determining when school districts can be found liable under Federal law for a teacher's sexual harassment of a student."[91] In the case in question, high school teacher Frank Waldrop led a book discussion group, to which an eighth-grade student, Alida Star Gebser, was assigned in 1991. Waldrop, who was known to make sexually suggestive comments to students, eventually made sexual advances toward Gebser, with whom he initiated a sexual relationship. Waldrop was arrested, fired, and had his teaching license revoked in 1993 after a police officer discovered him having sex with the underage student. Later that year, Gebser and her mother sought damages under Title IX against the Lago Vista School District. After a district court ruled in favor of the school district, the Supreme Court agreed to review the opinion of the lower court (known legally as granting certiorari). Justice Sandra Day O'Connor delivered the opinion of the Supreme Court in 1998, saying that "damages may not be recovered in those circumstances unless an official of the school district who at a minimum has authority to institute corrective measures on the district's behalf has actual notice of, and is deliberately indifferent to, the teacher's misconduct."[92] The court reasoned that, while the harassment of students by teachers is "all too common" and "reprehensible," they did not think it appropriate to attribute "the independent misconduct of a teacher" to the school district that employs him under Title IX, which they said was primarily designed to prevent "recipients of federal financial assistance from using the funds in a discriminatory manner."[93] Writing for the dissenting justices, though, Justice Stevens said that "the majority's policy judgment about the appropriate remedy in this case thwarts the purposes of Title IX" and "ranks protection of the school district's purse above the protection of immature high school students."[94]

Justice Stevens concluded his dissenting opinion by saying that failing to hold the school district liable was "not faithful to the intent of the policymaking branch of our government. . . . It is not clear to me why," he continued, "the well-settled rules of law that impose responsibility on the principal for the misconduct of its agents should not apply in this case," especially since the students harmed in such cases "are members of the class for whose special benefit Congress enacted Title IX."[95] But that very fact may actually explain why the court would make such a policy choice. As a precursor to her discussion of testimonial injustice as hierarchy preservation, Kate Manne notes that we "have a tendency to pardon the hitherto historically dominant," and "that power does not tend to be granted to historically subordinate people vis-à-vis the dominant without a fight."[96] Those subjected to harassment in workplaces and schools are often from historically subordinate groups, including women, people of color, and workers dependent on a paycheck. Standards that constrain the scope of who can be held responsible for workplace harassment, such as defined in the original parameters of Title VII and subsequent court decisions like *Vance*, can be understood as being concerned with preserving the power of the historically dominant—employers, men, and white people, who have overwhelmingly been the authors of such standards—more so than with righting injustices experienced by those with weak political power, who are also often defined by negative social constructions and have been historically socially subordinate. Without sufficient recourse to address harassment in the workplace or educational institutions, members of such subordinate groups can be expected to continue to experience burdens that limit their ability to transcend that subordinate status and achieve more proportional representation in positions of power and privilege.

Gatekeepers, including Supreme Court justices like Thomas, as well as the people whom their policy decisions impact, are characterized by complex intersecting identities that influence their own beliefs and choices, as well as how they are affected by the systems in which they are situated. Justice Thomas, an African American man, is, at the time of this writing, the second of only two African Americans to serve on the court since it was founded. He is also a JD graduate of Yale Law School, the top ranked law school in the United States.[97] He was nominated to the court by Republican president George H. W. Bush, who considered both Thomas's race and conservative credentials in choosing him to fill Justice Thurgood Marshall's place upon his retirement from the court in 1991.[98] Thomas is a noteworthy figure for his status as the most conservative justice on the court since the 1930s, the first of two justices to be accused of sexual harassment or impropriety during his confirmation hearing, and for being the longest serving justice, with three decades spent honing his identity as the court's most right-wing member.[99] Though it is impossible to say with certainty what aspects of identity, whether ideological persuasion or individual experience, might have the most influence on Thomas or any other justice's decision-making, it is our intent here to illustrate just how influential any given gatekeeper can be in maintaining patriarchal order, which we take to include historical race and class, as well as gender, supremacy.

As a man notoriously accused of workplace sexual harassment himself, Thomas voted in Gebser to make the job of addressing sexual harassment in schools more difficult, by making the school district liable only if a supervising employee knows of the abuse, has authority to intervene, and fails to do so.[100] With the power differential between students, especially underage ones, and teachers, who are the ultimate authority figures in the classroom, most victims of sexual harassment by teachers are afraid to report; they may be uncertain of how or to whom to report; they may fear being disbelieved or the possibility of facing condemnation from parents or peers; they may even harbor misplaced feelings of shame or responsibility for what transpired.[101] These factors, and a liability standard that relies upon official knowledge of harassment "would effectively immunize school districts much of the time" according to the National Women's Law Center.[102] And the number of those affected is not insubstantial; according to a report made available through the Office of Justice Programs' National Criminal Justice Reference Service in 2017, "an estimated 10 percent of K–12 students will experience sexual misconduct by a school employee by the time they graduate from high school."[103]

PA State Police v. Suders, 2004, established the right to sue for sexual harassment even if the employee didn't initially report it, with Justice Thomas penning the sole dissent. The case involved a police dispatcher, Nancy Drew Suders, who quit her job after enduring persistent sexual harassment for months, including "obscene gestures, lewd comments, and humiliation," from her supervisors.[104] Suders subsequently brought suit in federal district court, claiming that she had been forced to quit due to intolerable working conditions (known in legal parlance as a case of "constructive discharge"),[105] but the court determined that she could not bring suit since she had not used the employer's set process for reporting, and the employer had not taken any overt "tangible employment action against her."[106] On appeal, though, the district judge's decision was overturned, and the Third Court of Appeals ruled that the police were, in fact, responsible for her quitting, since the harassment had been so bad. As Justice Ruth Bader Ginsburg wrote in the eight-to-one Supreme Court decision, "a reasonable person in the employee's position would have felt compelled to resign."[107] As the sole dissenter, Thomas wrote that in an "*alleged* constructive discharge" resulting "*only* from a hostile work environment, an employer is liable *if* negligent" (italics added for emphasis); Thomas wrote that Suders, as the respondent, had "not adduced sufficient evidence of an adverse employment action taken because of her sex, nor . . . proffered any evidence that petitioner knew or should have known of the alleged harassment."[108]

Thomas's dissent[109] might be construed as downplaying or doubting the harassment reported by Suders by calling her quitting an "*alleged* constructive discharge"—in effect calling into question the veracity of the intolerable nature of her working conditions. Thomas elaborated that in such an act of quitting, if *only* a hostile work environment is the cause (perhaps implying that there might be other reasons for the employee to have quit, or that a hostile work environment in and of itself might not be sufficient grounds for quitting), an employer is only liable *if* they can be shown to be negligent. But the catch here, as in so many cases of women reporting harassment or assault, is that their evidence is routinely deemed insufficient based on the policy mechanisms in place. In Thomas's view,[110] the aggrieved employee here did not provide sufficient evidence of "an adverse employment action taken against her because of her sex" or provide any evidence that the petitioner—the Pennsylvania State Police Department, her employer—"knew or should have known about the *alleged* harassment," when, in fact, three of her supervisors evidently not only knew about the harassment but perpetrated it themselves.

The facts of the *PA State Police v. Suders* case, as summarized by the Court of Appeals and recited in the opinion of the Supreme Court by Justice Ginsburg,[111] include the following: one of Suder's Pennsylvania State Police supervisors, Sergeant Eric D. Easton, who served as station commander, would bring up the subject of people having sex with animals whenever Suder entered his office. He also told a colleague, in Suder's presence, that young girls should be taught how to gratify men with oral sex, and he would sit near her wearing spandex shorts and spread his legs apart. Another of her supervisors, Patrol Corporal William D. Baker, would grab his genitals and shout out a "vulgar comment inviting oral sex" five to ten times a night when Suders was on shift, sometimes jumping on a chair while he was so gesturing; he would also "rub his rear end in front of her and remark 'I have a nice ass, don't I?'"[112]

During the Supreme Court confirmation process for then judge Clarence Thomas in 1991, Anita Hill's testimony before the Senate Judiciary Committee outlined similar comments (though not gestures) on the part of Thomas when he was Hill's supervisor at both the Department of Education and the Equal Employment Opportunity Commission. Thomas, who, according to Hill's testimony, repeatedly asked Hill to see him socially outside of work, would describe to her "in vivid detail" pornography he had seen that involved women having sex with animals and rape scenes, among other scenarios.[113] He also, according to Hill, boasted about his own "sexual prowess," once mentioning a porn star named "Long Dong Silver," and spoke about his own penis size.[114]

Sociologists Angela Hattery and Earl Smith note that institutions that are sex segregated are characterized by hypermasculinity, in which "rape jokes are commonly told" and "women are sexually objectified."[115] These institutions include police departments, fraternities, the military, and we argue here, all bastions of societal power from which women had been historically barred and in which they are, more recently, substantially underrepresented, including the legislature and the judiciary at state and federal levels. In such hypermasculine cultures, Hattery and Smith say, men often engage in gender-based violence—which we argue includes harassment in the form of aggressive, sexually charged derision and verbal harassment—to demonstrate their masculinity and reinforce women's inferiority. Such put-downs can have a dehumanizing quality aimed at undermining women's perceived competence[116] and serve a gatekeeping function to (continue to) exclude women from positions of power.

In addition to the overt sexual harassment endured by Suders while in the employ of the Pennsylvania State Police, her supervisors also took more direct aim at her professional competence. Supervisor Corporal Eric B. Prendergast told her that "the village idiot could do her job" as a police dispatcher.[117] And, after Suders repeatedly took a required computer skills exam to fulfill a job requirement, she was told by her supervisors each time that she had failed; she subsequently discovered her ungraded exams in a drawer in the women's locker-room and concluded that they had never been officially forwarded for grading. After she took the tests, which she considered to be her own property, from the locker-room, her supervisors, though never bringing official theft charges against her, apprehended, handcuffed, and interrogated her, at first refusing to release her, despite her stated desire to tender her previously prepared statement of resignation.[118]

Questioning women's competence and trustworthiness are hallmarks of testimonial injustice.[119] Subjecting women to denigrating rhetoric and behavior, then casting doubt on their motives for reporting such injustices—or questioning the very veracity of their statements about them—serves to perpetuate the systems in which women's voices are effectively silenced or blunted. When Anita Hill came forward as a character witness for Judge Thomas, lawmakers cast about for motives Hill might have had for reporting the harassment. Senator Howell Heflin (D-AL) asked her if she was "a scorned woman" or "a zealot civil rights believer," whether she had a "militant attitude relative to the area of civil rights" or a "martyr complex."[120] Hill demurred that she did not seek or enjoy the attention that Heflin implied that she was courting by bringing forth her testimony; to this charge she replied that she did not enjoy the attention, but that even if she did, she would not lie to get it.[121] Senator Patrick Leahy (D-Vermont) asked Hill if she had anything to gain by coming to the hearing; "Has anybody promised you anything for coming forth with this story now?"[122] he asked. Women are often subject to accusations of self-promotion or profit seeking for bringing accusations of sexual harassment or assault. Hill's response to Leahy typified the experience of many women in similar circumstances when she replied, "I have nothing to gain here. This has been disruptive of my life, and I have taken a number of personal risks. I have been threatened, and I have not gained anything except knowing that I came forward and did what I felt that I had an obligation to do and that was to tell the truth."[123]

Senator Arlen Specter (R-PA) questioned the reliability of Hill's testimony at the hearings in 1991, which took place eight or ten years after the interactions between herself and Thomas had occurred. "Federal law is very firm on a six-month period of limitation; how sure can you expect this committee to be on the accuracy of your statements?" Specter asked.[124] Yet, statutes of limitations are known to work in the favor of those who do the harassing or engage in any form of gender-based violence, since it is a well-understood psychological phenomenon that victims are often reticent to come forward and may delay doing so for extended periods of time due to shame, denial, minimization, and fear of the consequences of reporting.[125] As feminist legal scholar Catherine MacKinnon described, statutes of limitations "disappear" the legal existence of possible claims,[126] diminishing the possibility of accountability and promulgating the authority of those in power who can continue to take advantage of their position with impunity. Hill herself explained, when questioned by Senator Alan Simpson (R-WY) during Thomas's confirmation hearings as to how she could have continued a professional relationship with Thomas after his behavior in the early 1980s, "I was afraid of retaliation. I was afraid of damage to my professional life . . . this type of response is not atypical, and I can't explain . . . it takes an expert in psychology to explain how that can happen."[127] Ironically, the next woman to testify about experiencing sexually harassing behavior before a Supreme Court confirmation hearing would bear just such a credential, when psychology professor Dr. Christine Blasey Ford later spoke of Brett Kavanaugh assaulting her when the two were high school students.

In addition to rules limiting the time period and circumstances under which one's testimony might be given, another tactic that can diminish or discredit women is the suggestion that they are mentally or emotionally unstable. When Hill took a lie detector test intended to substantiate the credibility of her statements, Senator Alan K. Simpson (R-WY) suggested that she could have passed the polygraph due to being delusional.[128] Even though the FBI had asked Professor Hill if she would be willing to submit to a lie detector test during their initial interrogation, once she submitted the results of such a test, various male gatekeepers in the confirmation process were at pains to downplay their importance or reliability. Senator Orrin G. Hatch (R-UT) questioned their integrity, saying, "You can find a polygraph operator for anything you want them for."[129] Senator Arlen Specter (R-PA) declared such tests inadmissible in court, calling them unreliable. And Committee Chair Senator Joseph Biden, Jr. (D-PA) said it would be a "sad day for the civil liberties of this country" if we were to admit such tests in Judiciary Committee proceedings.[130] When asked if Thomas, as nominee, should take a lie detector test, President Bush replied, "I think it's a stupid idea." If the intent is to use the test to challenge "the word of one over another"—in this case, Hill over Thomas—"I reject it," Bush asserted.[131]

In both the *PA State Police v. Suders* case and Judge Thomas's confirmation hearing, we see overlapping systems at play that disadvantaged the women who came forward to report having been harassed and advantaged the men so accused. In both cases, the women reporting the harassment described language that objectifies and demeans women. Such language, of the ilk famously described by former President Donald Trump as "locker-room talk," we argue, has been "implicated in the perpetuation of unjust social hierarchies," enacting "norms constitutive of harm."[132] Mary Kate McGowan, professor of metaphysics and philosophy of language and law at Wellesley College, describes how "what might seem like harmless fun" to some, "what is taken to be mere male bonding, and what functions as ordinary banter might also be an act of oppression."[133] Such language can be spoken with hostile intent, meant to metaphorically mark territory where women are warned against treading, including traditional bastions of male authority like police stations or federal agencies. It can wield particular power when uttered by supervisors or others with authority over its rhetorical targets. But even absent such intent or authority, the use of such language has the potential to do harm.[134] The harm of greatest concern to us here is the role it plays in ostracizing women from positions of power and professional influence that ultimately perpetuate, or at least slow ascent from, their historically subordinate status. This can be accomplished by the creation of hostile working conditions that may compel women to leave and thus become impediments to their career progression. Such language can also signal to others that women are unwelcome or unfit by raising objectifying or sexualized stereotypes that can undermine their perceived competency, credibility or appropriateness for particular roles or workplaces.

Both Suders and Hill may well have been expected to remain silent by their accused harassers, given that each exercised professional authority over them that, in Suder's case, caused her to quit and in Hill's caused her to stay silent until Thomas stood to attain a lifetime appointment to the nation's highest court. Not only did Suders and Hill endure the original insult and injury of verbal harassment, but reporting it required them to repeat objectionable and embarrassing utterances that would open them to derision and disbelief and forever affiliate their names with their accusations of sexual harassment against powerful men. In the process of reporting, Hill was asked to repeat some uncomfortable details of her testimony for the potentially prurient interest of her all-male interrogators on the Senate Judiciary Committee.

According to a CBS News report, in response to Hill's reporting that Thomas has spoken about pornography and women with large breasts, Senator Arlen Specter (R-PA) suggested that discussing the latter was common workplace behavior, saying, with a smirk, "This is not too bad—women's large breasts. That is a word we use all the time."[135] He then goaded Hill to say "large breasts" a second time, after having already asked her about the comment.[136] In her opening statement, Hill recounted an incident in which she said Thomas asked her who had put a pubic hair on his can of Coke; half an hour later, during questioning, Biden asked, "Can you describe it, once again, for me please?"[137]

Thomas's dissent in the Suders case might be inferred as having been influenced both by his ideological leanings and his personal experience as one accused of sexual harassment by Hill long after the harassment occurred. The court's decision in the Suders case established the right to sue for sexual harassment, even if the employee didn't initially report it. This represented a material gain for women by eliminating a procedural boundary to reporting and bringing suit for sexual harassment, in spite of Thomas's lone dissent. Given the eight-to-one decision, it is reasonable to consider how consequential such a dissenting opinion is likely to be in the four total cases where Thomas penned or joined dissents or, more, broadly in sexual harassment cases.

In a lecture on the topic of dissenting opinions published in 2011, Justice Ginsburg noted that dissents could have both an "in house" and wider impact. Among colleagues in the court, she said, an impressive dissent could lead to the refinement or clarification of the majority opinion circulated in initial draft or even, on occasion, attract the votes needed to become the opinion of the court.[138] Externally, according to Ginsburg, dissents could attract public attention and be used to propel legislative change. Yale Law Professor Akhil Amar said in an interview with NPR's Nina Totenberg in 2019 that while Thomas himself had "not written many high-visibility majority opinions for the court" he had introduced "many new ideas into the conversation," some of which eventually win.[139] Such power of persuasion could prove to be much more consequential "if the new conservative Supreme Court majority starts rethinking major and long-established precedents in other areas" with Thomas, the longest serving justice on the court, with no plans to retire,[140] leading the way. When Totenberg considered the topic in 2011, she asked experts whether Thomas, whose voice had not been deemed central to the biggest decisions of the court in the last quarter century, could actually be considered influential; it was his dissents that were attention grabbing, she suggested.[141] Supreme Court advocate Tom Goldstein replied, "I think he's planting flowers in a garden that he thinks are going to bloom a long time from now. And whether that's going to happen is going to depend on the court's membership."[142]

The Suders decision in 2004, with Thomas's noted dissent, furthered "the objectives and policy considerations" promoted in earlier "pathmarking opinions," including the dual 1998 decisions in *Burlington Industries, Inc. v. Ellerth* and *Faragher v. City of Boca Raton*,[143] with Thomas dissenting and Scalia joining the dissent in both cases. In these opinions, the Supreme Court technically lowered the bar for workers to make a case that they had been sexually harassed, saying, in the former, that employers are vicariously liable for supervisors who create hostile working conditions for those over whom they have authority and, in the latter, that an employer is vicariously liable under Title VII of the Civil Rights Act of 1964 for discrimination caused by a supervisor.[144] Despite having been considered advancements, though, these two cases are also seen as being responsible for making workplace sexual harassment lawsuits particularly difficult to file.[145] This is because the "Fargher-Ellerth defense" allows employers to escape liability for actionable sexual harassment if they can show that they have a sexual harassment policy in place that includes some procedure for reporting.[146] An "Open Statement on Sexual Harassment from Employment Discrimination Law Scholars" published in the *Stanford Law Review* in 2018 argued that the "Fargher-Ellerth defense" is thus responsible for sexual or hostile-work-environment harassment being treated differently than other forms of discrimination, where supervisors *can* be held liable whether "higher-ups" knew about it or not.[147] Requiring victims of sexual or hostile-work-environment harassment to show that they have first gone through the internal complaint process in their workplace ignores the fact that most victims never formally report for fear of losing their jobs or other retaliation from employers due to shame or the belief that the workplace where they are experiencing harassment is unlikely to take constructive action to address the problem.[148] Further, the requirement expressed in these cases for hostile-work-environment harassment victims to prove that the conduct they were subjected to was sufficiently "severe or pervasive" creates an unduly high standard that "prevents many victims from having their day in court, let alone winning."[149] Even with these constraints, Thomas's dissents in these cases expressed the desire to further constrain the ability of victims to report and to strengthen the advantage of employers. Thomas wrote that "an employer should be liable if, and only if, the plaintiff proves that the employer was negligent in permitting the supervisor's conduct to occur" in *Burlington Industries v. Ellerth;* in *Faragher v. Boca Raton*, Thomas took issue with the majority opinion that the city "should be liable as a matter of law" *merely*, Thomas said, "because it did not disseminate its sexual harassment policy."[150]

In *Davis v. Monroe County Board of Education* Thomas joined the dissent to the court's 1999 ruling that public schools could be sued for damages if they failed to stop sexual harassment by students.[151] The case involved a fifth-grade girl, LaShonda Davis, whose classmate repeatedly groped her breasts and genitals. Teachers to whom she reported the behavior did nothing to stop it, and eventually the girl's grades began to slip, and she became suicidal. Her parents filed a criminal complaint against the classmate, who ultimately pled guilty to sexual battery and moved to a different school district; her parents also brought suit against the school district, leading to the Supreme Court case.[152] While the majority opinion, written by Justice Sandra Day O'Connor, held that school districts should be responsible for such student misconduct, it stipulated that the misconduct must be so "'severe, pervasive, and objectively offensive' that it makes it impossible for students to receive the benefits of their public education."[153] The stringent standard was expressly established to avoid legal action being taken in cases where a student has been merely "'teased' or 'called offensive names,'" O'Connor wrote, but dissenting Justices Kennedy, Scalia, Thomas, and Rehnquist inveighed against the specter of federal intrusion into "day-to-day classroom logistics and interactions" and what Kennedy's dissent characterized as overreaction to behaviors that were what he called "routine problems of adolescence."[154] Justice O'Connor concluded her announcement of the court's decision by directly addressing the dissenters' implication that "the ruling would 'teach little Johnny a perverse lesson in federalism.'" Rather, she said, the majority believed the decision "assures that little Mary may attend class."[155]

Justice Kennedy's dismissal of sexual harassment as a "routine problem of adolescence" for which federal intervention would be an overreach inadvertently conveys one important element of truth, and that is that sexual harassment in "just part of the school day" for many middle and high school students in the United States, about half of whom experience such harassment and its negative effects.[156] Girls are more likely to be sexually harassed in person and online; are harassed more frequently, physically, and intrusively than boys; and are also more likely to experience negative effects of harassment, including trouble sleeping, decreased productivity, and increased absenteeism.[157] O'Connor's comment about "little Mary" attending class acknowledges that sexual harassment can be a barrier to girls' access to education as early as primary school. And, in keeping with the overarching thesis of our present analysis, we argue that such setbacks, set in motion in the early years of education, can have a stunting effect on the educational advancement of girls, with potential long-term consequences for their educational and professional advancement, and thus their wider representation in positions of authority. Further, allowing young perpetrators of such harassment to act with impunity while on their own unfolding educational and professional paths enables that pattern of behavior to continue in spheres of power, creating continuing obstacles for young girls and women.

In addition to his four notable dissents in sexual harassment cases that were decided in ways that we interpret as at least nominally advancing women's rights, Thomas voted with the court in four such sexual harassment cases that were decided unanimously. In 1992 and 1993, his first two full years on the court, Thomas joined unanimous decisions in favor of the individuals over the organizations named in cases involving sexual harassment. The first of these, *Franklin v. Gwinnet County Public Schools* in 1992, allowed that monetary damages are available under Title IX to remedy the violation of the federal right to access education. *Harris v. Forklift Systems, Inc., 1993* decided that sexual harassment need not "seriously affect [an employee's] psychological well-being" in order to create an "abusive work environment" that violates Title VII of the Civil Rights Act of 1964.[158] In 2001, he delivered the unanimous opinion in *Pollard v. E. I. du Pont de Nemours & Company* "that front pay is not an element of compensatory damages under the Civil Rights Act of 1991 and thus is not subject to the damages cap imposed by the Act."[159] Finally, though he voted with the unanimous court in *Crawford v. Nashville* in 2009 to extend the antiretaliation provision of Title VII to people who speak out to "oppose" sexually obnoxious behavior, he was joined by Justice Alito in a separate concurring opinion stipulating that the plain meaning of "oppose" should not include "silent opposition," thus favoring some limitation on that extension.[160]

The cases that we coded as extending women's rights may effectively advance their voice and power by identifying legal protections, with some limitations, for those reporting sexual harassment in the workplace, and expanding the legal mechanisms for seeking compensatory damages for hostile work conditions based on sex. Employers or school boards facing legal action or monetary damages for sexually harassing behavior in the workplaces or learning environments that they oversee are thus more likely to be held accountable and incentivized to prevent it. This can be seen as a benefit to women, who have historically been subjected to such behavior without recourse, and as an imposition of some measure of burden on those who previously faced no consequences for engaging in or tolerating sexual harassment.

In sum, Justice Thomas rendered legal interpretations that favored organizations or employers over individuals in ways that we interpret as constraining rather than advancing women's rights in six out of ten cases dealing with sexual harassment brought before the court (see table 4.1). In one of the four cases where he joined unanimous decisions favoring the

Table 4.1 Ten Harassment/Sexual Harassment Supreme Court Decisions with Thomas Vote between 1992 and 2020[i,*]

Constraining Women's Rights/Pro Employer	Advancing Women's Rights/Pro Employee/ Student
Vance v. Ball State, 2013 • **Thomas wrote concurring opinion, 5–4** • **Decision:** Narrow definition of supervisor for determining liability for workplace harassment • RBG dissent says decision ignores conditions of the modern workforce and that a more workable definition of a supervisor would be that offered by the Equal Employment Opportunity Commission (EEOC)	*Crawford v. Nashville*, 2009 • *Unanimous decision: Thomas and Alito filed a separate concurring opinion on this unanimous opinion that the plain meaning of "oppose" should not include "silent opposition" (limiting)* • **Decision:** Anti-retaliation provision of Title VII extends to people who speak out . . . includes people who "oppose" sexually obnoxious behavior by merely disclosing the violation and need not initiate the disclosure
Gebser v. Lago Vista Independent School District, 1998 • **Thomas voted with the majority**, *5-4* • **Decision:** The court held that two criteria must be met in order for an aggrieved party to recover sexual harassment damages under the Title IX of the Education Amendments of 1972	*PA State Police v. Suders*, 2004 • **Thomas sole dissent** • **Decision:** Right to sue for sexual harassment even if didn't initially report. RBG opinion—a "reasonable person . . . would have felt compelled to resign"
	Pollard v. E. I. du Pont de Nemours & Company, 2001 • *Unanimous opinion delivered by Justice Clarence Thomas* • **Decision:** Front pay is not an element of compensatory damages under the Civil Rights Act of 1991 and, thus, is not subject to the damages cap imposed by the Act
	Davis v. Monroe County Board of Education, 1999 • *Thomas joins dissent, written by Kennedy, with Chief Justice Rehnquist, and Scalia also voting no, 5-4 opinion* • **Decision:** Private damage actions may lie against schools that act with deliberate indifference to harassment that is severe enough to prevent victims from enjoying educational opportunities

(Continued)

Table 4.1   (*Continued*)

Constraining Women's Rights/Pro Employer	Advancing Women's Rights/Pro Employee/ Student
	***Burlington Industries, Inc. v. Ellerth*, 1998** • **Scalia and Thomas dissenting**, 7-2 opinion • **Decision:** The court held that employers are vicariously liable for supervisors who create hostile working conditions for those over whom they have authority
	Faragher v. City of Boca Raton*, 1998** • ***Scalia and Thomas dissenting, 7-2 opinion • **Decision:** An employer is vicariously liable under Title VII of the Civil Rights Act of 1964 for actionable discrimination caused by a supervisor
	***Harris v. Forklift Systems, Inc.*, 1993** • *Unanimous decision* • **Decision:** Justice O'Connor wrote, "Certainly Title VII bars conduct that would seriously affect a reasonable person's psychological well being, but . . . there is no need for it also to be psychologically injurious (in order to find that it violates Title VII)."
	***1992. Franklin v. Gwinnet County Public Schools*, 1992** • *Unanimous decision (Scalia special concurrence to imply limitations)* • **Decision:** Monetary damages are available under Title IX because there is a presumption that any appropriate relief is available to remedy the violation of a federal right

[i] Case details in table 4.1 from www.oyez.org/cases.

* Thomas opinions, votes or dissents that favor organizations or employers over individuals and can be seen as constraining rather than advancing women's rights are bolded and italicized (in six of the ten cases here); in one additional case (*Crawford v. Nashville*) his concurring opinion is interpreted as constituting a limitation on such a right even though he voted with the unanimous opinion of the court to confer that right.

plaintiff (*Crawford*), he filed a separate concurring opinion that can be viewed as a limitation on that right.

Thomas's Decisions on Violence against Women

While we consider Thomas's opinions on cases related to sexual harassment most pertinent to our analysis, we also consider three additional categories of importance to women's autonomy, beginning with violence against women. Though this category contains just two cases on which Thomas voted during his tenure on the court during the observed time period, they serve as relevant examples of women's constrained testimonial authority and access to justice.

A unanimous decision of the court made in June 2006 in *Davis v. Washington* determined that statements made to police during the investigation of a crime could be admitted in court without allowing defendants to cross-examine the person who made the original statements.[161] The decision would allow such a woman's voice, in the form of the call transcript, to be heard as evidence in court without necessitating that it be considered "testimony," thus sparing her the burdensome need to appear and be cross-examined, an especially onerous prospect in cases of intimate partner violence. In the original case, a woman named Michelle McCottry called 911 to report that she had been beaten by her former boyfriend, who had then fled the scene.[162] When the 911 call was offered as evidence at trial, the accused had objected that his Sixth Amendment right to confront his accuser had been violated. Justice Thomas wrote a separate opinion for the nine-to-zero decision, both concurring and dissenting in part, saying in the latter case that "though McCottry's statements were not testimonial, the court should not 'guess' at the primary motive behind the statements," a dissent that seems to express some concern to limit the breadth of the decision expressed by the court and the attendant power of the evidence introduced against the accused abuser.[163]

In the earlier case of *United States v. Morrison*, the court held in May 2020 that Congress did not have the authority to enact the Violence Against Women Act of 1994 (VAWA) under either the Commerce Clause or Fourteenth Amendment.[164] Christy Brzonkala, who had been raped as a student at Virginia Tech by fellow students (varsity football players Antonio Morrison and James Crawford), sought redress through this avenue after one of her assailants received a light punishment that was ultimately set aside, and the other received no punishment at all. In the majority five-to-four opinion, Chief Justice Rehnquist said that "if the allegations here are true, no civilized system of justice could fail to provide [Brzonkala] a remedy for the conduct of . . . Morrison. But under our federal system that remedy must be provided by the Commonwealth of Virginia, and not by the United States."[165] Justice Thomas concurred. Yet, in his dissent, Justice Souter said that VAWA contained a "mountain of data assembled by Congress . . . showing the effects of violence against women on interstate commerce."[166]

Rehnquist's statement suggests that he either believed that the system of justice over which he himself prevailed was not "a civilized system of justice" or that the allegations on which the case was based were not true, despite Morrison having twice been found guilty under the university's administrative system, through which Brzonkala had filed a complaint under Virginia Tech's Sexual Assault Policy.[167]

Thomas's Rulings on Reproductive Rights

We identified seven key Supreme Court cases on reproductive rights between 1992 and 2020 on which Thomas voted, joined an opinion, or registered a concurrence or dissent. Of these, five cases either preserve or advance women's rights, and two cases restrict women's autonomy in their reproductive decisions. As seen in table 4.2, six of these cases addressed women's right to abortion, and one case dealt with employer-mandated coverage of contraceptives through the Affordable Care Act. In these seven cases, Thomas dissented in four that preserved or advanced women's reproductive rights. Thomas joined the majority in three cases, two of which restricted women's reproductive rights (*Gonzales v. Carhart* and *Burwell v. Hobby Lobby Stores*). In one case (*Ayotte v. Planned Parenthood of Northern New England*), Thomas joined his fellow eight justices in issuing a unanimous decision upholding women's access to abortion while also giving lower courts declaratory and injunctive relief in portions of legislation they deem unconstitutional.

Thomas's record on women's reproductive rights, as in the previously examined categories, favors restricting women's autonomy. His votes on reproductive rights were in agreement with other conservatively appointed men on the court but differed with those of the women justices, including the first female justice, Sandra Day O'Connor, who, as a Reagan appointee, was usually relied upon to vote conservatively. On the three reproductive cases O'Connor heard while serving on the court, though (*Planned Parenthood of Southern Pennsylvania v. Casey, Stenberg v. Carhart,* and *Ayotte v. Planned Parenthood of Northern New England*), she

Table 4.2 Supreme Court Decisions on Reproductive Rights and Sex and Workplace Discrimination with Thomas Vote 1992–2020[i], [*], [**]

Reproductive Rights	Sex and Workplace Discrimination
***Planned Parenthood of Southeastern Pennsylvania v. Casey*, 1992** Issue area: Abortion Roe upheld but states may impose regulations if no "undue burden" imposed 5-4 decision for Planned Parenthood, plurality opinion written by Justices O'Connor, Kennedy, and Souter: O'Connor, Kennedy, Souter, Blackmun, Stevens **Dissent: Scalia, Rehnquist, White, Thomas**	***J.E.B. v. Alabama ex rel. T.B.*, 1994** Issue area: Equal protection clause, Fourteenth Amendment Excluding jurors based on their gender alone is a violation of the equal protection clause of the Fourteenth Amendment 6-3 decision for J.E.B., majority opinion written by Justice Blackmun: Blackmun, Stevens, O'Connor, Souter, Ginsburg Concurrence: O'Connor, Kennedy **Dissent: Rehnquist, Scalia, Thomas**
***Stenberg v. Carhart*, 2000** Issue area: Abortion Nebraska's partial birth abortion ban struck down, upholding Roe and Casey 5-4 decision for Carhart, majority opinion written by Justice Breyer: Breyer, Stevens, O'Connor, Souter, Ginsburg **Dissent: Rehnquist, Scalia, Kennedy, Thomas**	***United States v. Virginia*, 1996** Issue area: Equal protection clause, Fourteenth Amendment Virginia Military Institute (VMI)'s male-only admissions policy found to be unconstitutional 7-1 decision, majority opinion written by Justice Ginsburg: Ginsburg, Stevens, O'Connor, Kennedy, Souter, Breyer Concurrence: Rehnquist Dissent: Scalia Recused: Thomas (son attending VMI)
***Ayotte v. Planned Parenthood of Northern New England*, 2006** Issue area: Abortion Court held that New Hampshire parental notification law would be unconstitutional in a very small percentage of cases Unanimous decision for Ayotte, majority opinion written by Justice O'Connor: O'Connor, Roberts, Stevens, Scalia, Kennedy, Souter, Thomas, Ginsburg, Breyer	***Kolstad v. American Dental Association*, 1999** Issue area: Federal antidiscrimination protection An employer's conduct does not have to be "egregious" or "outrageous" to sustain a punitive damages award under Title VII of the 1964 Civil Rights Act 5-4 decision, majority opinion written by Justice O'Connor: O'Connor, Scalia, Kennedy Concurrence: Rehnquist, Thomas Dissent: Stevens, Souter, Ginsburg, Breyer

(Continued)

Table 4.2   (*Continued*)

Reproductive Rights	Sex and Workplace Discrimination
Gonzales v. Carhart,* 2007* Issue area: Abortion Partial-Birth Abortion Ban Act of 2003 found not to be unconstitutional or constitute an undue burden 5-4 decision for Gonzales, majority opinion written by Justice Kennedy: Kennedy, Roberts, Scalia, Thomas, Alito **Concurrence: Thomas, Scalia** Dissent: Ginsburg, Stevens, Souter, Breyer	***Pollard v. E.I. du Pont de Nemours & Company,* 2001** Issue area: Compensatory damages, Civil Rights Act of 1991 "Front pay" awarded for lost compensation is not subject to a statutory cap on compensatory damages under Title VII of the Civil Rights Act of 1991 Unanimous decision for Pollard, majority opinion written by Justice Thomas: Thomas, Rehnquist, Stevens, Scalia, Kennedy, Souter, Ginsburg, Breyer Recused: O'Connor
Burwell v. Hobby Lobby Stores,* 2014* Issue area: ACA contraceptive mandate The Religious Freedom Restoration Act of 1993 allows for companies to deny health coverage of contraception for employees based on owner's religious objections **5-4 decision for Hobby Lobby, majority opinion written by Justice Alito: Alito, Roberts, Scalia, Kennedy, Thomas** Concurrence: Kennedy Dissent: Ginsburg, Sotomayor, Breyer, Kagan	***Ferguson v. City of Charleston,* 2001** Issue area: Unreasonable search, Fourth Amendment Diagnostic tests constitute an unreasonable search for evidence of criminal misconduct if a patient has not consented 6-3 decision for Ferguson, majority opinion written by Justice Stevens: Stevens, O'Connor, Souter, Kennedy, Ginsburg, Breyer Concurrence: Kennedy **Dissent: Scalia, Rehnquist, Thomas**
***Whole Woman's Health v. Hellerstedt,* 2016** Issue area: Abortion Courts should consider the extent to which abortion restrictions actually promote health 5-3 decision for Whole Woman's Health, majority opinion written by Justice Breyer: Breyer, Kennedy, Ginsburg, Sotomayor, Kagan Concurrence: Ginsburg **Dissent: Alito, Thomas, Roberts**	***Swierkiewicz v. Sorema,* 2002** Issue area: Employment Discrimination An employment discrimination lawsuit need not contain specific facts establishing a prima facie case of discrimination Unanimous decision for Swierkiewicz, majority opinion written by Justice Thomas: Thomas, Rehnquist, Stevens, O'Connor, Scalia, Kennedy, Souter, Ginsburg, Breyer

(*Continued*)

Table 4.2 (*Continued*)

Reproductive Rights	Sex and Workplace Discrimination
June Medical Services LLC v. Russo, **2020**	*Nevada Department of Human Resources v. Hibbs,* **2003**
Issue area: Abortion	Issue area: Family Medical Leave Act of 1993
Reverses a Louisiana law that requires abortion providers to hold admitting privileges at local hospitals	Individuals may sue for monetary damages in federal court if a State doesn't comply with provisions of the Family and Medical Leave Act of 1993
5-4 decision for June Medical, plurality opinion written by Justice Breyer: Breyer, Ginsburg, Sotomayor, Kagan	6-3 decision for Hibbs, majority opinion written by Justice Rehnquist: Rehnquist, O'Connor, Souter, Ginsburg, Breyer
Concurrence: Roberts	Concurrence: Stevens
Dissent: Thomas, Alito, Gorsuch, Kavanaugh	**Dissent: Kennedy, Scalia, Thomas**
	Jackson v. Birmingham Board of Education, **2005**
	Issue area: Title IX, Education Amendments of 1972
	Suits that allege retaliation for reporting sex discrimination are allowed under Title IX
	5-4 decision for Jackson, majority opinion written by Justice O'Connor: O'Connor, Stevens, Souter, Ginsburg, Breyer
	Dissent: Thomas, Rehnquist, Scalia, Kennedy
	Fitzgerald v. Barnstable School Committee, **2009**
	Issue area: Title IX, Education Amendments of 1972
	Claims filed under Title IX do not preclude further constitutional claims for sex discrimination under 42 U.S.C. Section 1983
	Unanimous decision for Fitzgerald, majority opinion written by Justice Alito: Alito, Roberts, Stevens, Scalia, Kennedy, Souter, Thomas, Ginsburg, Breyer

(*Continued*)

Table 4.2   (*Continued*)

Reproductive Rights	Sex and Workplace Discrimination
	Ledbetter v. Goodyear Tire & Rubber Company*, 2007*
	Issue area: Salary discrimination lawsuit, 180-day statutory limitations, Title VII of the Civil Rights Act of 1964
	Salary discrimination lawsuits under Title VII of the Civil Rights Act of 1964 are time bound by the established statutory limitation period
	5-4 decision for Goodyear, majority opinion written by Justice Alito: Alito, Roberts, Scalia, Kennedy, Thomas
	Dissent: Ginsburg, Stevens, Souter, Breyer
	Wal-Mart Stores, Inc. v. Dukes, et al.*, 2011*
	Issue area: Class-action lawsuit
	A small group of women who initiated a class action lawsuit could not represent a class of 1.5 million, including all Wal-mart employees
	5-4 decision for Walmart, majority opinion written by Justice Scalia: Scalia, Roberts, Kennedy, Thomas, Alito
	Concurrence and Dissent in Part: Ginsburg, Breyer, Sotomayor, Kagan

[i] Case details in table 4.2 from www.oyez.org/cases.

*Thomas's opinions, concurrences or dissents that favor restricting women's autonomy in reproductive rights cases (six of the seven reproductive rights decisions here) or that do not favor the rights of individuals/employees in sex and workplace discrimination cases (six of eleven cases here; in a seventh case, *United States v. Virginia*, 518 U.S. 515, Thomas recused himself) are noted in boldface type.

**Cases decided in a way that we interpret as setting back women's autonomous rights.

voted in favor of advancing women's autonomy and right to abortion. In the *Planned Parenthood of Southeastern Pennsylvania v. Casey* case, Justice O'Connor—who jointly wrote the opinion with Kennedy and Souter—said in her opinion, "some of us as individuals find abortion offensive to our most basic principles of morality but that can't control our decision.

Our obligation is to define the liberty of all, not to mandate our own moral code."[168] Thomas, who had joined the court months before the oral arguments for *Planned Parenthood of Southeastern Pennsylvania v. Casey* were heard, joined Rehnquist in his dissenting opinion, which stated, "Justice White, Justice Scalia, Justice Thomas and I are of the opinion that the court did err in Roe when it determined that the Constitution includes a fundamental right to abortion,"[169] a sentiment which Thomas later echoed. In his dissenting opinion for *June Medical Services LLC v. Russo*, Thomas wrote that earlier decisions of the court had "created the right to abortion out of whole cloth, without a shred of support from the Constitution's text. Our abortion precedents are grievously wrong and should be overruled."[170]

In 2019, the court heard arguments in *Box v. Planned Parenthood of Indiana and Kentucky* in which two questions were presented: the first concerned how fetal remains could be disposed of by abortion providers and the second considered whether Indiana "may prohibit the knowing provision of sex-, race-, and disability-selective abortions by abortion providers."[171] The court did not express a view on the second question, as it had only been considered by the Seventh Circuit Court and they chose to "follow [their] ordinary practice of denying petitions insofar as they raise legal issues that have not been considered by additional Courts of Appeal."[172] In Thomas's eighteen-page concurring opinion, he discussed the second question, the merit of which the court had chosen not to consider. In his concurring opinion, Thomas wrote that the Constitution is actually silent on what he called "putative right to abortion"[173] and said that since the court created that right through *Roe* it was "dutybound to address its scope."[174] Thomas further made clear his fundamental disavowal of a right to abortion in equating it to eugenic manipulation.[175] Some scholars have suggested that the arguments Thomas made in this concurrence could pave the way for the Supreme Court to reconsider their previous decisions on women's right to abortion, since, under the principle of stare decisis, "Roe v. Wade, cannot be overruled simply because a majority of the current Court disagrees with it"; such a seismic reversal would require a "special justification" and Thomas's association of abortion with eugenics constructs the case that racial injustice is the "special justification" that warrants overruling Roe.[176] In April 2021, the Sixth Circuit Court upheld Ohio's law prohibiting abortion providers from performing an abortion if the reason for the abortion is a prenatal diagnosis of Down syndrome.[177] The conservative justices argued that the law was not restricting abortion but rather "combatting eugenics by protecting disabled fetuses from discrimination," a nod to the opinion espoused in Thomas's concurrence.[178]

Thomas's Decisions on Sex and Workplace Discrimination

We identified eleven Supreme Court cases relating to sex and workplace discrimination on which Thomas voted between 1994 and 2011. Nine of these cases dealt with discrimination based on sex. Two of these cases dealt with issues that have implications for *future* discrimination claims on the basis of sex (*Swierkiewicz v. Sorema N.A.*, which came from a case of discrimination based on national origin, and *Nevada Department of Human Resources v. Hibbs*, concerned with compliance with the provisions of the Family and Medical Leave Act of 1993). Of all the discrimination cases with Thomas votes, Thomas dissented in four cases that were decided in ways that advanced women's rights in cases of gender discrimination (*J. E. B. v. Alabama ex re TB*; *Ferguson v. City of Charleston*; *Jackson v. Birmingham Board of Education*; and *Jackson v. Birmingham Board of Education*), and had recused himself in one case (*United States v. Virginia* 518 U.S. 514). In two of the eleven discrimination cases during the observed time period (1992–2020), the court voted unanimously, with Thomas delivering the opinion, and both of these unanimous decisions can be seen as advancing the position of employees in relation to their employers (*Pollard v. E. I. du Pont de Nemours & Company* and *Swierkiewicz v. Sorema*). In *Pollard v. E. I. du Pont de Nemours & Company*, the court ruled that front pay does not constitute compensatory damages and therefore cannot be capped.[179] (We also considered this case in the analysis of Justice Thomas's rulings on sexual harassment above, since the petitioner, Pollard, said that she had been subjected to discrimination in the workplace based on her sex in the form of coworker sexual harassment.[180]) In *Swierkiewicz v. Sorema*, the court ruled that employment discrimination cases "need not include specific facts establishing a prima facie case," allowing for a flexible evidentiary standard.[181] In *Kolstad v. American Dental Association*, Thomas concurred with the majority opinion that an employer's conduct does not have to be "egregious" or "outrageous," in order for an employee to be awarded punitive damages under Title VII of the 1964 Civil Rights Act—a win for employees—but that employers may not face punitive damages if they acted to prevent bias.[182]

Of the two workplace discrimination cases we identified (*Ledbetter v. Goodyear Tire & Rubber Company* and *Wal-Mart Stores Inc v. Dukes, et al.*), Thomas voted with the majority opinion in both instances, where rulings favored employers. In *Ledbetter v. Goodyear Tire & Rubber Company*, Thomas joined the majority opinion finding that Ledbetter's claim—that Goodyear paid her a lower salary due to her gender—was time-barred, as her claim for discriminatory intent fell outside of the limitation period (180 days of a discriminatory salary decision).[183] In *Wal-Mart Stores Inc v. Dukes, et al.*, Thomas joined the opinion ruling that the five women who filed a class-action lawsuit—alleging that Wal-Mart policies led to unequal pay and longer waits for managerial positions—did not have enough commonalities to constitute a class-action lawsuit.[184] In both cases, the decisions were based on technicalities of rules that favor employers, such as we identified in our analysis of sexual harassment cases above, including time limitations that constrain women's ability to report or act upon injustices.

Kavanaugh's Nascent Legacy

Justice Brett Kavanaugh, who joined the Supreme Court in October of 2018, had only ruled on one Supreme Court case within the scope of our analysis at the time of our writing in 2021. He had, however, been vocal about his quite limited view of constitutional protections for personal liberty rights during his twelve years on the D.C. Court of Appeals, where he had the first- or second-most conservative voting record in every area of policy. In a speech given at the American Enterprise Institute in September 2017, Kavanaugh praised former Chief Justice Rehnquist for "stemming the general tide of free-wheeling judicial creation of unenumerated rights that were not rooted in the nation's history and tradition," notably referencing *Roe v. Wade*.[185]

The one Supreme Court case with a Kavanaugh vote during the time frame of our study, relevant due to its bearing on women's autonomy, was *June Medical Services LLC v. Russo*. In that case, the court majority—including conservative Chief Justice Roberts—voted to reverse a judgment of the Fifth Circuit Court that had upheld a Louisiana law requiring abortion providers to have admitting privileges at local hospitals.[186] The judgment was based on a 2016 ruling of the Supreme Court in *Whole Woman's Health v. Hellerstedt*, which found there was no medical benefit to women for the admitting privileges requirement, and it further ruled in declaring the requirement unconstitutional, imposed a substantial burden on patients and abortion providers.[187] Kavanaugh authored a dissenting opinion, adding his own voice to a chorus of other dissents issued by Gorsuch, Thomas, and Alito. Kavanuaugh argued that the Louisiana law should be allowed to stand, based on the Fifth Circuit's judgment that it may not, in fact, be unduly burdensome on women's right to abortion, because, they said, the plaintiffs did "not adequately demonstrate that the three relevant doctors (Does 2, 5, and 6)" could not obtain admitting privileges—in other words, according to this point of view, the doctors just had not tried hard enough to seek surgical privileges that the Supreme Court had already ruled unnecessary and unduly burdensome in *Whole Woman's Health v. Hellerstedt*.[188] Kavanaugh's dissent was seen by some proponents of abortion rights as nothing less than a "declaration of war" on *Roe v. Wade*, demonstrating Kavanaugh's willingness to side with states imposing restrictions.[189]

Kavanaugh's propensity to support restrictions on access to abortion was also demonstrated a year prior to his appointment to the Supreme Court, while on the U.S. Court of Appeals for the District of Columbia Circuit, when, as part of a three-judge panel, he supported the Trump administration's efforts to prevent an undocumented minor from accessing an abortion by refusing to grant her leave from the Office of Refugee Resettlement (ORR) shelter where she was staying.[190] When the case was reheard by the full court and the panel's ruling was overturned, allowing the seventeen-year-old to get an abortion, Kavanaugh dissented, saying that she did not have a right to "abortion on demand."[191] When asked about this case during his confirmation hearings, Kavanaugh said that "he would have allowed the Trump administration to require the young woman be placed with an 'immigration sponsor,'" which ostensibly would have allowed her the freedom to access the abortion she was seeking.[192] What he didn't say was that finding such a sponsor usually takes months, and the minor in the case was sixteen weeks pregnant in a state where abortion is banned after twenty weeks of pregnancy, making it highly unlikely that she would have been able to secure an abortion in such a scenario.[193] In both this case and *June Medical Services*, Kavanaugh's dissents focused on procedural points that would have the practical effect of thwarting abortion access if his suggested course of action were followed. Though professing to be a staunch follower of precedent in his judicial opinions, Kavanaugh seems to have maneuvered precedent and some procedural points in these cases in the service of his conservative ideology, to the detriment of women's autonomy.[194]

During his confirmation process in 2018, the National Women's Law Center (NWLC) published a report on "The Record of Brett M. Kavanaugh on Critical Legal Rights for Women" after two months of examining his public record with regard to the rights and well-being of women and girls. The report focused on "the constitutional right to liberty and personal decision-making, including the rights to abortion and birth control, and on antidiscrimination protections, including prohibitions against sex discrimination under the Equal Protection Clause or statutory provisions that protect against discrimination in education and employment, and beyond."[195] Some noteworthy conclusions of the report include that Kavanaugh's record suggests that he would weaken workplace rights and antidiscrimination protections and continue to rule routinely in favor of employers, since he tended to take the view that being covered by civil rights protections made workers less desirable as employees.[196] Further, NWLC predicted that a Kavanaugh placement on the court would lead to the denial of many meaningful legal protections from sexual harassment (which includes sexual assault) and other forms of workplace discrimination. NWLC reported that Kavanaugh regularly dissented from the majority while on the D.C. Circuit Court of Appeals, with opinions that would make antidiscrimination protections "inapplicable or unenforceable for the plaintiffs before him."[197] A *Washington Post* analysis of hundreds of Kavanaugh's votes while he was on the D.C. Circuit Court concluded that his judicial record was more conservative than almost every other judge there.[198]

Of particular note from the point of view of our own analysis, Kavanaugh exhibited what NWLC deemed a possible "personal tolerance for sexual harassment," noting his clerkship and subsequent close relationship with Judge Alex Kozinski of the Ninth Circuit, who retired suddenly in 2017 after allegations of sexual harassment from more than a dozen former clerks and professional contacts.[199] Kozinski's behavior, including showing women pornography in his chambers, groping or fondling women or ogling them, and making suggestive comments, was considered a widely known open secret for years, begging the question of what Kavanaugh knew and when, and what his reaction had been.[200] Kavanaugh himself described the closeness between a judge and clerk as "the most intense and mutually dependent one outside of marriage, parenthood, or a love affair," suggesting a deep level of kinship and familiarity between the two.[201] Yet he categorically denied being aware of allegations of crude or inappropriate behavior on the part of Kozinksi, saying under oath at his confirmation hearing that he had known nothing about Kozinksi's reputation for ribald humor—which Kozinski had shared widely for years on his "Easy Rider gag list" listserv with colleagues, friends, and even journalists.[202] Allegations of sexual assault against Kavanaugh himself by Christine Blasey Ford did not come to light until after the NWLC report was completed and would, no doubt, have added to the sense of urgency expressed in its assessment that Kavanaugh's lifetime appointment to the Supreme Court would represent a threat to pivotal rights and legal protections for women for no less than "generations to come."[203]

Despite the accusations made against him and his association with Kozinski, Kavanaugh's record in supporting women clerks and colleagues was called "exemplary" by White House officials.[204] After being tapped by Trump for the Supreme Court position, Kavanaugh spoke of his pride in the fact that the majority of his law clerks had been women, eighteen of whom signed a letter in the summer of 2018 lauding Kavanaugh for making the legal field "fairer and more equal."[205] Once on the court, Kavanaugh was praised by Justice Ginsburg for making history with his "all-female law clerk crew," helping the court to reach the milestone of having more women than men as law clerks for the first time ever.[206] One former law clerk from the DC Circuit who credits Kavanaugh for championing her career advancement in the male-dominated legal profession described him as a mentor who "couldn't be a better advocate for women in his actual day-to-day life."[207] Yale law professor Amy Chua (of *Tiger Mom* fame) called Kavanaugh, whose Supreme Court nomination she strongly endorsed, "an exceptional mentor to his female clerks and a champion of their careers"; she called it one of her "proudest moments as a parent" when she learned that her own daughter would clerk for Kavanaugh.[208] Yet when mentoring students on how to win a Kavanaugh clerkship, she included advice on their physical appearance, saying it was "not an accident" that his female law clerks all "looked like models."[209] Chua's husband, who is also a Yale law professor, Jed Rubenfeld, advised another prospective clerk that "Kavanaugh liked a certain 'look.'"[210] Though these comments received a lot of coverage in the press, there have been no allegations made that Kavanaugh had sexually harassed or assaulted anyone in his professional life. The three or four women who came forward to accuse Kavanaugh of sexual misconduct all pointed to incidents that were alleged to have occurred when he was a student, either in high school at Georgetown Prep or as an undergraduate at Yale.[211]

Most Republicans, including the majority of Republican women, wanted Kavanaugh to take his seat on the bench despite the allegations against him, just as they had remained Trump loyalists even after the revelation, in October 2016, of the Access Hollywood tape of Trump's infamous boasting about grabbing women's genitals.[212] Republican women are nearly as likely as Republican men to deny or minimize sexism. A nationally representative poll conducted in 2017 found that the majority of all Republicans agreed with the statement, "Most women interpret innocent remarks or acts as being sexist."[213] Some prominent conservative women used their positions of authority to voice doubt about the veracity of Blasey Ford's testimony about being assaulted by Kavanaugh at a high school party. Fox News host Laura Ingraham called her "hysterical," an age-old trope used to trivialize the statements of women—and Trump attorney and former federal prosecutor Sidney Powell described the incident in which Ford related that she feared Kavanaugh might accidentally kill her as he jumped on top of her and put his hand over her mouth to stifle her screams, as a mere "fumbled attempt to make out with a girl at a party."[214]

Conservative men may valorize and support conservative women, insofar as their elevation to positions of power serves to edify and advance the status quo of predominant male authority, and as long as those women "have a certain look" and toe the party line—that sexism isn't really a problem and that traditional social structures benefit women as well as men. This expression of conservative antifeminist thought echoes Phyllis Schlafly, conservative activist and opponent of the Equal Rights Amendment in the 1970s, who also argued that legal measures to protect women from domestic violence and harassment encouraged divorce and hatred of men. While individual women, such as law clerks from prestigious schools, may benefit from the career boost afforded by association with powerful men like Kavanaugh, women in general stand to suffer barriers or setbacks to their rights and ability to exercise individual autonomy in the workplace and in their personal lives as a result of his judicial decisions. If women have a limited ability to make decisions regarding their own health and reproductive lives and are constrained in their capacity to address barriers to career advancement in the form of harassment and discrimination in the workplace, their underrepresentation in positions of authority in the public sphere can be expected to continue.

Conclusion

"The Supreme Court has an enormous impact on women's ability to live their lives with dignity and equality. It affects individual liberty, including women's right to make decisions about their own bodies."[215] But on the court, as elsewhere in public life, women have long been underrepresented, and their ability to be heard has been constrained by convention and mediated by active, ongoing interpretation of the rules of the game in the form of case law. The legal opinions rendered by Justices Thomas and Kavanaugh often served to defend the status quo of power through legal technicalities or procedural boundaries, like limiting employer liability in *Vance*, creating hurdles to addressing sexual harassment in *Gebser*, allowing employers to escape liability for actionable sexual harassment (the "*Fargher-Ellerth* defense") if they merely have a policy in place for reporting, or creating the almost impossibly high standard for misconduct that is "severe, pervasive, and objectively offensive" before it must be addressed in public education, as decided in *Davis*. So, from their earliest days in the education system, through the arc of their professional careers, women face considerable legal hurdles to addressing injustices that they confront in the form of harassment or unequal treatment.

When Lily Ledbetter sued to rectify the injustice of having been paid less and reviewed more harshly than her male coworkers over the course of her career at Goodyear Tire and Rubber Company, the court ruled that the case for salary discrimination could not be brought under Title VII of the Civil Rights Act of 1964, not because the case lacked merit but because of the 180-day statutory limitations period.[216] When Anita Hill testified as to Thomas's harassing behavior a decade earlier, Senator Specter, rather than addressing the substance of her concerns, raised the "very firm" federal requirement for a six-month period of limitation for reporting and cast doubt on the accuracy of her statements. As suggested by MacKinnon, the strictures of statutes of limitations serve to suppress the possible existence of claims for justice based on the technicality of arbitrary and constraining time limits, thus perpetuating the authority of those historically holding authority.

That authority, encoded in law through means such as statutes of limitations, is further supported by the tacit tenets of testimonial injustice, where women are seen as less competent and trustworthy than men, lessening their testimonial authority when they do speak up to address injustices. And, since historically, mostly men have been making the law, it is not surprising that they are not welcoming of or persuaded by women who speak up to challenge that authority. The principle of homophily explains how men in power find others like themselves to be more credible and relatable, undergirding the proverbial "old boys' club," where the alleged "locker-room talk" and actions of men like Kozinski, Kavanaugh, and Thomas might easily be overlooked or excused by their "brothers" and others who still view them as legitimate standard bearers of authority.

The individual experiences and ideological predilections of judges at all levels—especially the highest—have been shown to influence judicial decision-making. Combined with the power of established law and embedded cultural and individual beliefs about the legitimacy of male versus female power, these factors constitute a formidable collective barrier to women being given a full hearing and achieving full representation in the law when addressing issues like sexual harassment and factors integrally affecting their autonomy, like equal pay and reproductive rights.

Notes

1. Anita Hill, *Speaking Truth to Power* (New York: Anchor Books, 1998).

2. Emma Brown, "California Professor, Writer of Confidential Brett Kavanaugh Letter, Speaks Out about Her Allegation of Sexual Assault," *Washington Post*, September 16, 2018, https://www.washingtonpost.com /investigations/california-professor-writer-of-confidential-brett-kavanaugh-letter-speaks-out-about-her-allegation-of-sexual-assault/2018/09/16/46982194 -b846-11e8-94eb-3bd52dfe917b_story.html.

3. Brown, "California Professor Speaks Out."

4. Brown, "California Professor Speaks Out."

5. Vicki Schultz, "Open Statement on Sexual Harassment from Employment Discrimination Law Scholars," *Stanford Law Review*, June 18, 2018, https:// www.stanfordlawreview.org/online/open-statement-on-sexual-harassment-from -employment-discrimination-law-scholars/.

6. David Cohen, "Roberts: Judicial Branch 'Not Immune' from Sexual Harassment Issues," *POLITICO*, December 31, 2017, https://politi.co/2zTMVhL.

7. Cohen, "Judicial Branch 'Not Immune.'"

8. Matt Zapotosky, "Nine More Women Say Judge Subjected Them to Inappropriate Behavior, Including Four Who Say He Touched or Kissed Them," *Washington Post*, December 15, 2017, sec. National Security, https: //www.washingtonpost.com/world/national-security/nine-more-women -say-judge-subjected-them-to-inappropriate-behavior-including-four-who -say-he-touched-or-kissed-them/2017/12/15/8729b736-e105-11e7-8679 -a9728984779c_story.html.

9. Vanessa Romo, "Federal Judge Kozinski Retires Following Sexual Harassment Allegations," *NPR*, December 18, 2017, sec. America, https://www.npr.org /sections/thetwo-way/2017/12/18/571677955/federal-judge-retires-in-the-wake -of-sexual-harassment-allegations.

10. Caitlin Oprysko, "Chief Justice Praises Progress on Sexual Harassment Policies for Judiciary," *POLITICO*, December 31, 2018, https://politi.co /2EYHLqM.

11. Mason Schar School, *Glass Houses and Glass Ceilings: Congressional Ethics in the #MeToo Era*, 2020, https://vimeo.com/444925325.

12. Frank Dobbin and Alexandra Kalev, "Training Programs and Reporting Systems Won't End Sexual Harassment. Promoting More Women Will,"

Harvard Business Review, November 15, 2017, https://hbr.org/2017/11 /training-programs-and-reporting-systems-wont-end-sexual-harassment -promoting-more-women-will.

13. Kate Manne, *Down Girl: The Logic of Misogyny* (Oxford: Oxford University Press, 2018), 185.

14. Angela Nicole Johnson, "Intersectionality, Life Experience & Judicial Decision Making: A New View of Gender at the Supreme Court Note," *Notre Dame Journal of Law, Ethics & Public Policy* 28, no. 1 (2014): 353–354.

15. Adam Glynn and Maya Sen, "Identifying Judicial Empathy: Does Having Daughters Cause Judges to Rule for Women's Issues?" *American Journal of Political Science* 59, no. 1 (2015): 52; Catherine I. Bolzendahl and Daniel J. Myers, "Feminist Attitudes and Support for Gender Equality: Opinion Change in Women and Men, 1974–1998," *Social Forces* 83, no. 2 (December 1, 2004): 759–789, https://doi.org/10.1353/sof.2005.0005.

16. Adam Bonica and Maya Sen, "Estimating Judicial Ideology," *Journal of Economic Perspectives* 35, no. 1 (February 2021): 98, https://doi.org/10.1257 /jep.35.1.97.

17. Jeffrey J. Rachlinski, Andrew J. Wistrich, and Chris Guthrie, "Judicial Politics and Decisionmaking: A New Approach," *Vanderbilt Law Review* 70, no. 6 (2017): 2051–2104.

18. Rachlinski, Wistrich, and Guthrie, "Judicial Politics and Decisionmaking."

19. Christopher Zorn and Jennifer Barnes Bowie, "Ideological Influences on Decision Making in the Federal Judicial Hierarchy: An Empirical Assessment," *The Journal of Politics* 72, no. 4 (2010): 1214, https://doi .org/10.1017/s0022381610000630.

20. Christopher Zorn and Jennifer Barnes Bowie, "Ideological Influences on Decision Making in the Federal Judicial Hierarchy: An Empirical Assessment," *The Journal of Politics* 72, no. 4 (2010): 1213.

21. Alma Cohen and Crystal S. Yang, "Judicial Politics and Sentencing Decisions," *American Economic Journal: Economic Policy* 11, no. 1 (February 2019): 160–191, https://doi.org/10.1257/pol.20170329.

22. Adam Bonica and Maya Sen, "Estimating Judicial Ideology," *Journal of Economic Perspectives* 35, no. 1 (February 2021): 110, https://doi.org/10.1257 /jep.35.1.97.

23. Manne, *Down Girl*, 185.

24. Jessica Campisi and Brandon Griggs, "Of the 114 Supreme Court Justices in US History, All but 6 Have Been White Men," *CNN*, September 26, 2020, https://www.cnn.com/2020/09/25/politics/supreme-court-justice -minorities-history-trnd/index.html.

25. Pat Ralph and Shayanne Gal, "Who's on the Senate Judiciary Committee Now and Who Was On It in 1991," *Business Insider*, September 27, 2018, https://www.businessinsider.com/senate-judiciary-committee-members-anita -hill-christine-blasey-ford-kavanaugh-2018-9.

26. Campisi and Griggs, "All but 6 Have Been White Men."

27. Pat Ralph and Shayanne Gal, "3 of the Same Senators Who Were on the Judiciary Committee When Anita Hill Testified Are Still On It. Here's What the Make-Up Was Then Compared to Now," *Business Insider*, September 27, 2018, https://www.businessinsider.com/senate-judiciary-committee-members -anita-hill-christine-blasey-ford-kavanaugh-2018-9.

28. Campisi and Griggs, "All but 6 Have Been White Men."

29. OpenSecrets, "Reelection Rates Over the Years," OpenSecrets, accessed June 13, 2021, https://www.opensecrets.org/elections-overview/reelection-rates.

30. Jane Mayer, "What Joe Biden Hasn't Owned Up to about Anita Hill," *The New Yorker*, April 27, 2019, https://www.newyorker.com/news/news -desk/what-joe-biden-hasnt-owned-up-to-about-anita-hill.

31. Mayer, "What Joe Biden Hasn't Owned Up to about Anita Hill."

32. Julia Jacobs, "Anita Hill's Testimony and Other Key Moments from the Clarence Thomas Hearings," *The New York Times*, September 20, 2018, sec. U.S., https://www.nytimes.com/2018/09/20/us/politics/anita-hill-testimony -clarence-thomas.html.

33. Mayer, "What Joe Biden Hasn't Owned Up to about Anita Hill."

34. Julia Jacobs, "Anita Hill's Testimony and Other Key Moments from the Clarence Thomas Hearings," *The New York Times*, September 20, 2018, sec. U.S., https://www.nytimes.com/2018/09/20/us/politics/anita-hill-testimony -clarence-thomas.html.

35. Miller McPherson, Lynn Smith-Lovin, and James M. Cook, "Birds of a Feather: Homophily in Social Networks," *Annual Review of Sociology* 27 (2001): 415–444, https://doi.org/10.1146/annurev.soc.27.1.415.

36. Mayer, "What Joe Biden Hasn't Owned Up to about Anita Hill."

37. Isaac Chotiner, "Kate Manne on the Costs of Male Entitlement," *The New Yorker*, September 4, 2020, https://www.newyorker.com/news/q-and-a /kate-manne-on-the-costs-of-male-entitlement.

38. Chotiner, "The Costs of Male Entitlement."

39. Chotiner, "The Costs of Male Entitlement."

40. Manne, *Down Girl*, 188.

41. Jessica Gresko, "Deja Vu: What These Senators Said Then and What They Say Now," *AP NEWS*, September 27, 2018, sec. Clarence Thomas, https:// apnews.com/article/ea7caea1332e4897b3f22e804423392e.

42. Eleanor Clift, "Republicans and Democrats Dismissed Anita Hill. Christine Blasey Ford Won't Be So Easy to Ignore," *The Daily Beast*, September 25, 2018, sec. politics, https://www.thedailybeast.com/republicans-and-demo crats-dismissed-anita-hill-christine-blasey-ford-wont-be-so-easy-to-ignore.

43. Timothy Phelps, "I Broke the Anita Hill Story. Here's What We Need to Learn from Her Treatment," *Los Angeles Times*, September 18, 2018, sec. Opinion, https://www.latimes.com/opinion/op-ed/la-oe-phelps-anita-hill-christine-blasey -ford-kavanaugh-20180918-story.html.

44. Allie Malloy, Kate Sullivan, and Jeff Zeleny, "Trump Mocks Christine Blasey Ford's Testimony, Tells People to 'Think of Your Son,'" *CNN*, October 3, 2018, https://www.cnn.com/2018/10/02/politics/trump-mocks-christine -blasey-ford-kavanaugh-supreme-court/index.html.

45. Jamie Ducharme, "'Indelible in the Hippocampus Is the Laughter.' The Science Behind Christine Blasey Ford's Testimony," *Time*, September 27, 2018, https://time.com/5408567/christine-blasey-ford-science-of-memory/.

46. Ducharme, "'Indelible in the Hippocampus Is the Laughter.'"

47. C-SPAN, *Supreme Court Nomination Announcement* (Washington, D.C., 1991), https://www.c-span.org/video/?18649-1/supreme-court-nomination -announcement.

48. Mayer, "What Joe Biden Hasn't Owned up to about Anita Hill"; Brown, "California Professor Speaks Out"; Phelps, "I Broke the Anita Hill Story."

49. Elise Viebeck, "Here's What Happened When Anita Hill Testified against Clarence Thomas in 1991," *Chicagotribune.Com*, September 27, 2018, sec., Nation & World, https://www.chicagotribune.com/nation-world /ct-anita-hill-clarence-thomas-20180927-story.html.

50. Jacobs, "Anita Hill's Testimony."

51. Viebeck, "Here's What Happened When Anita Hill Testified."

52. Jill Smolowe, "Sex, Lies and Politics: He Said, She Said," *Time*, October 21, 1991, https://content.time.com/time/magazine/article/0,9171,974096,00 .html.

53. Haley Sweetland Edwards, "The Kavanaugh Hearing Showed Why the Myth of Nice Girls and Tough Guys Persists," *Time*, September 28, 2018, https:// time.com/5409351/christine-blasey-ford-brett-kavanaugh-gender-dynamics/.

54. Chotiner, "The Costs of Male Entitlement."

55. Sweetland Edwards, "The Myth of Nice Girls and Tough Guys Persists."

56. Sarah Banet-Weiser, "'Ruined' Lives: Mediated White Male Victimhood," *European Journal of Cultural Studies* 24, no. 1 (February 1, 2021): 60–80, https:// doi.org/10.1177/1367549420985840.

57. Jen Kirby, "Brett Kavanaugh's Angry, Emotional Opening Statement," *Vox* (blog), September 27, 2018, https://www.vox.com/2018/9/27/17911256 /brett-kavanaugh-christine-blasey-ford-senate-hearing.

58. Kirby, "Brett Kavanaugh's Angry, Emotional Opening Statement."

59. Clarence Thomas quoted by Kevin Liptak, "The FBI Did Investigate Anita Hill's Accusation, and It Took 3 Days," *CNN*, September 19, 2018, par. 22, https://www.cnn.com/2018/09/19/politics/anita-hill-clarence-thomas -allegations-timeline/index.html; Julia Jacobs, "Anita Hill's Testimony."

60. Smolowe, "Sex, Lies and Politics."

61. Ralph and Gal, "Who's on the Senate Judiciary Committee."

62. Jacobs, "Anita Hill's Testimony."

63. Kate Manne, *Entitled: How Male Privilege Hurts Women* (New York: Crown, 2020).

64. Chotiner, "The Costs of Male Entitlement."

65. Chotiner, "The Costs of Male Entitlement."

66. Manne, *Male Privilege Hurts Women*, 4–5.

67. Manne, *Male Privilege Hurts Women*, 6.

68. Malloy, Sullivan, and Zeleny, "Trump Mocks Christine Blasey Ford's Testimony."

69. Renae Reints, "Trump Calls Christine Blasey Ford a 'Very Credible Witness,'" *Fortune*, September 28, 2018, https://fortune.com/2018/09/28/trump-ford-credible-witness/.

70. Malloy, Sullivan, and Zeleny, "Trump Mocks Christine Blasey Ford's Testimony."

71. Banet-Weiser, "'Ruined' Lives."

72. Romo, "Federal Judge Kozinski Retires."

73. Avi Selk, "How the FBI's Flawed Investigation of Clarence Thomas Became a Model for Kavanaugh's," *Washington Post*, October 4, 2018, https://www.washingtonpost.com/politics/2018/10/02/fbis-anita-hill-investigation-quick-professional-flawed/.

74. Kevin Liptak, "The FBI Did Investigate Anita Hill's Accusation, and It Took 3 Days," *CNN*, September 19, 2018, https://www.cnn.com/2018/09/19/politics/anita-hill-clarence-thomas-allegations-timeline/index.html.

75. German Lopez, "The FBI Investigation of Kavanaugh Was Doomed from the Start," *Vox*, October 5, 2018, https://www.vox.com/policy-and-politics/2018/10/5/17940738/fbi-investigation-kavanaugh-thorough-limits.

76. Kate Kelly, "Details on F.B.I. Inquiry Into Kavanaugh Draw Fire from Democrats," *The New York Times*, July 22, 2021, sec. U.S., https://www.nytimes.com/2021/07/22/us/politics/kavanaugh-fbi-investigation.html.

77. Jeremy Wanderer, "Addressing Testimonial Injustice: Being Ignored and Being Rejected," *The Philosophical Quarterly* 62, no. 246 (2012): 148–169, https://doi.org/10.1111/j.1467-9213.2011.712.x.

78. American Civil Liberties Union, "Timeline of Major Supreme Court Decisions on Women's Rights" (New York: American Civil Liberties Union, 2018).

79. National Women's Law Center, "The Record of Brett M. Kavanaugh on Critical Legal Rights for Women" (National Women's Law Center, 2018), https://nwlc.org/wp-content/uploads/2018/09/NWLC-Kavanaugh-Report-FINAL-5.pdf.

80. Manne, *Down Girl; Miranda Fricker, Epistemic Injustice: Power and the Ethics of Knowing* (Oxford: Oxford University Press, 2007), 188, https://doi.org/10.1093/acprof:oso/9780198237907.001.0001.

81. Legal Information Institute, "Vance v. Ball State University," LII / Legal Information Institute, accessed June 9, 2021, https://www.law.cornell.edu/supct/cert/11-556.

82. Legal Information Institute, "Vance v. Ball State University," LII / Legal Information Institute, accessed June 9, 2021, https://www.law.cornell.edu /supct/cert/11-556.

83. Oyez, "Vance v. Ball State University," Oyez, accessed June 9, 2021, https://www.oyez.org/cases/2012/11-556.

84. Oyez, "Vance v. Ball State University."

85. Oyez, "Vance v. Ball State University."

86. Oyez, "Vance v. Ball State University."

87. Adaku Onyeka-Crawford, "Vance v. BSU Anniversary: A Case of the Terrible Twos," National Women's Law Center, June 24, 2015.

88. Onyeka-Crawford, "Vance v. BSU Anniversary."

89. Pat Garofalo, "Supreme Court Sides with Business in Vance v. Ball State Harassment Case | Thomas Jefferson Street | US News," *US News & World Report*, June 24, 2013, https://www.usnews.com/opinion/blogs/pat -garofalo/2013/06/24/supreme-court-sides-with-business-in-vance-v-ball -state-harassment-case.

90. Caroline Fairchild, "Roberts' Supreme Court Is More Pro-Business Than Any Other Court Since WWII, Study," *HuffPost*, May 6, 2013, sec. Business, https://www.huffpost.com/entry/supreme-court-pro-business_n_3223608.

91. Linda Greenhouse, "School Districts Are Given a Shield in Sex Harassment," *The New York Times*, June 23, 1998, sec. U.S., https://www.nytimes .com/1998/06/23/us/school-districts-are-given-a-shield-in-sex-harassment.html.

92. Greenhouse, "School Districts Are Given a Shield in Sex Harassment."

93. Greenhouse, "School Districts Are Given a Shield in Sex Harassment."

94. Justice Stevens, "Alida Star Gebser and Alida Jean McCulLough, Petitioners v. Lago Vista Independent School District," 1998, https://www.law .cornell.edu/supremecourt/text/524/274.

95. Stevens, "Alida Star Gebser and Alida Jean McCulLough, Petitioners v. Lago Vista Independent School District."

96. Manne, *Down Girl*, 184–185.

97. Jeff Schmitt, "Yale Law (Again) Ranks as the Top Law School," Tipping the Scales, March 20, 2020, https://tippingthescales.com/2020/03/yale-law -again-ranks-as-the-top-law-school/.

98. Linda Greenhouse, "The Power of Supreme Court Choices," *The New York Times*, December 6, 2018, sec. Opinion, https://www.nytimes .com/2018/12/06/opinion/bush-supreme-court-thomas.html.

99. Nina Totenberg, "Clarence Thomas: From 'Black Panther Type' to Supreme Court's Conservative Beacon," *NPR.org*, July 15, 2019, https://www .npr.org/2019/07/14/740027295/clarence-thomas-from-black-panther-type -to-supreme-court-s-most-conservative-mem.

100. Greenhouse, "The Power of Supreme Court Choices."

101. Joyce Li and Wendy M. Craig, "Adolescent Sexual Harassment, Shame, and Depression: Do Experiences of Witnessing Harassment Matter?" *The*

Journal of Early Adolescence 40, no. 5 (May 1, 2020): 712–737, https://doi .org/10.1177/0272431619870610; Eunkyung Yoon, Roni Stiller Funk, and Nancy P. Kropf, "Sexual Harassment Experiences and Their Psychological Correlates Among a Diverse Sample of College Women," *Affilia* 25, no. 1 (February 1, 2010): 8–18, https://doi.org/10.1177/0886109909354979.

102. Greenhouse, "School Districts Are Given a Shield in Sex Harassment."

103. Billie-Jo Grant, Stephanie B. Wilkerson, deKoven Pelton, Anne Cosby, and Molly Henschel, "A Case Study of K–12 School Employee Sexual Misconduct: Lessons Learned from Title IX Policy Implementation" (Charlottesville, VA: Magnolia Consulting, September 15, 2017).

104. Amal Bass, "Pennsylvania State Police v. Suders: Turning a Blind Eye to the Reality of Sexual Harassment," *Harvard Journal of Law & Gender* 28, no. 1 (2005): 195.

105. Legal Information Institute, "Constructive Discharge Definition," LII / Legal Information Institute, accessed June 6, 2021, https://www.law.cornell.edu /wex/constructive_discharge.

106. Oyez, "Pennsylvania State Police v. Suders," Oyez, accessed June 5, 2021, https://www.oyez.org/cases/2003/03-95.

107. Ruth Bader Ginsburg, Pennsylvania State Police v. Suders (Opinion of the Court), 542 U.S. 129 (U.S. Supreme Court 2004).

108. Thomas, Pennsylvania State Police v. Suders (Thomas, J., dissenting), 542 U.S. 129 (U.S. Supreme Court 2004).

109. Thomas, Pennsylvania State Police v. Suders.

110. Thomas, Pennsylvania State Police v. Suders.

111. Ginsburg, Pennsylvania State Police v. Suders.

112. Ginsburg, Pennsylvania State Police v. Suders.

113. Julia Jacobs, "Anita Hill's Testimony."

114. Julia Jacobs, "Anita Hill's Testimony"; Grace Segers, "Here Are Some of the Questions Anita Hill Answered in 1991," September 19, 2018, https://www .cbsnews.com/news/here-are-some-of-the-questions-anita-hill-fielded-in-1991/.

115. Angela Hattery and Earl Smith, *Gender, Power and Violence* (Lanham: Rowman & Littlefield, 2019), 16–17.

116. Manne, *Down Girl*, 175,186.

117. Ginsburg, Pennsylvania State Police v. Suders.

118. Ginsburg, Pennsylvania State Police v. Suders.

119. Manne, *Down Girl*, 186.

120. Segers, "Some of the Questions Anita Hill Answered."

121. Segers, "Some of the Questions Anita Hill Answered."

122. Segers, "Some of the Questions Anita Hill Answered."

123. Segers, "Some of the Questions Anita Hill Answered."

124. Segers, "Some of the Questions Anita Hill Answered."

125. Beverly Engel, "Why Don't Victims of Sexual Harassment Come Forward Sooner," *Psychology Today*, November 16, 2017, https://www

.psychologytoday.com/us/blog/the-compassion-chronicles/201711/why
-dont-victims-sexual-harassment-come-forward-sooner.

126. Catharine A. MacKinnon and Durba Mitra, "Ask a Feminist: Sexual Harassment in the Age of #MeToo," *Signs: Journal of Women in Culture and Society* 44, no. 4 (June 1, 2019): 1027–1043, https://doi.org/10.1086/702290.

127. Segers, "Some of the Questions Anita Hill Answered."

128. Jacobs, "Anita Hill's Testimony."

129. Martin Tolchin, "The Thomas Nomination; Hill Said to Pass a Polygraph Test," *The New York Times*, October 14, 1991, sec. U.S., https://www.nytimes .com/1991/10/14/us/the-thomas-nomination-hill-said-to-pass-a-polygraph -test.html.

130. Tolchin, "Hill Said to Pass a Polygraph Test."

131. Tolchin, "Hill Said to Pass a Polygraph Test."

132. Wellesly College, "Mary Kate McGowan," Wellesley College, accessed June 11, 2021, https://www.wellesley.edu/philosophy/faculty/mcgowan.

133. Mary Kate McGowan, "On Locker Room Talk and Linguistic Oppression," *Philosophical Topics* 46, no. 2 (2018): 167.

134. McGowan, "On Locker Room Talk and Linguistic Oppression."

135. Segers, "Some of the Questions Anita Hill Answered."

136. "User Clip: Sector: Large Breasts," C-SPAN, September 19, 2018, https:// www.c-span.org/video/?c4750136/user-clip-spector-large-breasts.

137. Jacobs, "Anita Hill's Testimony."

138. Hon. Ruth Bader Ginsburg, "The Role of Dissenting Opinions," *MINNESOTA LAW REVIEW*, July 2011.

139. Totenberg, "Clarence Thomas: From 'Black Panther Type.'"

140. Nicholas Wu, "Supreme Court Justice Clarence Thomas Jokes 'I Cause Stress,' Addresses Retirement Rumors," *USA TODAY*, June 4, 2019, https://www.usatoday.com/story/news/politics/2019/06/04/clarence-thomas -addresses-supreme-court-retirement-rumors/1336998001/.

141. Nina Totenberg, "Clarence Thomas' Influence on the Supreme Court," *NPR.Org*, October 11, 2011, https://www.npr.org/2011/10/11/141246695 /clarence-thomas-influence-on-the-court.

142. Totenberg, "Clarence Thomas' Influence."

143. Erin Hendricks, "The Supreme Court Gets Constructive: A Case Note on Pennsylvania State Police v. Suders," *Saint Louis University Law Journal* 50, no. 4 (January 1, 2006), https://scholarship.law.slu.edu/lj/vol50/iss4/18.

144. Olivia Waxman, "The Surprising Consequences of the Supreme Court Cases that Changed Sexual Harassment Law 20 Years Ago," *Time*, June 26, 2018, https://time.com/5319966/sexual-harassment-scotus-anniversary/; Oyez, "Burlington Industries, Inc. v. Ellerth," Oyez, 1998, https://www.oyez.org /cases/1997/97-569; Oyez, "Faragher v. City of Boca Raton," 1998, https:// www.oyez.org/cases/1997/97-282.

145. Waxman, "Supreme Court Cases that Changed Sexual Harassment."

146. Elizabeth Potter, "When Women's Silence Is Reasonable: Reforming the Faragher/Ellerth Defense in the #MeToo Era," *Brooklyn Law Review* 85, no. 2 (April 29, 2020), https://brooklynworks.brooklaw.edu/blr/vol85/iss2/9.

147. Waxman, "Supreme Court Cases that Changed Sexual Harassment Law."

148. Potter, "When Women's Silence Is Reasonable."

149. Waxman, "Supreme Court Cases that Changed Sexual Harassment Law."

150. Clarence Thomas, Burlington Industries, Inc. v. Ellerth dissent, U.S. (U.S. Supreme Court 1998).

151. Joan Biskupic, "Schools Liable for Harassment," *Washington Post*, May 25, 1999, https://www.washingtonpost.com/wp-srv/national/longterm /supcourt/stories/court052599.htm.

152. Nan Stein, "Supreme Court Rules in Davis Case That Schools Are Responsible for Student-To-Student Sexual Harassment," National Violence Against Women Prevention Research Center, 2000, https://mainweb-v.musc .edu/vawprevention/policy/daviscase.shtml.

153. Biskupic, "Schools Liable for Harassment."

154. Stein, "Supreme Court Rules in Davis Case."

155. Linda Greenhouse, "The Overview: Court Rules Schools Can Be Liable for Unchecked Sexual Harassment," *New York Times*, May 25, 1999, https://archive.nytimes.com/www.nytimes.com/library/politics/scotus /articles/052599harassment.html.

156. American Association of University Women, "Crossing the Line: Sexual Harassment at Schools," November 9, 2011, https://web.archive.org /web/20111109163013/http://www.aauw.org/learn/research/crossingtheline .cfm.

157. American Association of University Women, "Sexual Harassment at Schools."

158. Oyez, "Harris v. Forklift Systems, Inc.," Oyez, accessed August 30, 2021, https://www.oyez.org/cases/1993/92-1168.

159. Oyez, "Pollard v. E. I. Du Pont de Nemours & Company," Oyez, accessed March 14, 2021, https://www.oyez.org/cases/2000/00-763.

160. Oyez, "Crawford v. Nashville and Davidson County, TN," Oyez, accessed March 14, 2021, https://www.oyez.org/cases/2008/06-1595.

161. Oyez, "Davis v. Washington," Oyez, accessed March 14, 2021, https: //www.oyez.org/cases/2005/05-5224.

162. Lexis Nexis, "Case Brief: Davis v. Washington" (LexisNexis), accessed March 14, 2021, https://www.lexisnexis.com/community/casebrief/p /casebrief-davis-v-washington-2112476927.

163. Lexis Nexis, "Case Brief: Davis v. Washington"; Oyez, "Davis v. Washington."

164. Oyez, "United States v. Morrison," Oyez, accessed March 14, 2021, https://www.oyez.org/cases/1999/99-5.

165. Oyez, "United States v. Morrison."

166. Oyez, "United States v. Morrison," Oyez, accessed March 14, 2021, https://www.oyez.org/cases/1999/99-5.

167. Oyez, "United States v. Morrison."

168. "Planned Parenthood of Southeastern Pennsylvania v. Casey," Oyez, accessed August 30, 2021, https://www.oyez.org/cases/1991/91-744.

169. "Planned Parenthood of Southeastern Pennsylvania v. Casey," Oyez.

170. "June Medical Services L.L.C. v. Russo, 591 U.S. ___ (2020)," Justia Law, accessed August 30, 2021, https://supreme.justia.com/cases/federal/us/591/18-1323/.

171. Kristina Box, Commissioner, Indiana Department of Health, et al. v. Planned Parenthood of Indiana and Kentucky, INC., et al., No. 18-483 (Supreme Court of the United States May 28, 2019), 3.

172. Box, Commissioner, Indiana Department of Health, et al. v. Planned Parenthood of Indiana and Kentucky, 3.

173. "Whole Woman's Health v. Hellerstedt, 579 U.S.," *Justia Law*, accessed March 13, 2022, https://supreme.justia.com/cases/federal/us/579/15-274/.

174. Box, Commissioner, Indiana Department of Health, et al. v. Planned Parenthood of Indiana and Kentucky, 20.

175. Box, Commissioner, Indiana Department of Health, et al. v. Planned Parenthood of Indiana and Kentucky, 9.

176. Melissa Murray, "Race-Ing Roe: Reproductive Justice, Racial Justice, and the Battle for Roe v. Wade," *Harvard Law Review* 134, no. 2025 (April 12, 2021), https://harvardlawreview.org/2021/04/race-ing-roe/.

177. Mark Joseph Stern, "Conservative Judges Are Manipulating the History of Eugenics to Overturn Roe v. Wade," *Slate Magazine*, April 15, 2021, https://slate.com/news-and-politics/2021/04/sixth-circuit-clarence-thomas-abortion-eugenics.html.

178. Stern, "Conservative Judges Are Manipulating the History of Eugenics."

179. Oyez, "Pollard v. E. I. Du Pont de Nemours & Company," Oyez, accessed August 30, 2021, https://www.oyez.org/cases/2000/00-763.

180. Oyez, "Pollard v. E. I. Du Pont de Nemours & Company."

181. Oyez, "Swierkiewicz v. Sorema N.A.," Oyez, accessed August 30, 2021, https://www.oyez.org/cases/2001/00-1853.

182. "Kolstad v. American Dental Association," Oyez, accessed August 30, 2021, https://www.oyez.org/cases/1998/98-208.

183. Oyez, "Ledbetter v. Goodyear Tire and Rubber Company," Oyez, accessed August 30, 2021, https://www.oyez.org/cases/2006/05-1074.

184. Oyez, "Wal-Mart Stores, Inc. v. Dukes," Oyez, accessed August 30, 2021, https://www.oyez.org/cases/2010/10-277.

185. National Women's Law Center, "The Record of Brett M. Kavanaugh on Critical Legal Rights for Women" (National Women's Law Center, 2018), https://nwlc.org/wp-content/uploads/2018/09/NWLC-Kavanaugh-Report-FINAL-5.pdf, 4–5.

186. Oyez, "June Medical Services LLC v. Russo," Oyez, accessed August 30, 2021, https://www.oyez.org/cases/2019/18-1323.

187. Mark Joseph Stern, "Brett Kavanaugh Just Declared War on Roe v. Wade," *Slate Magazine*, February 7, 2019, https://slate.com/news-and -politics/2019/02/brett-kavanaugh-june-medical-services-louisiana-john -roberts.html.

188. Stern, "Brett Kavanaugh Just Declared War on Roe v. Wade."

189. Stern, "Brett Kavanaugh Just Declared War on Roe v. Wade."

190. National Women's Law Center, "The Record of Brett M. Kavanaugh on Critical Legal Rights for Women."

191. Jessica Spitz, "How Kavanaugh Ruled on Gun Control, Health Care, and Other Hot-Button Issues," *NBC News*, July 10, 2018, https://www.nbcnews .com/politics/supreme-court/how-kavanaugh-ruled-gun-control-health-care -other-hot-button-n890381.

192. Scott Horsley, "Kavanaugh Defends Controversial Abortion, Gun-Control Dissents." *Washington Post*, 2018, https://www.npr.org /2018/09/05/644615158/kavanaugh-hearings-day-2-senators-questions-to -take-center-stage.

193. Stern, "Brett Kavanaugh Just Declared War on Roe v. Wade."

194. Stern, "Brett Kavanaugh Just Declared War on Roe v. Wade."

195. National Women's Law Center, "The Record of Brett M. Kavanaugh."

196. National Women's Law Center, "The Record of Brett M. Kavanaugh."

197. National Women's Law Center, "The Record of Brett M. Kavanaugh."

198. Kevin Cope and Joshua Fischman, "It's Hard to Find a Federal Judge More Conservative than Brett Kavanaugh," *Washington Post*, September 5, 2018, https://www.washingtonpost.com/news/monkey-cage/wp/2018/09/05 /its-hard-to-find-a-federal-judge-more-conservative-than-brett-kavanaugh/.

199. National Women's Law Center, "The Record of Brett M. Kavanaugh."

200. National Women's Law Center, "The Record of Brett M. Kavanaugh"; Akela Lacy, "What Did Brett Kavanaugh Know about His Mentor Alex Kozinski's Sexual Harassment? A Timeline Suggests an Awful Lot," *The Intercept* (blog), September 20, 2018, https://theintercept.com/2018/09/20 /alex-kozinski-brett-kavanaugh-judge-9th-circuit/.

201. National Women's Law Center, "The Record of Brett M. Kavanaugh," 20.

202. Lacy, "What Did Brett Kavanaugh Know about His Mentor Alex Kozinski's Sexual Harassment?"

203. National Women's Law Center, "The Record of Brett M. Kavanaugh," 23.

204. Elana Schor, "Dems Zero in on Kavanaugh Ties to Judge in Sexual Harassment Scandal," *POLITICO*, August 6, 2018, https://politi.co/2nfPJlg.

205. Schor, "Dems Zero in on Kavanaugh Ties to Judge in Sexual Harassment Scandal."

206. John Bowden, "Ginsburg Credits Kavanaugh for Helping Boost Number of Female Supreme Court Clerks," *The Hill*, June 8, 2019, https:

//thehill.com/blogs/blog-briefing-room/447576-ginsburg-credits-kavanaugh
-for-helping-boost-number-of-female.

207. Kelsey Bolar, "Why His Female Law Clerks Are among Kavanaugh's
Biggest Advocates," *The Daily Signal*, July 11, 2018, https://www.dailysignal
.com/2018/07/11/why-his-female-law-clerks-are-among-brett-kavanaughs
-biggest-advocates/.

208. Stephanie Kirchgaessner and Jessica Glenza, "'No Accident' Brett
Kavanaugh's Female Law Clerks 'Looked like Models', Yale Professor Told
Students," *The Guardian*, September 20, 2018, sec. US news, https://www
.theguardian.com/us-news/2018/sep/20/brett-kavanaugh-supreme-court
-yale-amy-chua.

209. Kirchgaessner and Glenza, "'No Accident' Brett Kavanaugh's Female Law
Clerks 'Looked like Models.'"

210. Kirchgaessner and Glenza, "'No Accident' Brett Kavanaugh's Female Law
Clerks 'Looked like Models.'"

211. Christine Hauser, "The Women Who Have Accused Brett Kavanaugh,"
The New York Times, September 26, 2018, sec. U.S., https://www.nytimes
.com/2018/09/26/us/politics/brett-kavanaugh-accusers-women.html.

212. Amanda Marcotte, "Think Republican Women Will Turn on Brett
Kavanaugh—Or Donald Trump? Think Again," Salon, October 2, 2018,
https://www.salon.com/2018/10/02/think-republican-women-will-turn-on
-brett-kavanaugh-or-donald-trump-think-again/.

213. Marcotte, "Think Republican Women Will Turn on Brett Kavanaugh—
Or Donald Trump?"

214. Marcotte, "Think Republican Women Will Turn on Brett Kavanaugh—
Or Donald Trump?"

215. National Women's Law Center, "The Record of Brett M. Kavanaugh."

216. Oyez, "Ledbetter v. Goodyear Tire and Rubber Company," Oyez,
accessed August 2, 2021, https://www.oyez.org/cases/2006/05-1074.

5

Congressional Culpability and Legislative Legacy

Combine a milieu that is historically (and currently) heavily male, entitled and powerful men, a system that allows members to keep claims quiet and mostly hidden, and a business in which victims are particularly reluctant to speak out for fear of reprisal, and the result is an atmosphere that is catastrophically overrun with sexual harassment.[1]—(David Graham, *The Atlantic*, 2017)

In every building, down every hallway, and behind every door in Congress are good, honest people—often young people—working long hours for little pay in hopes of making our country and the world fairer and more just. And they have chosen to do so for and with you. It is impossible to describe how meaningful it is to work there. But for too many of us, the work was tainted by harassment and abuse nurtured by a culture of secrecy and an unforgiving, flawed system that protects those in power rather than those who need protection most. And in every instance, our current jobs and future careers in politics were integrally tied to our willingness to stay quiet.[2]—(Letter to Congressional Leadership from former staff that survived harassment and assault, September 20, 2018)

Introduction

Congresswoman Jackie Speier (D-CA) released a YouTube video on October 27, 2017, in which she described the sexual assault she had experienced as a congressional staffer forty years earlier. She encouraged others to come forward and share their own similar stories using the #MeToo-Congress hashtag, calling Congress "a breeding ground for a hostile work environment."[3] Her request followed actress and activist Alyssa Milano's entreaty two weeks earlier for victims of sexual harassment and assault to tweet "me too" to validate and amplify the collective experience of women whose careers and personal lives had been impacted by a sub-rosa culture of harassment and abuse. On the same day that Speier's video was released, *The Washington Post* published an article highlighting a history of systemic sexual misconduct and silencing of victims on Capitol Hill. As *The Washington Post* related, "Congress makes its own rules about the handling of sexual complaints against members and staff. . . . The result is a culture in which some lawmakers suspect harassment is rampant. Yet victims are unlikely to come forward."[4]

The spotlight of the MeToo movement made it clear that sexual harassment, discrimination, and retaliation had plagued Congress, like so many other sectors, for decades, though the full scope of the misconduct would remain unknown. One study commissioned in 1994 found that "44% of federal employees had experienced sexual harassment during the preceding two years."[5] The study also found that over half of all staffers in the House of Representatives feared that they would be unable to find another job on Capitol Hill if they reported sexual harassment, and almost half of the respondents feared retaliation if they spoke about harassment.[6] One of the main challenges in providing workplace protections and rights on Capitol Hill had been the lack of a central office for managing complaints. "House and Senate member offices operate as a federation of independent offices, each with their own policies and latitude when setting pay scales and time-off policies."[7] This lack of oversight or centralized management arguably contributed to enabling a hierarchical power structure rife with the potential for abuse and exploitation.

Revelations continued in the weeks and months following Representative Speier's call for a #MeTooCongress movement. In the wake of Speier's and myriad other testimonials, dozens of legislators, staffers, and political appointees, both Democrat and Republican, at the federal and state level, were publicly accused of various forms of sexual assault and harassment, seemingly fueled by the election of Donald Trump, the revelations of abuse by movie mogul Harvey Weinstein, and the cascade of subsequent

MeToo activism across sectors. In 2018 alone, twelve Republicans and thirteen Democrats campaigning for political office were compelled to end their campaigns, while several sitting congressmen resigned as they found themselves the subject of #MeToo allegations.[8] "In all, there were complaints against more than a dozen sitting members of Congress, as well as against two chiefs of staff, for their role in covering up complaints."[9]

Though the Congressional Accountability Act of 1995 had established some previously nonexistent procedures for contending with the problem of harassment, numerous and prominent instances of abuse were in evidence after its implementation. The MeToo era set the stage for the Congressional Accountability Act of 1995 Reform Act, passed in 2018 to provide further antidiscrimination and anti-harassment protections for legislative branch staff members.

In this chapter, we take a look at the congressional context where, as in other venues of governmental authority, women are underrepresented in the most powerful positions, are overrepresented in support roles, and have been systematically subjected to sexual harassment and misconduct that has been inadequately acknowledged or addressed. As in the foregoing chapters, we argue that this latter factor, in combination with the former circumstances, contributes to women's continued underrepresentation in positions of power, just as it results from their formerly disadvantageous position in society. This position is influenced by the regard with which women continue to be held, still beset by biases about women's relative competence and trustworthiness, in accord with the concept of testimonial injustice.

The Congressional Accountability Act of 1995 (CAA) and the CAA Reform Act that followed just over two decades later in 2018 are the primary policy mechanisms developed that contend with the problem of sexual harassment in the halls of Congress. We consider elements of the CAA and its Reform Act, including the conditions in which they were called for, the benefits and burdens they entailed, and for whom. We consider a sampling of cases of sexual misconduct brought to light during the decades spanning the two acts, and the financial implications of harassment and discrimination as measured by an accounting of settlement payouts precipitated by the misbehavior of congressional transgressors.

Congressional Accountability Act of 1995

Prior to 1995, Congress and legislative branch entities were exempt from federal workplace laws, which provided various protections for employees at public and related private institutions. Senator Grassley

(R-IA), who introduced the Congressional Accountability Act of 1995 in the U.S. Senate, said he considered the passage of the act, the first law passed by the 104th Congress, to be one of the greatest achievements of that body during his long tenure in Congress.[10] The law covered, but was not primarily concerned with, issues of sexual harassment and gender inequality; it aimed, generally, to make members of Congress subject to the laws that it makes and by which other citizens must live, in accordance with James Madison's admonition in Federalist 57 that a law that is not "obligatory on the legislature as well as on the people" debases the very spirit of the law (which Madison, paradoxically for our purposes, called "a vigilant and manly spirit which nourishes freedom").[11] Grassley did note later, however, that the Clarence Thomas-Anita Hill hearings of 1991 were a pivotal event that brought attention to the lack of workplace protections for employees of the legislative branch, saying explicitly that had "Anita Hill been a Congressional employee, she would have had no legal recourse to pursue her claims had she chosen to do so."[12] Ultimately, the Congressional Accountability Act of 1995 (CAA) passed in the House of Representatives by a vote of 429-0, and in the Senate by a vote of 98-1.[13] Only one senator, Robert C. Byrd (D-WV), voted against the bill for fear that it would allow executive and judicial branch interference,[14] while Senator Jay Rockefeller (D-WV), did not vote on the bill.[15]

With nearly unanimous support, the CAA then applied thirteen existing labor, civil, and workplace safety laws to the legislative branch, providing protection for employees of Congress, the U.S. Capitol Police, the Office of the Architect of the Capitol, the Congressional Budget Office, and the Office of the Attending Physician.[16] The independent Office of Compliance (OOC), now the Office of Workplace Rights (OCWR) was established to administer the Act,[17] with the self-described mission of the OOC articulated as being to "provide a safe and accessible legislative branch that is free from unlawful harassment and discrimination."[18]

The CAA also set up a three-stage—and some might say labyrinthian—process for filing a complaint, inclusive of sexual misconduct: an employee wishing to file a complaint first had to go through mandatory counseling for thirty days. If they wished to proceed with their complaint after the counseling stage, the individual, and their employing office, were required to undergo mediation for thirty days.[19] After sixty days, if the dispute had not been resolved by counseling or mediation, the employee had the option to choose to either lodge an administrative complaint or file a lawsuit in federal court. However, prior to any action being taken, there was a mandatory thirty-day wait period, referred to as the "cooling-off period."[20] Employees had to complete this ninety-day process within

180 days of the reported harassment incident.[21] While the ability to go forward with a complaint was an acknowledged advancement of the CAA, the bureaucratic burdens that the process imposed could well have dissuaded or derailed attempts at reporting by, in effect, substantially raising the cost of doing so.

The CAA provided civil rights, labor, and workplace protections for legislative branch employees, but the barriers to filing a lawsuit and the near immunity enjoyed by members of Congress contributed to the continuing "systemic issue of sexual misconduct on Capitol Hill."[22] In 2017, twenty-two years after the passage of the CAA, only 10 percent of women on Capitol Hill were aware of the processes for addressing sexual harassment that it had established, and those who were aware saw them as an "ordeal . . . prohibitively confusing, onerous, and endless."[23] Representative Jackie Speier identified the process as an "institution-protection process" rather than a victim-friendly process.[24]

Congressional Accountability Act of 1995 Reform Act

The Congressional Accountability Act of 1995 Reform Act ("CAA Reform Act") was passed in December 2018, expanding those to whom the workplace protections of the CAA were afforded and simplifying how claims would be handled and settled. Notably, the CAA Reform Act extended discrimination and harassment protections provided in the CAA to unpaid staff, changed the process for resolving claims, required antidiscrimination and anti-harassment training programs, and required members of Congress to be personally and financially liable for awards and settlements related to sexual harassment, misconduct, or retaliation.[25]

The original CAA had not provided workplace protections to all individuals working within the legislative branch. Unpaid staffs, notably the ubiquitous interns of Capitol Hill, were not afforded the same civil rights, labor, or workplace protections as paid employees. The total number of *paid* interns was reported in 2021 to be 3,822 (1,506 in the Senate and 2,316 in the House) based on a survey of House offices looking at congressional intern pay in the 116th Congress.[26] Internships have long been an important entrée into political professions, with some 63 percent of congressional staffers beginning their careers in politics as interns in Congress.[27] Some 66 percent of these were unpaid, according to a survey of congressional staffers conducted in 2017, before which time, only 10 percent of interns were paid. In 2018, Congress passed a bill allocating funds for the payment of legislative interns in the form of stipends, with $20,000 for House and $50,000 for Senate offices.[28] Given that each office is likely to have several interns, these stipends probably represented, at best, modest compensation for individual staffers. The youth, lack of pay or modest pay, and gender balance of interns and support staff—women outnumber men, "making up 56 percent of interns in the Senate and 51.3 percent in the House"—create the kind of power dynamics often associated with unchecked sexual harassment, so the provision of the CAA Reform Act to cover unpaid staff, including interns, any individuals detailed to the office, or those participating in a fellowship program,[29] represented an advancement in efforts to address the larger problem.

In addition to increasing working protections for staff—expanding the scope of inclusion to all Library of Congress employees, too—the CAA Reform Act overhauled the dispute resolution process for handling cases. Mandatory jurisdictional prerequisites of counseling and mediation for filing claims were removed. Through the CAA Reform Act, employees could opt to have a confidential advisor provide them with information and guidance regarding their rights.[30] Mediation remained as an available option but was no longer required unless requested and approved by both parties. In addition, the "cooling-off" period, which prevented victims from taking action for a minimum of thirty days following mediation, was eliminated.[31]

Another key component of the CAA Reform Act was the requirement that the OCWR track data, conduct workplace climate surveys, and provide education and training materials to legislative branch offices.[32] The Act required the OCWR to publish a one-time report accounting for awards and settlements paid out prior to the Act, and to issue annual reports on settlements moving forward.[33] It also required OCWR to conduct workplace climate surveys every two years to track key components of the work environment, such as "attitudes towards sexual harassment."[34] The CAA Reform Act also sought to increase workplace awareness and understanding of workplace protections by requiring OCWR to create training materials, such as posters, informing employees of their rights under the CAA.[35]

The passage of the CAA Reform Act was an important, though limited, milestone in protecting employees and unpaid workers from sexual harassment, discrimination, and retaliation. Following the passage of the Act, Representative Jackie Speier, one of its a cosponsors, stated that she was "proud to work across party lines" to address what she described as "the scourge of harassment and discrimination that thrives in the darkest recesses of the Capitol . . . Congress must send a strong message that Members, not taxpayers, will be held accountable for their actions and that staff will receive the robust rights and protections they deserve."[36] An aide for Representative Speier credited the momentum of the bill "to the sustained #MeToo movement and a shifting office culture on the issue."[37]

Analytic Approach

We consider the legislative context, in which members of Congress were for so long culpable but not accountable for sexual harassment and misconduct that, in addition to exacting individual harms, contributed to a system in which women systematically suffered personal and professional setbacks, creating a legacy that we argue has contributed to the continued predominance of male members of Congress in lawmaking.[38] In 2021, Congress included 26.7 percent women among its 535 members; 24 percent in the U.S. Senate and 27.2 percent in the U.S. House of Representatives.[39] The total number of women in the 117th Congress in 2021, at 143, had almost doubled since the 107th Congress two decades earlier in 2001, with a total of 72 women.[40]

Our analysis considers the culture of Congress in the Trump and MeToo era and the nature of demands for change, including the passage of the CAA Reform Act. Our assessment of the Act and the circumstances surrounding its appearance on the policy agenda were informed by John Kingdon's "Multiple Streams Framework." In Kingdon's framework, the possibilities for policy change occur when three streams—politics, policy, and problems—converge. We take a particular interest in two elements of this frame: the role of policy entrepreneurs and focusing events in bringing the streams together and pointing to particular policy solutions to the problem at hand.[41] The politics stream refers to the political context of an issue and is influenced by political actors, public pressure, and agenda setting. In the problem stream, a policy issue is identified and defined, while in the policy stream, solutions are recommended. When these three streams come together, often impelled by current events and shaped by the work of policy entrepreneurs advocating for change, a window of opportunity opens that assists in the realization of policy change.[42]

Drawing from existing research, we sought to identify the environment, actors, and key events that focused public attention and created pressure for change. First, we conducted preliminary Google searches for pertinent articles relevant to the #MeToo movement and sexual harassment and assault in Congress, which yielded articles from an array of publications, including *The Atlantic, The New York Times, The New Yorker, Politico, Roll Call, USA Today,* and *The Washington Post.* During this search, we discovered other pertinent articles and publications in the sources cited. Through this process, we created a timeline of prominent public misconduct allegations and identified key events that galvanized public awareness and attention. Next, we searched for newspaper coverage around the CAA Reform Act, looking at the key actors working inside and outside of the government, who were driving policy formation and advocating for its passage. Finally, we include for consideration an account of payment awards of settlements in cases of claims against members of Congress for workplace violations, inclusive of sexual harassment, to illustrate one measure of the tangible costs of misconduct, for which taxpayers, unbeknownst to them, had long been footing the bill.[43]

Sexual Misconduct on Capitol Hill in the MeToo Context

An exposé on sexual abuse in Hollywood hit the headlines of *The New York Times* on October 5, 2017.[44] Jodi Kantor and Megan Twohey's article detailing decades of sexual assault and harassment by Harvey Weinstein, cofounder of Miramax Films and The Weinstein Company, later became a book: *She Said*, with the subtitle, *Breaking the Sexual Harassment Story That Helped Ignite a Movement*. The public seemed primed for protest against male heavyweights (in the metaphorical and literal sense) who wielded disproportionate power; recall the unprecedented protest[45] that had sent women surging into the streets following Donald Trump's inauguration as president in January 2017 after his boasting about grabbing women "by the p—" at will and barnstorming his way through the election cycle with a barrage of bullying insults directed at women. In the weeks that followed Kantor and Twohey's incendiary piece, some eighty-seven women—including prominent and beloved actresses—came forward with accusations of sexual misconduct by Harvey Weinstein.[46] It was revealed that Weinstein had engaged in sexual harassment, assault, stalking, and threatening of women for years, while he and others in his orbit silenced his victims and anyone who sought to expose his abuse publicly. Weinstein's behavior was long rumored and considered an open secret to many in Hollywood.[47] As journalist Ronan Farrow described, for more than two decades, "too few people were willing to speak, much less allow a reporter to use their names, and Weinstein and his associates used nondisclosure agreements, payoffs, and legal threats to suppress their accounts."[48] Weinstein's outsized power to serially assault and harass women with impunity and without fear of disclosure was attributable to the power he wielded as "a producer of some of the biggest culture-defining films" of the opening decades of the twentieth century and gatekeeper of career-defining roles for actresses.[49] As Donald Trump had notoriously noted, "When you're a star,"—or a producer, college athlete, judge, senator or congressman—"they let you do it. You can do anything."[50]

The scale of Harvey Weinstein's abuse, his coordinated efforts to silence victims, and the complicity of bystanders who had allowed him to operate with impunity for many years made the scandal relatable to women everywhere—including on Capitol Hill—who had suffered such harassment in silence themselves for fear of losing, or never attaining, the professional positions for which they were preparing their whole lives if they dared to break that silence. Many knew the indignity of being subjected to analogous insult and injury, and the stultifying sense of impotence that came from operating within a system where such powerful, sometimes abusive, men held sway. So breaking news of the Weinstein scandal, following on the heels of the Trump inauguration and Women's March in the first month of 2017, became inflection points—what Kingdon called focusing events—that impelled people to policy action. In this setting, a single tweet provided the spark that would make #MeToo the watchword of the year. On October 15, 2017, Hollywood actress Alyssa Milano tweeted, "If you've been sexually harassed or assaulted write 'me too' as a reply to this tweet."[51] The entreaty's roots reached back to a conversation that activist Tarana Burke—who was acknowledged as "The Woman Who Created #MeToo Long Before Hashtags"[52]—had in 1997 with a thirteen-year-old who was being sexually abused by her mother's boyfriend.[53] Within twenty-four hours of Milano's tweet, it went viral, with three hundred thousand women responding, sharing personal stories of sexual harassment, assault, and abuse,[54] and Google searches about sexual harassment hitting a record high.[55] At year's end, *Time Magazine's* Person of the Year was not a single individual, but rather a group of women—the voices credited with starting the MeToo movement, collectively deemed The Silence Breakers.[56]

In rapid succession, stories of a culture of abuse across a range of industries were unearthed that fall. By the end of October 2017, a month that began with the *New York Times* revelation of Weinstein's serial abuse, *The Washington Post* reported on the prevalence of sexual harassment on Capitol Hill. The coverage revealed that the U.S. Department of the Treasury had paid around $15.2 million between 1997 and 2014 in 235 settlements for workplace violations of the CAA (such as discrimination and sexual harassment) by members of Congress.[57] The extent of awards and settlements turned out to be even greater than reported at the time; eventually it was revealed that, over thirteen years, more than $18.2 million was paid out in 291 settlement awards, as illustrated in table 5.1. There was an average of twenty-two settlements a year between 1997 and 2014, with an average of $62,691 per settlement and $1.4 million in settlements per year. The fewest number of settlements occurred in 2017

Table 5.1   Settlement and Award Amounts for Discrimination and/or Harassment by Members of Congress[58]

Fiscal Year	Total Amount Paid	Number of Settlements
1997	45,729	7
1998	103,180	16
1999	72,350	6
2000	55,638	16
2001	121,400	7
2002	3,974,077	10
2003	730,071	11
2004	388,209	15
2005	909,872	14
2006	849,529	18
2007	4,053,274	25
2008	875,317	10
2009	831,360	13
2010	246,271	9
2011	437,465	16
2012	426,539	12
2013	334,823	14
2014	806,450	11
2015	483,529	13
2016	573,929	14
2017	934,754	8
2018	388,816	10
2019	600,363	16
Total Amount	18,242,945	291

(eight awards) for a total of $934,754 paid out, and the highest total amount paid in awards occurred in 2007 (twenty-five awards) for a total of $4,053,274 in settlements.

Rates of harassment and discrimination in the reported period were likely greater than the settlements awarded suggest. Far more cases began the dispute resolution process than went on to file an administrative complaint. As seen in table 5.2, the total number of filed administrative complaints was roughly 10 percent of the total number of requests for counseling, the first step in the dispute resolution process. The main issues raised during counseling were harassment, including sexual harassment, and hostile work environment. Details on the cases that filed an administrative complaint or were awarded a settlement before the CAA Reform Act were not publicly available.

The #MeToo movement focused public attention on a workplace environment where members of Congress, too, behaved with impunity, in a culture that enabled widespread sexual harassment. As with Weinstein, many men who were powerful in their own realms—in their congressional districts and Capitol Hill offices—had been able to act abusively for years with little pushback due to their outsized authority and own brand of political celebrity. At the apex of their own individual hierarchies, senators and congressman had often engaged in sexual misconduct, their behavior an open secret, rumored, but unaddressed. They collectively operated in a system in Congress where they made the rules for themselves and the laws for others, and so they remained largely unaccountable.

Revelations and details about which members of Congress engaged in sexual misconduct surfaced continuously in the years prior to 2017, as table 5.3 indicates, but they were arguably greeted with a more orchestrated impetus to change once a critical mass of #MeToo testimonials was aired and a lengthening stream of powerful perpetrators was publicly held to account. Table 5.3 identifies some of the known perpetrators of sexual misconduct reported in the press. A review of this table indicates that there are far fewer prominently known cases of sexual misconduct than there are settlements (outlined in table 5.1). The true extent of sexual harassment in the period prior to the CAA Reform Act remains unclear, in part because the number of settlements attributed to sexual harassment rather than other workplace violations (such as discrimination) is unclear. In addition, many of the victims who shared their experiences of sexual harassment and assault did not explicitly name the member of Congress responsible.

Table 5.2 Formal Requests for Counseling, Number of Harassment and Hostile Work Environment Issues Raised in Counseling, and Administrative Complaints Filed by Year

Year	Total Formal Counseling Requests Filed (initial inquiry stage)	Workplace Issues Raised in Counseling: General Harassment (more than one harassment issue may be filed in a counseling request)	Workplace Issues Raised in Counseling: Hostile Work Environment (more than one harassment issue may be filed in a counseling request)	New Administrative Complaints Filed (after mandatory counseling and mandatory mediation)
1996[i]	95	20	N/A	13
1997[ii]	152	19	N/A	6
1998[iii]	60	19	N/A	12
1999[iv]	330	11	N/A	9
2000[v]	105	15	N/A	5
2001[vi]	395	565	N/A	10
2002[vii]	82	29	N/A	13
2003[viii]	111	23	30	12
2004[ix]	84	34	36	14
2005[x]	60	12	23	9
2006[xi]	44	9	8	7
2007[xii]	52	21	8	7
2008[xiii]	82	11	13	12
2009[xiv]	108	17	20	10
2010[xv]	105	33	37	9
2011[xvi]	142	113		12
2012[xvii]	83	58		14
2013[xviii]	81	35		11
2014[xix]	57	48		19
2015[xx]	63	68		11
2016[xxi]	49	15		15
2017[xxii]	47	29		5

(Continued)

Table 5.2   (*Continued*)

Year	Total Formal Counseling Requests Filed (*initial inquiry stage*)	Workplace Issues Raised in Counseling: General Harassment (*more than one harassment issue may be filed in a counseling request*)	Workplace Issues Raised in Counseling: Hostile Work Environment (*more than one harassment issue may be filed in a counseling request*)	New Administrative Complaints Filed (*after mandatory counseling and mandatory mediation*)
2018[xxiii]	72	38		4
2019 (Pre-Reform Act)	65	45		14
Total	2,524	-		253

[i] Office of Compliance, "Section 301(H) Report to Congress: 1996," 1997.

[ii] Office of Compliance, "Section 301(H) Report to Congress: 1997," 1998.

[iii] Office of Compliance, "Section 301(H) Report to Congress: 1998," 1999.

[iv] Office of Compliance, "Section 301(H) Report to Congress: 1999," 2000.

[v] Office of Compliance, "Section 301(H) Report to Congress: 2000," 2001.

[vi] Office of Compliance, "Report to Congress on the Use of the Office of Compliance by Covered Employees (2002)," 2002.

[vii] Office of Compliance, "Report to Congress on the Use of the Office of Compliance by Covered Employees (2002)," 2003.

[viii] Office of Compliance, "Annual Report 2003," 2004.

[ix] Office of Compliance, "FY2004 Annual Report," 2005.

[x] Office of Compliance, "FY2005 Annual Report," 2006.

[xi] Office of Compliance, "FY2006 Annual Report," 2007.

[xii] Office of Compliance, "FY2007 Annual Report," 2008.

[xiii] Office of Compliance, "FY2008 Annual Report," 2009.

[xiv] Office of Compliance, "State of the Congressional Workplace (FY 2009 Annual Report)," 2010.

[xv] Office of Compliance, "State of the Congressional Workplace (FY 2010 Annual Report)," 2011.

[xvi] Office of Compliance, "FY 2011 Annual Report," 2012.

[xvii] Office of Compliance, "FY 2012 Annual Report," 2013.

[xviii] Office of Compliance, "FY 2013 Annual Report," 2014.

[xix] Office of Compliance, "FY 2014 Annual Report," 2015.

[xx] Office of Compliance, "State of the Congressional Workplace (FY 2015 Annual Report)," 2016.

[xxi] Office of Compliance, "2016 State of the Congressional Workplace," 2017.

[xxii] Office of Compliance, "FY2017 Annual Report," 2018.

[xxiii] Office of Compliance, "State of the Congressional Workplace (FY 2018 Annual Report)," 2019.

Table 5.3 A Sampling of Allegations of Sexual Misconduct against Members of Congress

Year	Member of Congress (Party)	Congressional District	Sexual Misconduct Summary
1992	Brock Adams (D)	WA	Did not seek reelection after accusations of sexual misconduct, ranging from sexual harassment to rape, became public.[i]
1995	Robert Packwood (R)	OR	Resigned after the Senate Ethics Committee voted to expel him following their investigation, which documented claims of sexual harassment, assault, and misconduct by 27 women.[ii]
1995	Mel Reynolds (D)	IL-02	Was convicted for statutory rape of a 16-year-old campaign counter and resigned from Congress.[iii]
2004	Don Sherwood (R)	PA-10	Lost re-election after his mistress accused him of abuse.[iv]
2006	Mark Foley (R)	FL-16	Resigned from Congress after accusations surfaced that he sent teenage male pages sexually explicit emails.[v]
2006	Jim Gibbons (R)	NV-02	While a sitting member of Congress and during his gubernatorial race, settled a civil lawsuit in which he was walking a waitress out to her car, pinned her to a wall, and sexually assaulted her. He won the gubernatorial race.[vi]
2007	Larry Craig (R)	ID	Did not seek reelection following a 2007 arrest on charges of lewd conduct inside the Minneapolis-Saint Paul International Airport bathroom. A federal judge ordered him to pay the U.S. Treasury $242,000 dollars after illegally using campaign funds to pay his legal defense.[vii]
2010	Eric Massa (D)	NY-29	Resigned following an investigation by the House Ethics Committee over ongoing sexually inappropriate behavior, including unwanted touching, toward male staff members.[viii]

(Continued)

Table 5.3 (*Continued*)

Year	Member of Congress (Party)	Congressional District	Sexual Misconduct Summary
2011	Chris Lee (R)	NY-26	Resigned after reports emerged that he used his congressional email to send sexually explicit emails to a woman via craigslist.[ix]
2011	Anthony Weiner (D)	NY-09	Resigned following his Twitter sexting scandal, in which he messaged women sexually explicit photographs.[x]
2011	David Wu (D)	NY-09	Resigned from Congress after allegations of an unwanted sexual encounter with an 18-year-old were made public.[xi]
2017	Joe Barton (R)	TX-06	Retired (did not seek reelection) after leaked nude photos he emailed surfaced.[xii]
2017	John Conyers Jr. (D)	MI-13	Resigned after allegations of sexual harassment and misconduct were made public.[xiii]
2017	Trent Franks (R)	AZ-08	Resigned after the House Ethics Commission launched an investigation for improper conduct. Female staffers alleged he asked them to serve as a surrogate for him and his wife.[xiv]
2017	Bobby Scott (D)	VA-03	Was accused in December of 2017 by a former aide of sexual misconduct on two instances in 2013. The staffer alleges she was fired after she rebuked his advances.[xv]
2017	Ruben Kihuen (D)	NV-04	Was accused of sexual misconduct, including unwanted sexual advances and inappropriate touching. Minority Leader Pelosi called on him to resign, but he refused, instead completing his term and choosing to not seek reelection.[xvi]
2018	Blake Farenthold (R)	TX-27	Resigned after an ethics inquiry was opened and reports emerged that he paid an $84,000 settlement for inappropriate behavior.[xvii]
2018	Al Franken (D)	MN	Admitted to kissing a woman without consent during a comedy skit and pretending to grope her while she was asleep. He resigned after several other women accused him of inappropriate behavior and the Senate Ethics Committee launched an investigation.[xviii]

(*Continued*)

Table 5.3   (*Continued*)

Year	Member of Congress (Party)	Congressional District	Sexual Misconduct Summary
2018	Pat Meehan (R)	PA-07	Reports emerged that he used taxpayer funds to settle with a former staffer, who alleged he created a hostile work environment after she rebuffed his advances. He resigned after a House Ethic Committee launched an investigation into sexual harassment allegations.[xix]
2019	Katie Hill (D)	CA-25	Resigned following a House Ethics Commission investigation was launched for sexually inappropriate relationships with staffers.[xx]
2020	Matt Gaetz (R)	FL-01	Investigated by the Department of Justice over violations of sex trafficking laws.[xxi]

[i] John Balzar, "Sex Charges Bring End to Brock Adams' Career: Congress: Senator Drops Reelection Bid after Publication of Allegations by 8 Women of Improprieties," *Los Angeles Times*, March 2, 1992, https://www.latimes.com/archives/la-xpm-1992-03-02-mn-2265-story.html.

[ii] Tamara Keith, "When Bob Packwood Was Nearly Expelled from the Senate for Sexual Misconduct," *NPR*, November 27, 2017, sec. Politics, https://www.npr.org/2017/11/27/566096392/when-bob-packwood-was-nearly-expelled-from-the-senate-for-sexual-misconduct.

[iii] Aamer Madhani, "Former U.S. Congressman Mel Reynolds Is Headed Back to Prison—And then Africa," *USA TODAY*, May 10, 2018, https://www.usatoday.com/story/news/2018/05/10/former-u-s-congressman-mel-reynolds-prison-tax-fraud/598489002/.

[iv] Alex Gangitano, "Don Sherwood Running for Another Kind of Seat," *Roll Call*, March 1, 2016, https://www.rollcall.com/2016/03/01/don-sherwood-running-for-another-kind-of-seat/.

[v] Kate Zernike and Abby Goodnough, "Lawmaker Quits Over Messages Sent to Teenage Pages," *The New York Times*, September 30, 2006, sec. U.S., https://www.nytimes.com/2006/09/30/us/30foley.html.

[vi] Steve Friess, "For Nevada GOP, One Spectacle Too Many," May 6, 2008, https://www.washingtonpost.com/wp-dyn/content/article/2008/05/05/AR2008050502205.html.

[vii] "Former Senator Larry Craig Owes U.S. Treasury $242,000 over Airport Sex-Sting Arrest, Judge Says," *Washington Post* (blog), accessed August 29, 2021, https://www.washingtonpost.com/blogs/in-the-loop/wp/2014/09/30/former-senator-larry-craig-owes-u-s-treasury-242000-over-airport-sex-sting-arrest-judge-says/.

[viii] Carol D. Leonnig, "Staffers' Accounts Paint More Detailed, Troubling Picture of Massa's Office," April 13, 2010, https://www.washingtonpost.com/wp-dyn/content/article/2010/04/13/AR2010041302257.html.

[ix] David A. Fahrenthold and Aaron Blake, "Rep. Chris Lee Resigns after Reports of Craigslist Flirtation," *Washington Post*, February 9, 2011, sec. Politics, https://www.washingtonpost.com/politics/rep-chris-lee-resigns-after-reports-of-craigslist-flirtation/2011/02/09/ABwspuQ_story.html.

[x] Raymond Hernandez, "Weiner Resigns in Chaotic Final Scene," *The New York Times*, June 16, 2011, sec. New York, https://www.nytimes.com/2011/06/17/nyregion/anthony-d-weiner-tells -friends-he-will-resign.html.

[xi] Aaron Blake, "Rep. David Wu (D-Ore.) Says He Will Resign after Report of Sexual 'Encounter,'" *Washington Post*, July 26, 2011, sec. Politics, https://www.washingtonpost.com/politics /rep-david-wu-d-ore-says-he-will-resign-after-report-of-sexual-encounter/2011/07/26/gIQALrQGbI _story.html.

[xii] Kyle Cheney, "Barton to Retire after Nude Selfie Fallout," *POLITICO*, November 20, 2017, https://politi.co/2AmdI83.

[xiii] Elise Viebeck and David Weigel, "Rep. John Conyers Jr. Resigns over Sexual Harassment Allegations after a Half-Century in Congress," *Washington Post*, December 5, 2017, sec. PowerPost, https://www.washingtonpost.com/powerpost/conyers-wont-seek-reelection-following-harassment -allegations-report-says/2017/12/05/17057ea0-d9bb-11e7-a841-2066faf731ef_story.html.

[xiv] Elaine Godfrey, Lena Felton, and Taylor Hosking, "The 25 Candidates for 2018 Sunk by #MeToo Allegations," *The Atlantic*, July 26, 2018, https://www.theatlantic.com/politics /archive/2018/07/the-25-candidates-for-2018-sunk-by-metoo-allegations/565457/.

[xv] Adam Edelman, "Former Aide Accuses Rep. Bobby Scott of Sexual Misconduct," *NBC News*, December 15, 2017, https://www.nbcnews.com/politics/congress/former-aide-accuses-rep-bobby -scott-sexual-misconduct-n830216.

[xvi] Heidi M. Przybyla, "A List: Members of Congress Facing Sexual Misconduct Allegations," *USA TODAY*, December 5, 2017, https://www.usatoday.com/story/news/politics/2017/12/05 /list-members-congress-facing-sexual-misconduct-allegations/923484001/.

[xvii] Politico Staff, "Farenthold Resigns from Congress," *POLITICO*, accessed August 29, 2021, https://politi.co/2GDpJwh.

[xviii] Elaine Godfrey, Lena Felton, and Taylor Hosking, "The 25 Candidates for 2018 Sunk by #MeToo Allegations," *The Atlantic*, July 26, 2018, https://www.theatlantic.com/politics /archive/2018/07/the-25-candidates-for-2018-sunk-by-metoo-allegations/565457/.

[xix] Godfrey, Felton, and Hosking, "The 25 Candidates for 2018 Sunk by #MeToo Allegations."

[xx] Heather Caygle, John Bresnahan, and Kyle Cheney, "Rep. Katie Hill to Resign amid Allegations of Inappropriate Relationships with Staffers," *POLITICO*, October 27, 2019, https://www .politico.com/news/2019/10/27/rep-katie-hill-to-resign-amid-allegations-of-inappropriate -relationships-with-staffers-000301.

[xxi] Jeremy Herb, Lauren Fox, and Ryan Nobles, "Gaetz Showed Nude Photos of Women He Said He'd Slept with to Lawmakers, Sources Tell CNN," *CNN*, April 1, 2021, https://www.cnn .com/2021/04/01/politics/matt-gaetz-photos-women/index.html.

Among those whose names would publicly and inextricably be tied to their sexually harassing behavior, Senator Bob Packwood (R-OR) was among the earliest offenders to receive in-depth scrutiny, ultimately resigning after the Senate Ethics Committee voted to expel him in 1992. As a respected chair of the Senate Finance Committee and powerful member of Congress, his Senate colleagues initially steadfastly supported him and opposed public hearings into his behavior.[59] From Packwood's perspective, the timing for the public airing of the accusations against him could not have been worse, coming as it did on the heels of Anita Hill's testimony against Supreme Court nominee Clarence Thomas, which had raised "the issue of sexual harassment to the forefront of the political agenda."[60] Others of his era bemoaned their bad luck. Senator Howell Heflin (D-AL), who had chaired the Ethics Committee on the case remarked, "We are trying Packwood on the mores of the 90s for conduct that occurred in the 1970s . . . there ought to be a statute of limitations. The passage of time dims memories; they are embellished; the embellishment becomes part of the issue. Packwood was a woman's issue."[61]

Heflin's comments highlight several notable themes raised by those in powerful positions, in Congress or elsewhere in society, who had formerly enjoyed more complete immunity from public scrutiny or accountability for their own sexual misconduct or other transgressions. First, he hints at what is felt by them to be the unfairness of being held to account for what had formerly been routine behavior. Second, he suggests a policy mechanism—a statute of limitations—for blunting the ability of accusers to speak out against and seek redress for offending behavior. And third, he casts doubt on the competence and trustworthiness of women, whose memories he suggests may be faulty, and who, he says, are likely to make more of reports of misconduct than is warranted, from the point of view of those accused. One might wonder how dim a senator's memory would likely be if someone at work grabbed his buttocks or crotch without warning or invitation or threatened to derail his career ambitions if he spoke out about it.

Focusing Events in #MeToo Era Demands for Change

In mid-November 2017 Paul McLeod and Lissandra Villa broke a story on *BuzzFeed News* detailing the experience of a former staffer who was sexually harassed by U.S. Representative John Conyers (D-MI).[62] The former staffer was awarded a $27,000 settlement after having been fired for not submitting to his sexual advances.[63] The disturbing revelation regarding Conyers, the longest-serving African American member of Congress, was just one example of similar instances that "exemplified entrenched male power."[64] Representative Conyers, who was revered within Congress and seen as a veritable icon,[65] had spent more than five decades championing liberal causes since he was first elected in 1964. When the initial allegation against him surfaced, congressional colleagues defended Conyers,[66] including Minority Leader Nancy Pelosi (D-CA), later to be Speaker of the House of Representatives, who said that Conyers had "done a great deal to protect women," noting his work on the Violence Against Women Act.[67] As the allegations and evidence against him mounted, though, suggesting decades of sexual assault, harassment, and retaliation by Conyers, members of Congress, including Speaker Paul Ryan (R-WI) and Pelosi, called for Conyers's resignation.[68] Conyers finally resigned on December 5, 2017, after a House Committee on Ethics investigation was launched.[69]

One problematic element of the sexual misconduct of members of Congress is their staying power in holding on to elective office—many incumbents, like Conyers, who was eighty-eight years old at the time of his resignation, serve for decades. Intent on keeping his legacy intact, Conyers insisted that he was retiring, not resigning, in the face of the allegations, and he endorsed his son, John Conyers III, to succeed him.[70] Conyers served for so long on the House Judiciary Committee that he had participated in the impeachment inquiries against both Presidents Richard M. Nixon in 1974 and Bill Clinton in 1998.[71] In Nixon's case, Conyers had said that after Watergate, a scandal involving the president's involvement in the break-in of the headquarters of the Democratic National Committee, impeachment was necessary "to restore to our government the proper balance of constitutional power and to serve notice on all future presidents that such abuse of power will never again be tolerated"; while in Clinton's case, Conyers said, "This is not Watergate. . . . It is an extramarital affair."[72] Conyers was not alone in his assessment that Clinton's transgression did not rise to the level of an impeachable offense—indeed, a "substantial majority" of Americans opposed his removal from office.[73] But, given the nature of the conduct in question for both Conyers and Clinton, it is not unreasonable to wonder whether such understanding might be routinely extended between other fellow lawmakers who don't see sexual interactions with younger subordinate staff members, consensual or otherwise, as problematic, thus perpetuating a congressional culture of misconduct and fraught power relations that can disadvantage women.

As the hundreds of settlement payments costing millions of dollars for cases of discrimination and sexual harassment by members of Congress during just over a decade ending in 2019 make clear, the problem of misconduct among members of Congress is not uncommon. In fact, incidences of sexual harassment and assault are likely higher than the number of known cases suggests. We know, for instance, according to a Justice Department analysis reported by the Brennan Center for Justice at New York University Law School, that some 80 percent of rapes and sexual assaults go unreported.[74] The U.S. Equal Employment Opportunity Commission reported that a similar number—about 75 percent—of people who are harassed at work don't ever file a complaint.[75] The most commonly cited reasons for not reporting include "not wanting to be seen as a victim or attention-seeker, the humiliation, the time it will likely take, including follow through, fear of negative consequences like being alienated or fired and being blamed as the victim."[76] A CQ Roll Call survey conducted in 2016 found that four in ten congressional staffers who are women reported perceiving sexual harassment as a problem on Capitol Hill, while one in six said they had been personally victimized.[77] Yet reporting is relatively rare because, "There is a sense that going forward with an allegation like this would be completely the end of any career working for anybody on the Hill—and it undoubtedly would be," according to Debra Katz, a Washington, D.C. employment attorney "who represents congressional aides in sexual harassment cases."[78]

Any individual case of sexual harassment or impropriety by a member of Congress might be seen as a focusing event that brings attention to the larger problem affecting the institution as a whole. The sampling of almost twenty complaints brought against members of Congress for allegations of sexual misconduct shown in table 5.3 spans several decades and categories of concern, including inappropriate relations with staffers (Hill); a hostile work environment (Meehan); unwanted sexual advances, including kissing and touching (Franken, Kihuen, Massa); and the sharing of nude photos or sexually explicit emails (Barton, Foley, Gaetz, Weiner). Allegations span levels of severity from rape/statutory rape (Adams, Reynolds) to sexual harassment (Adams, Packwood), sometimes serial in nature. In addition to the conduct or sexual harassment or assault itself, some extended their transgressions into the realm of questionable book-keeping; in 2018, Blake Farenthold (R-TX) paid an $84,000 settlement related to his own "inappropriate" behavior,[79] and Pat Meehan (R-PA) used taxpayer funds to settle with a former staffer who claimed that he had created a hostile work environment.[80]

Policy Entrepreneurs Pushing Reform

In late October, 2017, as allegations of sexual harassment and abuse of staffers emerged, Representative Jackie Speier revealed, for the first time in public, that as a young Capitol Hill staffer, she had been sexually assaulted: "A chief of staff held my face, kissed me, stuck his tongue in my mouth," she recounted.[81] After more than forty years of being silent, Representative Speier, believing that sexual misconduct continued to be a "rampant" problem on Capitol Hill, finally came forward, signaling that "the flood gates" had been opened and a tipping point had been reached.[82] Part of the flood of formerly untold stories were those recounted by women, like Speier, who had suppressed such memories and stories for decades, dating back to the early days of their careers, when reporting would have opened them to criticism, shaming, and possible job loss or the stymieing of their career advancement. "But in the midst of a burgeoning national conversation about misogyny, sexual harassment and assault" opened by the #MeToo movement, older women joined younger women in "revisiting their past experiences"[83] and asserting that the time for change was long past due.

Within a month of her revelation, Speier introduced *The Member and Employee Training and Oversight on (ME TOO) Congress Act (H.R. 4396)*[84] in the House, and Senator Kirsten Gillibrand introduced analogous legislation in the Senate (S. 2159).[85] The bills made the process of reporting instances of sexual harassment and assault less onerous, provided some supportive measures for victims, and extended coverage to more employees. They allowed employees to lodge formal complaints without mandatory counseling and training, created a victims' counsel to offer advice and provide legal representation, and ended required nondisclosure agreements. Where member perpetrators were concerned, the legislation eliminated their ability to use taxpayer funds to settle claims and required that all such claims be publicly disclosed, thereby eliminating the veil of secrecy they had formerly enjoyed in covering up their wrongdoing. Further, the Me Too Congress Act created an anonymous workplace survey to chronicle the incidence of harassment that could help to establish a baseline of information beyond the whispers and informally shared warnings of staff about the most egregious transgressors.[86] In February 2018, the Congressional Accountability Act of 1995 Reform Act, based on Speier's Me Too Congress Act, was introduced by Representative Gregg Harper (R-MS-03) and cosponsored by thirty-eight members, including Representative Speier.[87]

Following Representative Speier's public encouragement for past victims of assault to come forward, fifteen hundred former congressional staff members came together and formed CongressToo, a collective with the goal of ending sexual harassment on Capitol Hill.[88] On November 13, 2017, members of CongressToo delivered a letter to leaders in Congress, proposing policy changes to the CAA that would better protect those working in the legislative branch. Declaring Congress's policies for preventing and adjudicating complaints of sexual harassment to be inadequate and in need of reform, the group outlined actions beyond the mandatory sexual harassment training for all members and staff that the Senate had acted to require the previous week. CongressToo members collectively urged the House and Senate to change the policy requiring "mandatory in-person harassment training for all Members of Congress and Congressional staff" and instead to "make counseling and mediation voluntary for individuals wishing to file a complaint" with the Office of Compliance (OOC).[89] CongressToo took the position that "Members of Congress and Chiefs of Staff should be made aware of their responsibility for preventing and reporting cases of sexual harassment and the OOC should have the authority to investigate complaints of abuse or harassment." The group further argued that, every two years, congressional staff should be surveyed "in order to understand the rates of sexual harassment on Capitol Hill and determine the effectiveness of prevention and reporting programs."[90]

A key voice in CongressToo was Ally Coll, a recent Harvard Law School graduate and lawyer for a prestigious firm, who had also worked in the legal department of Hillary Clinton's presidential campaign.[91] Coll subsequently learned that her firm, Boies Schiller Flexner LLP, was employed by Hollywood mogul Harvey Weinstein, and it later came to light that in the course of their representation of Weinstein, the firm had contracted the services of Black Cube—a private investigation organization run in large part by former officers of Israeli intelligence agencies and Mossad[92]—to investigate claims and silence Weinstein's accusers.[93] "I found myself in an unexpected #MeToo moment in my workplace," she recounted.[94] Upon the revelation by *The New Yorker* that her law firm had retained these private investigators who targeted, lied to, and secretly recorded conversations with women coming forward with allegations against Weinstein, she faced a personal moment of reckoning that led her to alter the trajectory of her career path.

The Weinstein scandal had prompted conversations within Boies Schiller Flexner on the role of lawyers in the #MeToo movement.[95] Coll herself saw the #MeToo movement and the precipitating Weinstein scandal as a pivotal movement for change; "I was concerned that it may become just a moment of awareness-raising and wanted to ensure that it turned into a moment where we saw workplace policy change and also public policy change come out of it,"[96] she said before leaving Boies Schiller Flexner to start the Purple Campaign in 2018. The founding mission of the Purple Campaign was to end sexual harassment in the workplace, beginning with the first workplace Coll had known as a teen: Capitol Hill.[97]

The initial area of focus for the Purple Campaign was sexual harassment reform in Congress, informed by Coll's personal experience, which she had recounted in a *Washington Post* article on "How Congress Plays by Different Rules on Sexual Harassment and Misconduct," published on October 27, 2017. The story she shared was that at the age of eighteen, while serving as an intern herself, she was grabbed on the buttocks by a senator while attending the Democratic National Convention. Recalling the incident, she said, "I was in the position of having no choice but reacting in a way that was going to make a big deal out of it in front of his staff or his wife, or acting like nothing was happening. I chose the latter."[98] Coll's experience with the senator came as little surprise to those she confided in after the fact, as he apparently had a reputation on the Hill as being "handsy."[99]

As president and cofounder of the Purple Campaign, after her stints in one of the nation's very top law schools and employment at a self-described "elite litigation firm,"[100] Coll set out to provide outside pressure advocating for reform and building support for the CAA Reform Act. Coll's role was central to the campaign, in concert with the CongressToo network, to raise former staffers' voices. Using the Purple Campaign's platform, Coll created an organization with a simple but targeted roadmap for the legislation and offered the public a way to get engaged to pressure Congress to act.[101] Following her success in supporting change in Congress, she and the Purple Campaign widened their aspirations to addressing "the systemic problem of workplace sexual harassment that exists across every industry in the United States."[102] In July 2019, the campaign announced a partnership with Uber, Amazon, Airbnb, and Expedia for the purpose of developing a certification program to help corporations to establish workplace policy on harassment.[103]

Summing Up Sexual Harassment on the Hill

Though the problems of sexual harassment and assault are rife across society, they should be of particular concern as manifested in "the people's house." The "quality of representation the citizenry receives from its political leaders is central to evaluating the character of any democratic institution,"[104] and we argue that the widespread existence and acceptance of sexism, sexual harassment, and other sexual misconduct act as structural barriers to women's full participation and representation. Since women are underrepresented as a percentage of the population in the halls of Congress, one might wonder whether their interests are adequately represented in that body, which is meant, as its name implies, to be a House of Representatives. As asserted by the title of a report by the Center for American Women and Politics (CAWP) at Rutgers University, "Representation Matters."[105] "Women," the authors assert, "bring perspectives, priorities, and agendas that would be missing if women were not there to represent women and give voice to those who are too often left out of policymaking spaces."[106] In a representative democracy, the inclusion of women's voices can lead to better outcomes overall. It has been demonstrated that having "more women in public decision-making" leads to more "policies that benefit women, children and families in general."[107] Not only is advancing gender equality a matter of justice and fairness, it "is also a strategic imperative that reduces poverty and promotes economic growth, increases access to education, improves health outcomes,[108] advances political stability, and fosters democracy."[109]

As the social construction frame elucidates, those who are positively socially constructed and powerful are likely to receive policy benefits. This includes mostly male lawmakers, who have traditionally shared pedigrees as privileged graduates of prestigious schools that prepare them to assume positions of power. In this case, the policy that has benefited them the most might be said to have been the absence of any policy at all, since for most of the history of the country, there were no policies in place that would have constrained the behavior of lawmakers themselves where workplace harassment and discrimination were concerned. With the passage of the CAA in 1995, some strictures of accountability were introduced, but the process for reporting was seen to be so burdensome as to actually dissuade many from even attempting to negotiate its intricacies. And such burdens, as the social construction frame explains, are more likely to be experienced by those with less power and who might not be seen as positively or esteemed as highly, such as lower-level congressional staffers, mostly women, who have historically been targeted for sexual harassment or assault.

In this chapter, we have considered two policy mechanisms, the CAA of 1995 and its Reform Act in 2018, that were designed to address oversight of members of Congress, keeping them accountable to the public and affording some mechanisms of accountability and transparency, two watchwords of a well-functioning democracy. We considered two aspects of these policy solutions with regard to how they gained status on the policy agenda—the focusing events that garnered public attention and the policy entrepreneurs who helped define and advance those solutions.

This is just one possible analytical approach to advancing understanding about the problems at hand, which include women's underrepresentation in spheres of public authority, and the role of sexual harassment and other forms of sexual misconduct in creating barriers to their participation. In the course of describing the #MeToo context of sexual misconduct on Capitol Hill, we provide an account of settlements paid out for harassment and discrimination on the part of members of Congress over the course of two decades or so to give a sense of the direct tangible costs of such behavior. We also offer a sampling of related sexual misconduct and harassment cases to suggest some categories of concern and how they constitute setbacks to women's interests, individually and collectively.

The information that we feature suggests that sexual harassment is a bipartisan problem, with prominent examples of members from both parties engaging in egregious behavior. Many lawmakers engaged in such misconduct were repeat offenders, victimizing many women before their stories rose to the level of public attention or condemnation. Subordinate staffers seem to have been those most targeted for abuse, making them subject to testimonial injustice, with their accounts given less credence than those of the powerful elected officials for whom they worked. Many members accused of harassment, like the "handsy" senator who grabbed Ally Coll, observed few boundaries between themselves and the staffers they victimized, exhibiting a sense of entitlement to access to women's bodies and service far beyond what their official job descriptions or social propriety would imply. In addition to sticking their tongues down their throats and grabbing their breasts and buttocks, among other offenses, one member of Congress, Trent Franks (R-AZ), tried to prevail upon staffers to serve as gestational surrogates for him and his wife.[110]

Objectification of women by members of the legislature imposes individual harms and also arguably damages the status of women and the respect that they are afforded as a group. Some features of objectification that have been identified by philosopher Martha Nussbaum include instrumentality, "the treatment of a person as a tool for the objectifier's purposes," such as sexual gratification and violability, "the treatment of a person as lacking in boundary-integrity."[111] Additional features of objectification proposed by philosopher Rae Langton include reduction to body, reduction to appearance, and silencing.[112] When Bob Packwood and other elected perpetrators subjected women to their unwanted touch and gaze, they were engaging in just such objectification. When, more recently, Representative Matt Gaetz (R-FL), while on the House floor, showed photos of naked women whom he said he had slept with, to fellow lawmakers, he also promoted an objectifying view of women by reducing them to body and appearance.[113] To protect themselves from the repercussions of such behavior, lawmakers sometimes promote measures that contribute to silencing women, by requiring nondisclosure agreements or imposing statutes of limitations or other procedural hurdles that make reporting their misconduct so onerous that victims are disincentivized from going through the considerable trouble of coming forward. Less formally, at times implicitly, lawmakers may threaten retaliation for reporting or disparage women so as to undercut their credibility in case they do. These tactics can be observed beyond Capitol Hill, of course, and are evident wherever power disparities prevail.

Among offending lawmakers, federal elected representatives are not alone in their culpability. Since the start of 2017, *The Associated Press* has tallied at least 90 state lawmakers who have faced public allegations or repercussions over sexual misconduct claims.[114] One young woman who came forward in light of the #MeToo movement said of her own experience in making such a claim, "Because this happened so early on for me, I just assumed this was the way things worked and that I'd have to accept it."[115] Working to ameliorate the conditions that promote such discouragement and resignation, by reducing the burdens women face in the workplace from harassment and discrimination, will be necessary to further advance women's representation in the place that it may matter most: in legislatures where laws governing the shared existence of society are made.

Notes

1. David A. Graham, "The Dam of Congressional Sexual-Harassment Claims Cracks Open," *The Atlantic*, November 21, 2017, https://www.theatlantic .com/politics/archive/2017/11/is-the-dam-of-congressional-sexual -harassment-allegations-breaking/546479/.

2. Anna Kain, Rebecca Weir, Ally Coll Stele, Katherine Cichy, Winsome Packer, Melanie Sloan, and Lauren Green, "Harassment, Discrimination, and Reform in Congress," September 20, 2018, https://www.aclu.org/letter/letter -congressional-leadership-former-staff-survived-harassment-and-assault.

3. Sunlen Serfaty, "Congresswoman Describes Sexual Assault in #MeToo Video," *CNN*, October 27, 2017, https://www.cnn.com/2017/10/27/politics /jackie-speier-me-too-sexual-assault-harassment/index.html.

4. Michelle Ye Hee Lee and Elise Viebeck, "How Congress Plays by Different Rules on Sexual Harassment and Misconduct," *Washington Post*, October 27, 2017, sec. Politics, https://www.washingtonpost.com/politics

/how-congress-plays-by-different-rules-on-sexual-harassment-and-misconduct
/2017/10/26/2b9a8412-b80c-11e7-9e58-e6288544af98_story.html.

5. Jen Roesch, "Let's Talk about Biden and Sexual Harassment on Capitol Hill," *Age of Awareness* (blog), May 14, 2020, https://medium.com
/age-of-awareness/joe-biden-tara-reade-and-sexual-harassment-on-capitol
-hill-9c4eb1f88a90.

6. Jen Roesch, "Let's Talk about Biden and Sexual Harassment on
Capitol Hill," *Age of Awareness* (blog), May 14, 2020, https://medium.com
/age-of-awareness/joe-biden-tara-reade-and-sexual-harassment-on-capitol
-hill-9c4eb1f88a90.

7. Chris Cioffi and Katherine Tully-McManus, "The Opaqueness of
Congress' Workplace Rules Hangs over the Tara Reade Allegations about
Biden," *Roll Call*, May 7, 2020, https://www.rollcall.com/2020/05/07/the
-opaqueness-of-congress-workplace-rules-hangs-over-the-tara-reade
-allegations-about-biden/.

8. Elaine Godfrey, Lena Felton, and Taylor Hosking, "The 25 Candidates
for 2018 Sunk by #MeToo Allegations," *The Atlantic*, July 26, 2018, https:
//www.theatlantic.com/politics/archive/2018/07/the-25-candidates-for-2018
-sunk-by-metoo-allegations/565457/.

9. Roesch, "Let's Talk about Biden."

10. Charles Grassley and Jennifer Shaw Schmidt, "Practicing What We
Preach: A Legislative History of Congressional Accountability Policy Essay,"
Harvard Journal on Legislation 35, no. 1 (1998): 34.

11. Grassley and Schmidt, "Practicing What We Preach," 33.

12. Grassley and Schmidt, "Practicing What We Preach," 38–39.

13. Cioffi and Tully-McManus, "The Opaqueness of Congress' Workplace
Rules."

14. Cioffi and Tully-McManus, "The Opaqueness of Congress' Workplace
Rules."

15. United States Senator, "S.2 (Congressional Accountability Act of 1995):
Roll Call Vote," accessed August 27, 2021, https://www.senate.gov/legislative
/LIS/roll_call_lists/roll_call_vote_cfm.cfm?congress=104&session=1&vote
=00014.

16. Office of Compliance, "Congressional Accountability Act of 1995"
(Washington, D.C.: United States Congress, November 2016), iii.

17. Office of Compliance, "Congressional Accountability Act of 1995."

18. Office of Congressional Workplace Rights Training Video, ocwr.gov.

19. Office of Compliance, United States Congress, "Recommendations
for Improvements to the Congressional Accountability Act: An Analysis
of Federal Workplace Rights, Safety, Health, and Accessibility Laws That
Should Be Made Applicable to Congress and Its Agencies" (Washington,
D.C., December 2014), 5, https://www.ocwr.gov/sites/default/files/Section
%20102b%20Recommendations%20for%20the%20116th%20Congress.pdf.

20. Office of Compliance, United States Congress, "Recommendations for Improvements to the Congressional Accountability Act."

21. Benton Hughes, "Revisiting the 1995 Congressional Accountability Act: How Congress Granted Itself Practical Immunity from Sexual Misconduct and Learned to Stop Worrying about Allegations Student Articles," *Law & Psychology Review* 44 (2019–2020): 251.

22. Hughes, "Revisiting the 1995 Congressional Accountability Act," 260 –261.

23. Michelle Cottle, "Capitol Hill's Sexual Harassment Problem," *The Atlantic*, November 3, 2017, https://www.theatlantic.com/politics /archive/2017/11/capitol-hills-sexual-harassment-problem/544946/.

24. Lee and Viebeck, "How Congress Plays by Different Rules."

25. Office of Congressional Workplace Rights, United States Congress, "FAQ: What Is the Congressional Accountability Act of 1995 Reform Act?" January 2019: 1–2.

26. James R. Jones, Tiffany Win, and Carlos Mark Vera, "Who Congress Pays: Analysis of Lawmakers' Use of Intern Allowances in the 116th Congress," Pay Our Interns, 2021, https://payourinterns.org/wp-content /uploads/2021/03/Pay-Our-Interns-Who-Congress-Pays.pdf.

27. Tim LaPira and Alexander Furnas, "Paying Congress's Interns a Living Wage Is a Good Idea. Paying Professional Staff One Is Even Better," *Vox*, December 13, 2018, https://www.vox.com/policy-and -politics/2018/12/13/18139934/congress-intern-pay-ocasio-cortez-living -wage-staff.

28. Jones et al., "Who Congress Pays."

29. Office of Compliance, United States Congress, "Recommendations for Improvements to the Congressional Accountability Act."

30. Office of Compliance, United States Congress, "Recommendations for Improvements to the Congressional Accountability Act."

31. Office of Compliance, United States Congress, "Recommendations for Improvements to the Congressional Accountability Act," 6.

32. Government Accountability Office, "Office of Congressional Workplace Rights: Using Key Management Practices Would Help to Fully Implement Statutory Requirements" (Washington, D.C., December 2019): 8.

33. Government Accountability Office, "Office of Congressional Workplace Rights," 9.

34. Government Accountability Office, "Office of Congressional Workplace Rights," 9.

35. Government Accountability Office, "Office of Congressional Workplace Rights," 9.

36. "Reps. Speier, Byrne, Underwood, and Fitzpatrick Introduce Bipartisan Bill to Further Fix Congress' Broken Workplace Harassment

and Discrimination Rules," *Congresswoman Jackie Speier*, December 17, 2019, sec. Press Releases, https://speier.house.gov/2019/12/reps-speier -byrne-underwood-and-fitzpatrick-introduce-bipartisan-bill-to-further-fix -congress-broken-workplace-harassment-and-discrimination-rules.

37. Li Zhou, "Congress's Recently Passed Sexual Harassment Bill, Explained," *Vox*, December 20, 2018, https://www.vox.com/2018/12/20/18138377 /congress-sexual-harassment-bill.

38. Paul Cairney and Tanya Heikkila, "A Comparison of Theories of the Policy Process," in *Theories of the Policy Process*, 3rd ed., ed. Paul A. Sabatier and Christopher M. Weible (Boulder, CO: Westview Press, a member of the Perseus Books Group, 2014), 364–366.

39. Center for American Women and Politics (CAWP), 2021, https://cawp .rutgers.edu/women-us-congress-2021.

40. Center for American Women and Politics (CAWP), 2021.

41. John W. Kingdon, *Agendas, Alternatives, and Public Policies* (London: Longman, 2011).

42. Kingdon, *Agendas, Alternatives, and Public Policies*.

43. Jane Coaston, "There's a Little-Known Fund that Goes to Victims of Sexual Harassment on the Hill. You Pay for It." *Vox*, November 21, 2017, https://www.vox.com/policy-and-politics/2017/11/21/16679292/secret-fund -pays-victims-sexual-harassment-the-hill.

44. Jodi Kantor and Megan Twohey, "Harvey Weinstein Paid off Sexual Harassment Accusers for Decades," *The New York Times*, October 5, 2017, sec . U.S., https://www.nytimes.com/2017/10/05/us/harvey-weinstein-harassment -allegations.html.

45. Scott Malone and Ginger Gibson, "Women Lead Unprecedented Worldwide Mass Protests against Trump," *Reuters*, January 22, 2017, sec. Full coverage of the 2016 U.S. Election, https://www.reuters.com/article/us-usa -trump-women-idUSKBN15608K.

46. Sara M. Moniuszko and Cara Kelly, "Harvey Weinstein Scandal: A Complete List of the 87 Accusers," *USA TODAY*, accessed August 26, 2021, https://www.usatoday.com/story/life/people/2017/10/27/weinstein-scandal -complete-list-accusers/804663001/.

47. "Harvey Weinstein Timeline: How the Scandal Unfolded," *BBC News*, April 7, 2021, sec. Entertainment & Arts, https://www.bbc.com/news /entertainment-arts-41594672.

48. Ronan Farrow, "From Aggressive Overtures to Sexual Assault: Harvey Weinstein's Accusers Tell Their Stories," *The New Yorker*, October 10, 2017, https://www.newyorker.com/news/news-desk/from-aggressive-overtures-to -sexual-assault-harvey-weinsteins-accusers-tell-their-stories.

49. Reuters Staff, "Factbox: How Powerful Was Harvey Weinstein? His Film Legacy Paints a Picture," *Reuters*, February 14, 2020, sec. U.S. Legal

News, https://www.reuters.com/article/us-people-harvey-weinstein-factbox-movie-idUSKBN2081CJ.

50. Dara Lind and Dylan Matthews, "Vox Sentences: 'When You're a Star, They Let You Do It. You Can Do Anything.'—Donald Trump," *Vox* (blog), October 7, 2016, https://www.vox.com/2016/10/7/13206364/vox-sentences-trump-sexual-assault.

51. Alix Langone, "#MeToo and Time's Up Founders Explain the Difference Between the 2 Movements," *Time*, March 22, 2018, https://time.com/5189945/whats-the-difference-between-the-metoo-and-times-up-movements/.

52. Sandra E. Garcia, "The Woman Who Created #MeToo Long Before Hashtags," *The New York Times*, October 20, 2017, sec. U.S., https://www.nytimes.com/2017/10/20/us/me-too-movement-tarana-burke.html.

53. Langone, "#MeToo and Time's Up."

54. Langone, "#MeToo and Time's Up."

55. Karen Kaplan, "After Alyssa Milano's #MeToo Tweet, Google Searches about Sexual Assault Hit Record High," *Los Angeles Times*, December 21, 2018, https://www.latimes.com/science/sciencenow/la-sci-sn-metoo-google-searches-20181221-story.html.

56. Stephanie Zacharek, Eliana Dockterman, and Haley Sweetland Edwards, "TIME Person of the Year 2017: The Silence Breakers," *Time*, 2017, https://time.com/time-person-of-the-year-2017-silence-breakers/.

57. David A. Graham, "The Dam of Congressional Sexual-Harassment Claims Cracks Open," *The Atlantic*, November 21, 2017, https://www.theatlantic.com/politics/archive/2017/11/is-the-dam-of-congressional-sexual-harassment-allegations-breaking/546479/.

58. Office of Congressional Workplace Rights, "State of the Congressional Workplace: 2019 Annual Report," 2020.

59. Susan J. Tolchin and Martin Tolchin, *Glass Houses: Congressional Ethics and the Politics of Venom* (Boulder, CO: Westview Press, 2004).

60. Tolchin and Tolchin, *Glass Houses*, 86.

61. Tolchin and Tolchin, *Glass Houses*, 99.

62. Paul McLeod and Lissandra Villa, "She Said that a Powerful Congressman Harassed Her. Here's Why You Didn't Hear Her Story," *BuzzFeed News*, November 20, 2017, https://www.buzzfeednews.com/article/paulmcleod/she-complained-that-a-powerful-congressman-harassed-her.

63. Emily Stewart, "Report: Rep. John Conyers Settled a $27,000 Sexual Misconduct Complaint in 2015," *Vox*, November 21, 2017, https://www.vox.com/policy-and-politics/2017/11/21/16684606/john-conyers-settlement-buzzfeed.

64. Graham, "The Dam of Congressional Sexual-Harassment Claims Cracks Open."

65. Elise Viebeck and David Weigel, "Rep. John Conyers Jr. Resigns over Sexual Harassment Allegations after a Half-Century in Congress," *Washington Post*, December 5, 2017, sec. PowerPost, https://www.washingtonpost.com /powerpost/conyers-wont-seek-reelection-following-harassment-allegations-report-says/2017/12/05/17057ea0-d9bb-11e7-a841-2066faf731ef_story.html.

66. Anna North, "New Poll Shows Major Shifts in How Americans Think about Men in Power," *Vox*, September 27, 2019, https://www.vox.com /2019/9/27/20885011/trump-brett-kavanaugh-me-too-metoo-2020.

67. "Pelosi: Accused Congressman Conyers Deserves 'Due Process,'" *Meet the Press*, November 26, 2017, https://www.nbcnews.com/meet-the-press /video/nancy-pelosi-accused-congressman-john-conyers-is-an-icon-in-our -country-1103755843514.

68. Rebecca Shabad, "Nancy Pelosi, Paul Ryan Call on John Conyers to Resign from Congress," November 30, 2017, https://www.cbsnews.com/news /nancy-pelosi-calls-on-john-conyers-to-resign-from-congress/.

69. Ben Jacobs, "John Conyers Resigns from Congress after Sexual Harassment Allegations," *The Guardian*, December 5, 2017, sec. US news, https://www.theguardian.com/us-news/2017/dec/05/john-conyers-will-not -seek-re-election-amid-sexual-harassment-allegations.

70. Ben Jacobs, "John Conyers Resigns from Congress after Sexual Harassment Allegations," *The Guardian*, December 5, 2017, https://www .theguardian.com/us-news/2017/dec/05/john-conyers-will-not-seek-re -election-amid-sexual-harassment-allegations.

71. Adam Clymer, "John Conyers Jr., Longest-Serving African-American in Congressional History, Dies at 90," *The New York Times*, October 27, 2019, https://www.nytimes.com/2019/10/27/obituaries/john-conyers-jr-dead.html.

72. Clymer, "John Conyers Jr. Dies at 90."

73. Gary Jacobson, "Public Opinion and the Impeachment of Bill Clinton," *British Election and Parties Review* 10, no. 1 (2000): 1–31.

74. Cameron Kimble and Inimai M. Chettiar, "Sexual Assault Remains Dramatically Underreported," Brennan Center for Justice, October 4, 2018, https://www.brennancenter.org/our-work/analysis-opinion/sexual-assault -remains-dramatically-underreported.

75. Mona Patel, "Workplace Harassment: Why Women Don't Speak Up," *Forbes*, October 30, 2018, https://www.forbes.com/sites/yec/2018/10/30 /workplace-harassment-why-women-dont-speak-up/?sh=390e91b234b3.

76. Patel, "Why Women Don't Speak Up."

77. Emily Stewart, "Why Women on Capitol Hill Don't Report Sexual Harassment, Explained in 90 Seconds," *Vox*, November 20, 2017, https: //www.vox.com/policy-and-politics/2017/11/20/16679104/congress-sexual -harssment-process-explained.

78. Lee and Viebeck, "How Congress Plays by Different Rules."

79. Politico Staff, "Farenthold Resigns from Congress," *POLITICO*, accessed August 29, 2021, https://politi.co/2GDpJwh.

80. Elaine Godfrey, Lena Felton, and Taylor Hosking, "The 25 Candidates for 2018 Sunk by #MeToo Allegations," *The Atlantic*, July 26, 2018, https://www.theatlantic.com/politics/archive/2018/07/the-25-candidates-for-2018-sunk-by-metoo-allegations/565457/.

81. Sunlen Serfaty, "Congresswoman Describes Sexual Assault in #MeToo Video," *CNN*, October 27, 2017, https://www.cnn.com/2017/10/27/politics/jackie-speier-me-too-sexual-assault-harassment/index.html.

82. Sunlen Serfaty, "Congresswoman Describes Sexual Assault in #MeToo Video," *CNN*, October 27, 2017, https://www.cnn.com/2017/10/27/politics/jackie-speier-me-too-sexual-assault-harassment/index.html.

83. Caitlin Gibson, "Sharing Stories from Decades Ago, Older Women Find Their Place in #MeToo," *The Washington Post*, February 18, 2018, https://www.washingtonpost.com/lifestyle/style/sharing-stories-from-decades-ago-older-women-find-their-place-in-metoo/2018/02/16/c754838a-0db6-11e8-95a5-c396801049ef_story.html.

84. Jackie Speier, "H.R.4396—115th Congress (2017–2018): ME TOO Congress Act," legislation, November 15, 2017, https://www.congress.gov/bill/115th-congress/house-bill/4396.

85. Kirsten E. Gillibrand, "S.2159—115th Congress (2017–2018): ME TOO Congress Act," legislation, November 16, 2017, https://www.congress.gov/bill/115th-congress/senate-bill/2159.

86. Susan Davis, "'Me Too' Legislation Aims to Combat Sexual Harassment in Congress," *NPR*, November 15, 2017, sec. Politics, https://www.npr.org/2017/11/15/564405871/me-too-legislation-aims-to-combat-sexual-harassment-in-congress.

87. Gregg Harper, "H.R.4924—115th Congress (2017–2018): Congressional Accountability Act of 1995 Reform Act," Legislation, November 15, 2017, https://www.congress.gov/bill/115th-congress/house-bill/4924/cosponsors?q=%7B%22search%22%3A%5B%22Congressional+Accountability+Act+of+1995+Reform+Act+Gregg+Harper%22%2C%22Congressional%22%2C%22Accountability%22%2C%22Act%22%2C%22of%22%2C%221995%22%2C%22Reform%22%2C%22Gregg%22%2C%22Harper%22%5D%7D&r=2&s=2.

88. CongressToo, "CongressToo," accessed August 26, 2021, https://www.congresstoo.org.

89. CongressToo, "Nov. 2017 Letter," accessed August 26, 2021, https://www.congresstoo.org/our-letter.

90. CongressToo, "Nov. 2017 Letter," accessed August 26, 2021, https://www.congresstoo.org/our-letter.

91. "Ally Coll," The Purple Campaign, accessed March 13, 2022, https://www.purplecampaign.org/leadership.

92. Ronan Farrow, "Harvey Weinstein's Army of Spies," *The New Yorker*, November 6, 2017, https://www.newyorker.com/news/news-desk/harvey-weinsteins-army-of-spies.

93. Alex Gangitano, "Former Staffer's Nonprofit Strives to Combat Sexual Harassment," *Roll Call*, June 7, 2018, https://www.rollcall.com/2018/06/07/former-staffers-nonprofit-strives-to-combat-sexual-harassment/.

94. Ally Coll Steele, "Why I Left My Corporate Legal Job to Work Full-Time on #MeToo," *Washington Post*, January 25, 2018, https://www.washingtonpost.com/news/posteverything/wp/2018/01/25/why-i-left-my-corporate-legal-job-to-work-full-time-on-metoo/.

95. Gangitano, "Former Staffer's Nonprofit Strives to Combat Sexual Harassment."

96. Gangitano, "Former Staffer's Nonprofit Strives to Combat Sexual Harassment."

97. The Purple Campaign, "Our Mission," The Purple Campaign, accessed August 28, 2021, https://www.purplecampaign.org/our-mission.

98. Lee and Viebeck, "How Congress Plays by Different Rules."

99. Lee and Viebeck, "How Congress Plays by Different Rules."

100. Boies Schiller Flexner, accessed May 4, 2022, https://www.bsfllp.com/.

101. "#CAANow Action Campaign," The Purple Campaign, accessed August 28, 2021, https://www.purplecampaign.org/action-campaigns.

102. Soo Youn, "The Purple Campaign Partners with Uber, Amazon to Crack Down on Workplace Sexual Harassment," ABC News, July 17, 2019, https://abcnews.go.com/Business/purple-campaign-partners-uber-amazon-crack-workplace-sexual/story?id=64364049.

103. Youn, "The Purple Campaign Partners with Uber, Amazon."

104. Brian Frederick, "The People's Perspective on the Size of the People's House," *PS: Political Science & Politics* 41, no. 2 (April 2008): 329–335, https://doi.org/10.1017/S1049096508080517.

105. Kelly Dittmar, Kira Sanbonmatsu, Susan J. Carroll, Debie Walsh, and Catherine Wineinger, "Representation Matters: Women in the U.S. Congress" (Center for Women on Politics, Rutgers University, 2017).

106. Dittmar et al., "Representation Matters: Women in the U.S. Congress."

107. Marianela Jarroud, "Everyone Benefits from More Women in Power," Our World, March 7, 2015, https://ourworld.unu.edu/en/everyone-benefits-from-more-women-in-power.

108. Carles Muntaner and Edwin Ng, "The More Women in Government, the Healthier a Population," *The Conversation* (blog), accessed August 31, 2021, https://theconversation.com/the-more-women-in-government-the-healthier-a-population-107075.

109. The White House, "Executive Order on Establishment of the White House Gender Policy Council," The White House, March 8, 2021, https://www

.whitehouse.gov/briefing-room/presidential-actions/2021/03/08/executive
-order-on-establishment-of-the-white-house-gender-policy-council/.

110. Godfrey et al., "The 25 Candidates for 2018 Sunk by #MeToo Allegations."

111. Evangelia (Lina) Papadaki, "Feminist Perspectives on Objectification," in *The Stanford Encyclopedia of Philosophy*, ed. Edward N. Zalta (Stanford, CA: Metaphysics Research Lab, Stanford University, Spring 2021), https://plato .stanford.edu/archives/spr2021/entries/feminism-objectification/.

112. Papadaki, "Feminist Perspectives on Objectification."

113. Jeremy Herb, Lauren Fox, and Ryan Nobles, "Gaetz Showed Nude Photos of Women He Said He'd Slept with to Lawmakers, Sources Tell CNN," CNN, April 1, 2021, https://www.cnn.com/2021/04/01/politics/matt-gaetz -photos-women/index.html.

114. David A. Lieb, "#Metoo Movement Was Not 1-Year Phenomenon in State Capitols," AP NEWS, February 2, 2019, https://apnews.com/article /north-america-mo-state-wire-in-state-wire-wa-state-wire-id-state-wire-3f4e 4a2b95254467b1cbfa0752227d57.

115. Lieb, "#Metoo Movement Was Not 1-Year Phenomenon."

6

Epilogue

Only with the clout conferred by political and economic power can women turn the tide towards justice and rewrite the narrative that has silenced them for so long.—(Bonnie Stabile and Aubrey Grant in an op-ed in *The Hill* about U.S. Senate candidate Roy Moore, who was endorsed by President Trump in an Alabama special election after several women accused him of sexual assault and misconduct)[1]

We have argued that rape, sexual assault, and harassment are systemic impediments to women's advancement to positions of public authority. Rape culture encompasses various beliefs, attitudes, and practices that collectively conspire to keep women in more traditional gender roles, thus limiting the power they exercise in the public sphere. Such a culture includes sexist strictures about how women can and should comport themselves, embraces adversarial beliefs about relations between the sexes, and enacts hostility toward women. It also exhibits some level of acceptance of violence against women, as evidenced by the pervasive presence of such violence in popular culture, humor, and social media dialogue and the degree to which policy to prevent such violence is either absent or inadequate.

The election of Donald Trump, an inflection point blamed by many for coarsening political dialogue and setting back women's rights, also unleashed candid debate and demand for policy action in contexts across the country, from campuses to Congress. The 2016 election cycle gave new fervor to the movement to address persisting inequities in women's representation and confront long-ignored injustices of rape, sexual assault, and harassment. After 2017, hundreds of formerly untouchable public figures were publicly brought to account for sexual harassment and assault, with attendant calls for policy action. And as powerful men were prevailed upon to resign or face justice for previously undisclosed offenses, hundreds of women with no previous political experience threw their hats into the ring for public office, and state legislatures saw an uptick in bills addressing sexual harassment.

Women's representation matters for many reasons, from the practical to the philosophical. While there is evidence that women's presence contributes to better outcomes and greater productivity in organizations, governmental and otherwise, their proportional inclusion is also a matter of justice and fairness central to the articulated principles of democracy. Having identified these critically important criteria for caring about the problem of women's underrepresentation, we further follow the prescribed path of policy analysis by identifying contributing causal factors and assessing and suggesting alternatives to address the problem at hand. We identify rape culture as a major causal factor for women's underrepresentation. It is our hope that elucidating this connection might help raise awareness and inspire more robust policy solutions. The proximal goals of understanding and ameliorating various facets of rape culture, worthy in their own right, may also offer means of achieving the distal goal of more proportional representation of women in positions of power in the public sphere.

In the primary institutions of government authority and the campus context that prepares people for careers there, we observe that the pervasive problems of sexism, sexual harassment, and assault can set back women's interests, constraining their ability to get the traction needed to advance their careers individually and collectively make progress toward more proportional representation. Public policy as a field is concerned with identifying systemic causal factors that contribute to public problems, as well as assessing the viability of solutions that might fruitfully address such factors. Our analysis takes up these tasks by identifying and describing elements of rape culture that pervade the executive, judicial, and legislative branches of government and its germination on college campuses, examining both the content and context of various policy solutions.

In one case, we found that policy used to address sexual assault was of limited utility, in part because it was not designed for that purpose. Reliance on Title IX as a primary tool to contend with campus sexual assault fails to address the problem from two important perspectives: prevention and survivor services. Though designed to ensure equity in educational access, Title IX was neither intended for nor fully up to the task of addressing the problem of sexual assault to which it was interpreted to apply decades later. As applied by the Obama administration, Title IX was seen, from the perspective of survivors, as advancing their interests, though still an imperfect instrument. The Trump administration's rescission of modest Obama-era measures to facilitate reporting set those interests back. By privileging the position of the accused over accusers in enumerating reporting mechanisms, the latter policy change responded to rape myths rather than data in defining the problem and made it harder for women to report incidents of sexual assault on campus.

The Congressional Accountability Act of 1995 similarly gave with one hand while taking away with the other. The act represented an advancement from the perspective of protecting women's workplace rights, establishing reporting mechanisms for misconduct on the part of members of Congress where none had previously existed. But by making the reporting process unnecessarily cumbersome, it almost seemed designed to dissuade people from using it, and thus favored the position of members who would clearly prefer not to be investigated at all. The CAA Reform Act, passed in 2018, though not without shortcomings, made some strides in simplifying reporting and thus improving accountability.

As the social construction policy frame makes clear, those who have powerful, privileged positions are likely to see themselves protected in the policy process and experience policy benefits, and those who are less well thought of or are outsiders are more likely to experience burdens. This is, in large part, attributable to the fact that policy makers who are responsible for conferring those benefits and burdens look with favor on those who look like themselves. Before the CAA, members of Congress had avoided having any policy at all to hold themselves accountable for harassment and discrimination. When political conditions made it necessary for them to enact such accountability measures, they made them as palatable as possible for their own purposes. Without sufficient representation of women or other underrepresented groups to assert the importance of protections against such misconduct, stringent rules to address it are unlikely to be enacted, and those who experience discrimination or harassment are thus less likely to be heard.

Members of the judiciary also often exhibit a propensity to protect the powerful and those for whom they share an affinity. This was evident in the Senate Judiciary Committee's handling of the hearings in both the Clarence Thomas and Brett Kavanaugh Supreme Court nominations. The rules crafted and carried out by the committee contributed to scuttling the appearance of some witnesses that would have corroborated the testimony of the accusers and limiting the investigations in both cases. Once on the court, Thomas favored positions in cases of sexual harassment that privileged employers and supported limitations on the reporting of harassment.

The narrative used to justify the preference for policy mechanisms that limit reporting of sexual harassment and assault, thus privileging the perpetrators and enablers of such behavior, is predicated in part on the idea that women are not reliable witnesses. This is a narrative that President Trump's Twitter feed relentlessly related, often portraying women as mentally unstable, hysterical liars. Though not all lawmakers and justices would subscribe to the colorful characterizations that Trump promulgated, they may share the view, perhaps unconsciously, that women are not as trustworthy or competent as men. As the concept of testimonial injustice explains, those from historically privileged and powerful pedigrees—in this case men, mostly white—are likely to be afforded more credibility than those from historically subjugated groups, such as women and people of color. In each of the contexts that we examined, constraining policies could be said to trace their roots to some degree of acceptance of these sexist but pervasive tropes about women.

A companion concept to testimonial injustice is hermeneutical injustice, in which case "neither the harasser nor the harrassee" in situations such as these "has an adequate understanding of what is going on."[2] This seems to be the case for many operating in the policy process, who are ignorant, whether willfully or through little fault of their own, of the historical injustices and cultural factors influencing their own beliefs and behavior. But, while all labor under holes in understanding, only some are systematically and structurally disadvantaged by them. It would be "very much in" women's interest "to understand and make intelligible"[3] the factors that contribute to their continued mistreatment through subjection to harassment and sexual violence, as well as the limitations and indignities they often suffer in processes that thwart their interests through bureaucratic means. It is for this purpose that we hope our writing of this manuscript will prove useful.

> Women standing up and using their voices . . . standing up for each other in solidarity. . . . The collective pain we've felt has turned into a collective power. It's amazing.—(actress and activist Alyssa Milano)[4]

Notes

1. Bonnie Stabile and Aubrey Grant, "From Rape 'Myths' to Roy Moore: We Can't Continue to Blame Victims," *The Hill*, November 21, 2017, https://thehill.com/opinion/civil-rights/361436-from-rape-myths-to-roy-moore-we-cant-continue-to-blame-the-victim.

2. Rae Langton, "Epistemic Injustice: Power and the Ethics of Knowing. By Miranda Fricker," *Hypatia* 25, no. 2 (2010): 459–464, https://doi.org/10.1111/j.1527-2001.2010.01098.x.

3. Langton, "Epistemic Injustice."

4. Mary Pflum, "A Year Ago, Alyssa Milano Started a Conversation about #MeToo. These Women Replied," *NBC News*, October 15, 2018, https://www.nbcnews.com/news/us-news/year-ago-alyssa-milano-started-conversation-about-metoo-these-women-n920246.

Index

Note: Page numbers followed by *t* indicate tables and *f* indicate figures.

Abortion, 1, 50, 144, 145–147*t*, 148–149, 151–153
Access Hollywood tapes, 53, 154
Adams, Brock, 182*t*, 188
Alito, Samuel, 140, 141*t*, 146–148*t*, 151
Animals: reference to having sex with in incidents of harassment, 132, 133; Trump likening women to, 1, 34, 36, 39
AOC, 33, 42. *See also* O'Casio-Cortez, Alexandria
Ayotte v. Planned Parenthood of Northern New England, 144, 145*t*

Banet-Weiser, Sarah, 126
Barton, Joe, 183*t*, 188
Beard, Mary, 50
Biden, Joe, 9, 19, 39–40, 52, 82, 86, 121–122, 135, 136
Birth control, 153
Black Cube, 190
Blasey Ford, Christine, 53, 115, 121, 123–124, 125, 135, 153, 155
Bloomberg, Michael, 29

Boies Schiller Flexner LLP, 190
Bowie, Jennifer Barnes, 120
Bowser, Muriel, 45
Breastfeeding, 36–37
Brock, David, 123
Brownmiller, Susan, 4
Bully pulpit, 6, 17–20, 31, 52, 54, 56
Brzezinski, Mika, 32, 36, 40
Brzonkala, Christy, 143–144
Burke, Tarana, 2, 92, 177
Burlington Industries, Inc. v. Ellerth, 128, 137, 142*t*
Burwell v. Hobby Lobby Stores, 144, 146*t*
Bush, George H.W., 9, 116, 124, 130, 135
Byrd, Robert C., 172

Campus rape, 73, 74, 76, 93, 98, 104
Carson, Sage, 80*t*, 86, 100, 101–102
Celebrity Apprentice, 21, 32, 36
Center for American Women and Politics (CAWP), 192
Cher, 34
Chua, Amy, 154

Clery Act, 8, 90, 98, 104–105
Clery handbook, 90
Clinton, Bill, 3, 121, 187
Clinton, Hillary: appearance, 27, 33;
    competence questioned, 44, 51;
    "Crooked Hillary" moniker, 51;
    Democratic presidential primary,
    10; emails, 48; media portrayal of,
    55; "nasty," 35; Politifact assess-
    ment of, 52; popular vote, 1;
    presidential loss, 53, 55; public per-
    ception and trust, 50, 51, 52; pur-
    ported illness and stamina, 27–28;
    "revenge," 124; sexist attitudes and
    voting behavior toward, 22–23;
    "vicious," 39
Coffman, Katherine B., 22
Cohen, Michael, 48
Coll, Ally, 190–191, 193
Collins, Gail, 48
Comey, James, 30
Congressional Accountability Act
    (CAA) of 1995: legislation and pas-
    sage, 171–173; overview, 10, 192;
    settlements, 177–178; violations
    and reporting, 172–173, 192
Congressional Accountability Act of
    1995 Reform Act of 2018: advo-
    cacy for Act, 189, 191; legislation
    and passage, 173–175, 189; sum-
    mary, 171, 192, 205
CongressToo, 189–191
Contraception, 1, 146t
Conyers, John, 183t, 186–187
Coronavirus, 19, 41, 43, 46. See also
    COVID-19
Couric, Katie, 49
COVID-19, 47, 90. See also
    Coronavirus
Crawford v. Nashville, 140, 141t, 142t
Culture of Respect, 80t, 90
Cummings, Elijah, 38

Damore, James, 30–31
Daniels, Stormy, 17, 39
Data Feminism, 93, 104
Davis v. Monroe County Board of Edu-
    cation, 88, 128, 138, 141t
Davis v. Washington, 143
"Dear colleague letter," 82, 83, 87,
    89, 105
Department of Education (ED), 73,
    74, 100, 122, 133
Department of Justice (DOJ), 73, 82,
    100, 184t
DeVos, Betsy, 73–74, 76, 80, 83–85,
    87, 89, 95, 97, 100, 103
Dillon, Justin, 86, 95
Disgust, 35–38
Dissenting opinions, influence of,
    137–139
Dowd, Maureen, 40–41
Due process, 80, 95
Dunn, Laura, 79–82, 80t, 85, 89, 94,
    99, 101, 104
Duran, Gil, 54

Emotional state, 23, 24–26t, 40,
    43–44, 54
End Rape on Campus (EROC), 80t,
    88, 92
Equal Employment Opportunity
    Commission, 117, 122, 133,
    141t, 187
Equal Rights Amendment, 155
Eugenics, 149–150
Every Voice Coalition (EVC),
    79, 80t, 97, 99, 100, 101f,
    102–105

Fake news, 28, 48, 49, 51
False reports/accusations of rape or
    sexual assault, 73–74, 76, 84, 85
Families Advocating for Campus
    Equality (FACE), 83

Faragher v. City of Boca Raton, 128, 137, 138, 142*t*
Farenthold, Blake, 183*t*, 188
Farrow, Ronan, 176
FBI, 30, 32, 126, 135
Federalist, 57, 172
Feinstein, Diane, 124
Fiorina, Carly, 33
Focusing event, 2, 11, 175, 177, 186, 188, 192
Foley, Mark, 182*t*, 188
Franken, Al, 183*t*, 188
Franklin v. Gwinnet County Public Schools, 81, 140, 142*t*
Frederiksen, Mette, 35
Fricker, Miranda, 77–78, 84–85, 127

Gaetz, Matt, 3, 184*t*, 188, 193
Gallo, Nora, 79, 80*t*, 97–99, 101*f*, 102
Gebser v. Lago Vista Independent School District, 128, 129–130, 141*t*, 156
Gender-based violence, 88, 133, 134
Gender stereotypes, 22, 30, 40
Gillibrand, Kirsten, 17, 89, 189
Ginsburg, Ruth Bader, 28, 45, 121, 132, 137, 145–148*t*, 154
Gonzalez v. Carhart, 144, 146*t*
Graham, Lindsey, 125
Grassley, Chuck, 121, 171, 172

Haberman, Maggie, 48
Hardnett, Sukari, 122
Harris, Kamala, 45
Harris v. Forklift Systems, Inc., 140, 142*t*
Hatch, Orrin, 9, 121, 122, 123, 135
Hattery, Angela, 133
HBCU (historically Black college or university), 93

Heflin, Howell, 134, 186
Herasure, 54
Hermeneutical injustice, 78–79, 206
Hierarchy postulate, 120
Hill, Anita, 9–10, 115, 120–121, 122, 126, 133, 134, 156, 172, 186
Himpathy, 54, 94, 125
Historically Black college or university (HBCU), 93
Homophily, 9, 122, 156
Hostile sexism, 23
Huffington, Ariana, 32, 34
Hypermasculinity/hypermasculine, 133
Hysterical (women depicted as), 5, 6, 85, 155, 206

"I Can't Keep Quiet" ballad, 1
Imposter syndrome, 22
Incidence of rape and sexual assault on campus, 76
Ingraham, Laura, 155
Insurrection, 19, 21, 32, 38, 52. *See also* January 6th
Intelligence, 1, 7, 23, 24–26*t*, 30–32, 44, 54
Intersectional concerns, 91–92, 100, 104
It's On Us, 80*t*, 81, 83, 87, 92

Jackson, Candice, 74
James, Lebron, 33
James, Lily, 79, 80*t*, 98–100, 101*f*, 102, 104
January 6th, 19, 21, 32, 41. *See also* Insurrection
Jourdain, Rose, 122
June Medical Services LLC v. Russo, 147*t*, 149, 151, 152

Kagan, Elena, 121, 146–148*t*
Katz, Debra, 188

Kavanaugh, Brett: all-female law clerks, 154; confirmation, 126; relationship with Judge Kozinski, 9, 153–154; response to sexual misconduct accusations/allegations, 124, 125; sexual misconduct accusations/allegations, 3, 8, 53, 116, 117, 121, 123, 125–126, 135, 153, 154–155; voting record, 147–148*t*, 151–155

Kelly, John, 17

Kelly, Megyn, 36

Kennedy, Anthony, 128, 139, 141*t*, 145–148*t*, 148

Kennedy, John F., 7, 18

Kennedy, Ted, 3

Kihuen, Ruben, 183*t*, 188

Kingdon, John, 11, 177

Klum, Heidi, 34

Know Your IX, 80*t*, 86, 91

Kolstad v. American Dental Association, 145*t*, 150

Korman, Allison, 80*t*, 90–91, 99, 100–101, 105

Kozinksi, Alex, 9, 116, 153–154, 156

Lakoff, George, 27, 49, 54

Leahy, Partrick, 121, 124, 134

Ledbetter, Lily, 148*t*, 150–151, 156

Ledbetter v. Goodyear Tire & Rubber Company, 148*t*, 150–151

Lee, Harper, 78

Lemon, Don, 33

Lim, Connie, 1

Lipnic, Victoria, 117

Lisak, David, 76, 86

Loathsomeness, 7, 24–26*t*, 33

"Locker room talk," 3, 9, 53, 135

Looks, 7, 23, 24–26*t*, 33–36, 54

Machado, Alicia, 34

MacKinnon, Catherine, 95, 134, 156

Madison, James, 172

"Make America Great Again" (MAGA), 7, 18, 19, 46

Manne, Kate, 6, 20, 38, 75*t*, 77–78, 84–86, 92, 94, 95–97, 102, 123, 125, 130

Marco, Rubio, 28–29

Marcus, Ruth, 32

Markle, Meghan, 36

Massa, Eric, 182*t*, 188

Mattis, James, 41

Mayer, Jane, 121, 122

Meehan, Pat, 184*t*, 188

Mekanism, 87

Member and Employee Training and Oversight on (ME TOO) Congress Act, 189

Men's rights, 73–74, 80, 83, 86

Menstruation, 36, 37

#MeTooCongress, 170

MeToo era, 177, 186

MeToo movement, 2, 4, 10, 11, 92, 101*f*, 116, 170, 175, 177, 179, 186, 189, 190, 193, 194

Metzenbaum, Howard, 122

Midler, Bette, 34

Milano, Alyssa, 2, 87–88, 170, 177, 206

Miller, Chanel, 93–94

Minghella, Anthony, 78

Misogyny, 4, 6, 11, 20, 36, 95–96, 123, 189

Multiple streams framework, 11, 175

Murray, Patty, 89

NASPA, 80*t*, 90, 91

Nasty, 35–36

National Coalition for Men, 83

National Education Association (NEA), 89

National Network to End Domestic Violence, 82

National Women's Law Center (NWLC), 127, 128, 129, 152, 153
Navarro, Ana, 48–49
Necessary qualifications, 7, 24–26*t*, 44–45, 47, 54
Nessel, Dana, 41–42
Neurosexism, 30
Nevada Department of Human Resources v. Hibbs, 147*t*, 150
Noncarceral policy approach, 99, 100, 101*f*, 103, 105
Nondisclosure agreement, 35, 176, 189, 194
Noonan, Peggy, 32
Nussbaum, Martha, 20, 35, 37, 95, 193

Obama, Barack, 10, 21, 43, 45, 51, 52, 72, 74, 87, 121; Donald Trump attacks on Obama and administration, 43, 45, 51
Obama administration guidelines on Title IX, 7, 74, 82–84, 87, 89, 90, 95, 96, 105, 205
O'Casio-Cortez, Alexandria, 32, 37, 38, 42. *See also* AOC
O'Connor, Sandra Day, 121, 129, 139, 142*t*, 144, 145–148*t*, 148
O'Donnell, Rosie, 32, 39, 49
Office of Civil Rights (ED), 74, 83
Office of Compliance (OOC), 172
Office of Congressional Workplace Rights (OCWR), 10–11, 172, 174
Office of Management and Budget (OMB), 89
Office on Violence Against Women, 82
"Old boys" network or club, 9, 156
Omar, Ilhan, 33, 35, 37, 38, 39
Omarosa, 32, 35, 39, 41, 42
Onyeka-Crawford, Adaku, 128
Ott, Brian, 21

PA State Police v. Suders, 131–134
Packwood, Bob, 182*t*, 185–186, 188, 193
Parham, Kenyora, 80*t*, 89–90, 92–93
Patriarchy, defined, 6
Pelosi, Nancy: on John Conyers, 186–187; as object of Trump's ire, 28, 31, 32, 35, 41, 43, 44; on Ruben Kihuen, 183*t*
Picture a Scientist, 94
Planned Parenthood of Southeastern Pennsylvania v. Casey, 145*t*, 148–149
Pocohantas, 52
Policy entrepreneurs, 11, 188, 192
Policy process, 6, 11, 97, 103, 205, 206
Politifact, 23, 51–52
Pollard v. E. I. du Pont de Nemours & Company, 140, 141*t*, 146, 150
@POTUS, 21
Powell, Sidney, 155
Pressley, Ayanna, 33, 37, 102
Proud Boys, 32
Public policy process, 6
Purple Campaign, 190–191
"Pussyhat Project," 1

RAINN, 73
Rape, 34, 85, 92, 203; accusations/allegations, 1, 2, 83, 182*t*, 188; Clery Act response to, 104; Clery data reports on, 98; crisis centers, 98; defined as "sexual misconduct," 81; exemptions in abortion law, 50; jokes, 133; kits, 92; media messages about, 77; scenes, 133; survivors of, 74, 75, 76; threats of, 5. *See also* campus rape; false reports/accusations of rape or sexual assault; rape culture; rape myth
Rape culture, 4, 7, 11, 75, 84, 203, 204, 205

Rape myth, 8, 50, 51, 77, 205
@realDonaldTrump, 17, 18, 21
Red Zone, 86
Rehnquist, William, 128, 139, 141*t*,
    143–144, 145–147*t*, 149, 151
Reid, Joy, 49
Reproductive rights, 9, 119, 127,
    144, 145–148*t*, 157
Restorative justice, 100–102, 103*t*
Reynolds, Mel, 182*t*, 188
Roberts, John, 116, 117, 129,
    145–148*t*, 151
Roe v. Wade, 149, 151–152
Romney, Mitt, 39
Roosevelt, Franklin Delano, 7, 18
Roosevelt, Theodore, 6, 18, 54
Rosenthal, Lynn, 82
Rossello, Ricardo, 47
Rubenfeld, Jed, 154
Rubin, Jennifer, 31–32, 48
Rubio, Marco, 28–29
Russia, 30, 48

Safire, William, 18
Scarborough, Joe, 43
Schaffner, Brian, 23
Schlafly, Phyllis, 155
Schumer, Chuck, 29–30, 41
Sebelius, Kathleen, 45
Senate Judiciary Committee,
    8–9, 53, 121, 122, 123, 133,
    136, 205
#SendHerBack, 38
"Severe, pervasive and objectively
    offensive," 8, 75*t*, 88, 91, 138,
    139, 156
Sexism, defined, 5
Sexual assault, 3; accusations/allega-
    tions of Trump sexual assault, 34,
    53 (*see also* Trump, Donald, sexual
    harassment and assault allegations
    against); campus context, 2–5, 7, 8,
    74–75, 81–85, 86, 87, 90, 92, 94,

97, 98, 100, 101*t*, 103*t*, 104, 204;
    on Capitol Hill, 169, 170, 176,
    187; impediments to women, 203;
    in the Judiciary, 117, 118, 125,
    144, 153; myths, 50, 54, 85–86;
    survivors, 1, 8; testimonial injus-
    tice, 75*t*, 76, 78
Sexual harassment: Alex Kozinski,
    153, 157; Brett Kavanaugh sexual
    misconduct accusations/allegations
    and nomination process, 116,
    117, 119, 121, 123, 126, 153,
    154–155 (*see also* Kavanaugh,
    Brett); on Capitol Hill, 170, 171,
    172, 174, 175, 176, 177, 179,
    182–184*t*, 186, 187, 188, 189,
    190, 191, 192, 193 (*see also* Con-
    gressional Accountability Act of
    1995); Clarence Thomas sexual
    harassment accusations/allegations
    and nomination process, 9, 10,
    116, 117, 119, 122, 123, 133 (*see
    also* Thomas, Clarence); Donald
    J. Trump accusations/allegations,
    53; educational setbacks and career
    costs, 94–95; in the Judiciary,
    116, 117, 119, 122, 123, 126,
    153, 219–220; policy agenda,
    legislation, and laws, 2, 9, 73;
    policy options, 103*t*; rape culture,
    4, 53, 75; rates on campus, 99; in
    schools, 7, 8, 75, 76, 81, 82, 84,
    85, 88, 89, 92, 94, 95, 99, 103*t*;
    setback in education and profes-
    sional development, 94, 95; societal
    awareness, response, and tolerance,
    3, 9, 95, 170; stories, testimonies,
    and public accusations/allegations,
    2, 9, 203–204 (*see also* MeToo
    movement); Supreme Court cases,
    127–140, 141–142*t*, 143, 150,
    156; Supreme Court nomination
    hearings, 121–127; testimonial

injustice, 78, 84–85, 117, 118*f*, 206; Title IX, 7, 73, 76, 81, 82, 85, 88, 89, 92; in the workplace, 1, 116, 117

Sexual stratification hypothesis, 77

Shaw, Kate, 17, 18

SILENT mnemonic device, 7, 23, 24–26*t*

Simpson, Alan K., 135

Smith, Earl, 133

Social construction, 11, 75*t*, 77–79, 130, 192, 205

Social media, 5, 6, 19, 51, 77, 88, 203

Sommers, Christina Hoff, 84, 86

Sotomayor, Sonia, 28, 121, 146–148*t*

Souter, David, 144, 145–147*t*, 148

Specter, Arlen, 9, 134, 135, 136, 156

Speier, Jackie, 169–170, 173–175, 188–189

"The Squad," 37–38

Stahl, Lesley, 39

Stamina, 7, 23, 24–26*t*, 27, 44, 54–55

Stature, 7, 23, 24–26*t*, 27–28, 44, 54, 85

Statutes of limitations, 10, 134, 156, 194

Stevens, Justice, 129–130, 145–148*t*

Stop Abusive and Violent Environments (SAVE), 83–84

Summers, Lawrence, 30

SurvJustice, 79, 80*t*

Swierkiewicz v. Sorema N.A, 146*t*, 150

"Teflon Don," 2

Teigen, Chrissy, 35

Testimonial injustice, 11, 75*t*, 77–78, 84–85, 118*f*, 119, 122–123, 127, 130, 134, 193, 206

Thomas, Clarence: conservative credentials, 130–131; decisions on reproductive rights, 144, 145–148*t*, 149; decisions on sex and workplace discrimination, 150–151; decisions on sexual harassment cases, 127–140, 141–143*t*; decisions on violence against women, 143–144; dissenting opinions, 128, 131–132, 137–139, 149, 150; response to accusations/allegations, 124–125; sexual harassment accusations/allegations, 9, 116, 117, 121, 122, 123, 126, 133, 186

Thompson, Bennie, 38

"#TimesUp," 2

Title VII of the Civil Rights Act of 1964, 138, 140, 142*t*, 145*t*, 146*t*, 148*t*, 150, 156

Title IX, 2, 8, 73, 80, 81, 83, 204–205; activist criticism, 98, 99, 100, 103, 104; coverage, 82, 84, 87–88; interpretations, 7, 73, 74, 76, 82, 83, 85; purpose, 81, 91; rule changes, 89–91, 96, 97, 100; Supreme Court cases, 88–89, 129, 130, 140, 141–142*t*, 147*t*

Tlaib, Rashida, 33, 37

Tolchin, Martin, 5

Tolchin, Susan, 5

Toxic masculinity, 83

Trump, Donald, 1; "arrogant," 51; attacks on media, 48–49; calling women liars, 51–52; campus sexual assault policy, 8, 74, 83, 90, 105, 205; disparaging opponents, 1, 55; inauguration, 1, 11, 176, 177; lies, 50–51, 52; mocking, 123, 125; pandemic response, 41–42; presidential campaign and election, 1, 2, 21, 27, 28–29, 29, 30, 203; sexual harassment and assault allegations against, 2, 3, 53, 74; Supreme Court nomination, 116; tweets on competence, 44–50; tweets on emotional state, 40–43; tweets on intelligence,

Trump, Donald (*Continued*)
 31–33; tweets on looks and loathsomeness, 33–40; tweets on stature
 and stamina, 27–30; tweets on
 trustworthiness, 50–54; Twitter use,
 7, 21, 22, 23, 35, 44, 47, 206; use
 of bully pulpit, 18–20, 55–56
Trump Twitter Archive, 23
Trustworthiness, 7, 24–26*t*, 50, 54,
 134, 171, 186
Tur, Katy, 48
Turner, Brock, 93
2016 presidential election, 1, 2, 21,
 22, 28, 50, 51, 53, 170, 176, 203
2020 presidential election, 39, 52

United States v. Morrison, 143–144

Valenti, Jessica, 50
Vance v. Ball State, 128–129, 130,
 141*t*, 156
Vitchers, Tracey, 80*t*, 81, 83, 87–89, 92

Wallace, Nicolle, 39
Wal-Mart Stores Inc v. Dukes, et al.,
 148*t*, 151

Walsh, Debbie, 20
Wanderer, Jeremy, 78
Warren, Elizabeth, 31, 44–45, 52
Wasserman Schultz, Debbie, 40
Waters, Maxine, 31, 33
Weiner, Anthony, 183*t*, 188
Weinstein, Harvey, 2, 170,
 176–177, 190
Whitmer, Gretchen, 19, 42, 46
Whole Woman's Health v. Hellerstedt,
 151–152
Wilson, Frederica, 42
Witch hunt, 44
Women's March, 1, 4, 177
Women's underrepresentation, 3–4,
 11, 94, 118*t*, 118–119, 127, 133,
 155, 191, 193, 204
Wright, Angela, 122

Yale Law School, 122, 125, 130,
 137, 154
Yates, Sally, 45
Yulín Cruz, Carmen, 46–47

Zorn, Christopher, 120
Zuckerman Sivan, Ezra, 53

About the Authors

Bonnie Stabile, PhD, is associate professor and associate dean of student and academic affairs in the Schar School of Policy and Government at George Mason University, where she also serves as the director of the master of public administration (MPA) program and served for five years as director of the master of public policy (MPP) program. Professor Stabile was the 2019 recipient of the Schar School's Teaching Award and is the founding director of the Gender and Policy (GAP) Center at the Schar School. She is a graduate of Mount Holyoke College and holds master of public administration and PhD in public policy degrees from George Mason University.

Aubrey Leigh Grant, MPP, is a doctoral candidate at George Mason University. She served as editorial assistant for *World Medical & Health Policy*, an academic journal published by Wiley, and project coordinator for the Gender and Policy Center at the Schar School of Policy and Government. In 2019, she was awarded the Gender and Policy Leadership Award. Aubrey received her master of public policy (MPP) from American University and a bachelor of arts in political science from the University of North Carolina at Wilmington.

www.ingramcontent.com/pod-product-compliance
Lightning Source LLC
Chambersburg PA
CBHW050431280326
41932CB00013BA/2071